THIRD EDITION

On the Guard II

The YMCA Lifeguard Manual

YMCA of the USA

Library of Congress Cataloging-in-Publication Data

On the guard II : the YMCA lifeguard manual. -- 3rd ed.

    p.   cm.

    Includes bibliographical references (p. 257) and index.

    ISBN 0-88011-815-6

    1. Lifeguards--Training of.   2. Life-saving.   3. Aquatic sports-
-Safety measures.   I. YMCA of the USA.

    GV838.74.05   1997

    797.2'1'0289--dc21   97-14580

                                   CIP

Published for the YMCA of the USA by Human Kinetics Publishers, Inc.

The YMCA of the USA does not operate or manage any lifeguard training programs.

Item no.: Y5334

ISBN: 0-88011-815-6

Information in chapter 14 is from chapters 2-9 of *YMCA Pool Operations Manual*, Ralph L. Johnson, 1989, Champaign, IL: Human Kinetics. Chapters 3, 4, 6, and 8 and part of chapters 5 and 7 in *YMCA Pool Operations Manual* are adapted from chapters 5 and 13 in *Swimming Pools* (4th ed.) (pp. 65-76, 201-221) by M.A. Gabrielsen (Ed.), 1987, Champaign, IL: Human Kinetics. Copyright 1987 by the Council for National Cooperation in Aquatics. Adapted by permission.

Cover Design: Jack Davis

Illustrations: Line drawings, Keith Neely; Mac art, Gretchen Walters; Medical art, Marie Dauenheimer

Printed in the United States of America   10 9 8 7 6 5 4 3

Copies of this book may be purchased from the YMCA Program Store P.O. Box 5076, Champaign, IL 61825-5076, (800) 747-0089

CONTENTS

PREFACE

Lifeguarding is a serious and important undertaking. Although much of lifeguarding can be tedious, a matter of watching the same area for hours with little change, at any moment a guard may have to jump into action, quickly and efficiently, to save a life. Lifeguarding is a demanding task, requiring responsible, caring, and capable people who have been well trained in their duties.

On the Guard II is the YMCA's lifeguard training manual. It offers you up-to-date information on how to guard, anticipating and preventing problems before they occur, and taking action to help those in danger when necessary. But this information is always presented with the Y's mission in mind: How can we keep people safe in a caring, open way? How can we meet people's needs to have fun and to develop their aquatic skills within legal and moral constraints to keep aquatic environments as safe and pleasant as possible for everyone? The YMCA program tries to develop lifeguards who not only know a lot but also care a lot about lifeguarding and those they are trained to serve.

This third edition of *On the Guard II* includes many new features:

- A chapter on water park lifeguarding
- Sections on multiple victim/multiple guard rescues, character development, off-duty rescues, sizing and applying a cervical collar, and maintaining non-slip surfaces
- A section on the Aquatic Safety Assistant Course
- The description of minor changes in backboarding procedures and scuba rescue procedures
- Updates of CPR requirements and of minimum water depths for diving

After an introduction that explains the Y's historical involvement in aquatic safety and the lifeguarding requirements and aquatic courses available, *On the Guard II* (3rd edition) describes the safety and survival skills every swimmer needs to know. The next two chapters cover accident and incident prevention, with specifics on how to lifeguard and pool danger areas, along with suggested rules to protect patrons' safety. That's followed by the information you need to deal with emergencies, including rescue skills, emergency systems, first aid in aquatic environments, and spinal injury management. The chapters on rescue, first aid, and spinal injury contain step-by-step instructions on how to perform the appropriate procedures.

Chapters 10 and 11 tell you what you need to know for outdoor lifeguarding. Chapter 10 discusses weather and open water dangers and the precautions to take against them; chapter 11 highlights the specialized knowledge required for basic open water lifeguarding. Chapter 12 is the largest addition to *On the Guard II* (3rd edition). It explains the different aspects and techniques of the growing field of water park lifeguarding.

The next three chapters review some of the job-related responsibilities of lifeguards. The first explains basic legal terms and proceedings that might be relevant if you become involved in lawsuits against an aquatic facility. The next chapter addresses pool management concerns, such as pool chemistry and filtration and safety inspection; the final one includes guidance on how to seek and obtain a lifeguarding position and ideas for further training.

Each chapter begins with objectives to guide your reading and ends with review questions to check your knowledge of the main points. Some have special boxes that highlight guidelines or key points of procedures. Most skills and procedures are presented as numbered steps, with illustrations to clarify the instructions.

As you train at the YMCA to become a lifeguard, you should learn more than just skills. You should grow in both your ability and desire to help others. Lifeguarding is a perfect opportunity to develop leadership and service skills and to make a significant contribution to your community. We hope that as you read this manual and complete your training you develop an appreciation for the value of lifeguarding, for yourself and others.

ACKNOWLEDGMENTS

The YMCA of the USA would like to acknowledge the contributions of the following individuals to *On the Guard II* and the new lifeguard training, collectively known as the Lifeguard Project. Staff leadership for this project was coordinated by Laura Slane.

Lifeguard Project Technical Advisory Committee Members

Ronald K. Nelson, Chair	Grand Rapids Metropolitan YMCA, Grand Rapids, NE
Gerald DeMers, PhD	Associate Professor, California Polytechnic State University, San Luis Obispo, CA
Ralph L. Johnson, PhD	Director of Aquatics, Indiana University of Pennsylvania, Indiana, PA
Diane Knight	Garden Ranch YMCA, Colorado Springs, CO
Jay Newell	South Oklahoma City Branch YMCA, Oklahoma City, OK
Nancy W. Reece	Kankakee YMCA, Kankakee, IL
Laura J. Slane	YMCA of the USA, Chicago, IL
Steve Tarver	Suncoast Family YMCAs, Clearwater, FL

Lifeguard Project Field Test Group Members

Fred Doll	Ionia County YMCA, Ionia, MI
Pam Hendricks	Santa Barbara YMCA, Santa Barbara, CA
Ralph L. Johnson, PhD	Indiana University of Pennsylvania, Indiana, PA
Diane Knight	Garden Ranch YMCA, Colorado Springs, CO
Sandra Krol	Rich Port Branch YMCA, La Grange, IL
Jay Newell	South Oklahoma City Branch YMCA, Oklahoma City, OK
Brian Raymond	Sewickley YMCA, Sewickley, PA
Kathy Rhoads	Central Douglas County YMCA, Roseburg, OR
Richard Robinson	International Drive YMCA, Orlando, FL
Kay Smiley	Town North YMCA, Dallas, TX
Debbie Sutton	South Dekalb Family Branch YMCA, Decatur, GA
Steve Tarver	Suncoast Family YMCAs, Clearwater, FL
Cara Telleysh	International Drive YMCA, Orlando, FL
Melinda Vana	Marshalltown YMCA, Marshalltown, IA

Lifeguard Project Reviewers

Joe Ashworth	Jacksonville, FL
Bob Brucker	Phoenixville YMCA, Phoenixville, PA

Karen Bufalino	Aquatic and Physical Education Instructor, Health and Physical Education Department, Quaker Valley School District, Saxsonburg, PA
Paul Cerio	Aquatic Director, University of Nebraska-Omaha, Omaha, NE
Kathi Cook	Lombard, IL
Joe Cushing	Phoenixville YMCA, Phoenixville, PA
Douglas D'Arnall	Aquatic Safety Consulting, Huntington Beach, CA
Vernon Delpesce	YMCA of the USA, Columbus, OH
Terri Elder	Aquatics Coordinator, Wichita State University, Wichita, KS
Kevin Earnest	Oklahoma City, OK
John R. Fletemeyer, PhD	FIU-Sociology & Anthropology, College of Arts and Sciences, Miami, FL
Sam Freas, PhD	President, International Swimming Hall of Fame, Fort Lauderdale, FL
Millard Freeman	Atlanta, GA
Janet Gabriel	U.S. Diving, Fort Lauderdale, FL
Elaine Helm	Brandywine Branch YMCA, Wilmington, DE
Cheryl Houghtelin	Knoxville Metropolitan YMCA, Knoxville, TN
Janet M. Koran	McDermott, Will & Emery, Chicago, IL
Tom Massey	Director, Program Development, YMCA of the USA, Hattiesburg, MS
Efrank Mendoza, PhD	HPE Department, University of Puerto Rico, Mayaguez, Mayaguez, PR
Mike Miller	University of Missouri, Kansas City, Kansas City, MO
Clarence Moore	Assistant Chief, Cleveland Emergency Services, Cleveland, OH
Christopher Mould	General Counsel, YMCA of the USA, Chicago, IL
Robert Ogoreuc	Aquatic Director, Slippery Rock University, Slippery Rock, PA
Theresa Pagano	Ball State University, College of Applied Sciences & Technology, School of Physical Education, Muncie, IN
Frank Pia	Pia Consulting Services, Larchmont, NY
Jeff Scholten	St. Louis, MO
Duke H. Scott, MD	Medical Advisor, YMCA Scuba Program, Neptune Beach, FL
Glenda Short	Y-Services, Risk Management, YMCA of the USA, Chicago, IL
Charles E. Silvia	Springfield, MA
Donna-Bea Tillman, PhD	U.S. Consumer Product Safety Commission, Washington, DC
Kim Tyson	Texas Swim Center, University of Texas-Austin, Austin, TX
Allen Wagner	Director of Aquatics, East Allegheny H.S., North Versailles, PA
Hal Watz, MD	Colorado Springs, CO
Frankie Wingert	YMCA of the USA Scuba Program, Atlanta, GA
John Wingfield	Director of Aquatics, Ball State University, Muncie, IN
Mary Zoller	YMCA of the USA, Kenner, LA

Special thanks to Dr. Gerald DeMers not only for writing chapter 9 but also for his help, support, and countless contributions throughout this project.

Thanks also to Linda Bump, who wrote this manual, and to Patricia Sammann, who did the developmental editing.

CHAPTER 1

Introduction to YMCA Lifeguarding

YMCA aquatic professionals have led the crusade for improved aquatic safety for over 100 years, and they continue to improve the quality of millions of lives through YMCA instructional aquatic programs. This edition of *On the Guard II* provides personal safety and lifeguard training course material for those developing their aquatic skills.

IN THIS CHAPTER YOU ARE INTRODUCED TO

■ the importance of aquatic safety,

■ the Y's role in promoting aquatic safety,

■ the Y's program philosophy,

■ the Y's lifeguarding program, and

■ other Y aquatic safety programs.

THE IMPORTANCE OF AQUATIC SAFETY

In the past 25 years, interest in aquatic activities has exploded. With greater access to swimming facilities and water parks, people can easily include aquatic activities in their recreation and their fitness routines. Enthusiasts are found *on the water*, in activities like rafting, canoeing, sailing, and boating; *in the water*, in recreational and competitive swimming, synchronized swimming, water sliding, and water polo; *under the water*, through skin and scuba diving; and even *above the water*, as in parasailing. The popularity of aquatic activities has generated a new awareness of the need for aquatic education and safety for all age groups.

For those without awareness and proper training, the aquatic environment can be as dangerous as it is fun. And even those who don't participate in water sports may need water safety knowledge. Drowning is the fourth leading cause of accidental death in the United States, claiming about 4,300 lives each year, and most drowning victims are nonswimmers who never intended to go into the water. The scenarios include accidents in bathtubs, falling out of a boat, wading too far into the surf, falling off a fishing pier or into a backyard swimming pool, even plunging into a body of water inside an automobile.

In addition to those who die by drowning, untold numbers of people are injured in accidents in open water areas and at public, private, and residential pools. Carelessness, rough play, and unsafe head-first entries can lead to injury on pool decks, near starting blocks, and on or around diving boards.

THE Y'S ROLE IN AQUATIC SAFETY

The YMCA and other community agencies have taken on the challenge of providing swimming instruction and aquatic safety training for people of all ages. With programs like YMCA Skippers and YMCA Progressive Swimming, the national YMCA has developed swimming instruction to address the needs of preschoolers and advanced swimmers alike.

The YMCA has been teaching people to swim for over 100 years. Figure 1.1 traces the development of the YMCA contribution to aquatic safety.

1885-90	YMCA entered the aquatic arena by teaching individuals to swim.
1906	George Corsan, Sr. revolutionized swimming by teaching people in groups.
1908-09	The YMCA became the first organization to plan and carry out a national aquatic education program.
1909	The YMCA became the first organization to employ national field staff to carry out a national aquatic program.
1912	The YMCA developed the National YMCA Lifesaving Service.
1913	George E. Goss of the YMCA completed a systematic study of lifesaving in the United States.
1929	The YMCA *Lifesaving and Swimming Manual* was published.
1939	The YMCA, in cooperation with Drs. Thomas Cureton and Charles Silvia, published the first standardized examination of lifesaving and water safety knowledge and attitudes.
1949	The first edition of the *YMCA Lifesaving & Water Safety Instruction* text, written by Charles E. Silvia, was published. It was the first such text to advocate the use of mouth-to-mouth resuscitation.
1965	Charles Silvia's *YMCA Lifesaving & Water Safety Today* was published.

Figure 1.1

YMCA aquatic safety milestones.

(continued)

Figure 1.1
(continued)

1972	The YMCA Aquatic Safety & Lifesaving Program was launched. It was the first lifesaving program that divided lifesaving into levels (aquatic safety, advanced aquatic safety, senior lifesaving). The YMCA was the first national organization to develop a lifeguard training and certification program.
1974	James Cornforth's *YMCA National Lifeguard Manual* was released.
1986	The first edition of *On the Guard* was released.
1994	*On the Guard II* was released to meet the changing program needs of lifeguards.
1997	The third edition of *On the Guard II* was released.
	The YMCA Aquatic Safety Assistant Course was introduced.

THE Y'S PROGRAM PHILOSOPHY

Millions of people learn to swim through YMCA programs every year. But they take away more from those programs than just skills. Every Y program should meet the Y's mission to put Christian principles into practice to build a healthy spirit, mind, and body for all. To do this, every Y program should meet certain program objectives and incorporate the concept of character development.

✱ not "be prepared"

Program Objectives

In all YMCA programs, the prime objectives are to help participants

- grow personally by developing their self-esteem and self-reliance;
- strengthen positive values;
- improve their personal and family relationships by learning to care, communicate, and cooperate with others;
- appreciate people of different ages, abilities, races, religions, cultures, incomes, and beliefs;
- become better leaders and supporters by learning to work toward a common goal;
- develop specific skills through growth in spirit, mind, and body; and
- have fun.

These objectives, central to the Y's philosophy, make Y programs different from those offered by any other organization. Through this lifeguarding program, you'll have the opportunity to grow in all of these ways.

Character Development

Another part of all Y programs is character development. The Y's stated mission is "to put *Christian principles into practice* through programs that build healthy spirit, mind, and body for all." If we define principles as "a code of conduct; a basis for action" and Christian principles as "positive values," then challenging people to accept and demonstrate positive values is how we put them into practice. Our doing this is called "character development."

Values are the cornerstones that make our society safe and workable. They are the principles of thought and conduct that help distinguish right from wrong and provide a foundation for decision making. Values, which are sometimes referred to as *character*, are the basis of who we are, how we live, and how we treat others. The values we try to impart through character development are these four:

- Caring: to put others before yourself, to love others, to be sensitive to the well-being of others, to help others

- Honesty: to tell the truth, to act in such a way that I am worthy of trust, to have integrity, making sure my actions match my values
- Respect: to treat others as you would have them treat you, to value the worth of every person, including yourself
- Responsibility: to do what you should do, to be accountable for your behavior and obligations

If we believe that values are what makes society good, then it seems likely that inadequately defined values or a lack of values could be the source of many of today's problems: poor work ethics, lack of personal responsibility, lack of trust in our leaders and public officials, crime, violence, and substance abuse. In the long run, character development is an effective strategy that can help solve these problems. It fits the Y's continuing long-term goal to help people develop spirit, as well as mind and body.

Living with and acting on good values contributes to the development of a healthy self-esteem and overall personal happiness. The Y defines *self-esteem* as the positive valuing of oneself. The Y helps children and adults develop self-esteem by providing opportunities for them to become more capable and worthy. By *capable* we mean having practical abilities and competencies. The more capable a person is, the more confident that person is in his or her ability to think and to cope with life's basic challenges. By *worthy* we mean being able to act in a manner that is consistent with those principles a person has been taught are important, such as doing one's best or doing the right thing. As a person becomes more worthy, he or she also becomes more confident of the right to be successful and happy. It makes the person feel more deserving and entitled to assert his or her needs and wants, achieve his or her values, and enjoy the fruits of his or her efforts.

Because we have free will, we always have three choices when we act:

1. We may choose to act in ways that we know will earn and support our self-esteem.
2. We may choose to act in ways that will not earn and support our self-esteem.
3. We may close our eyes to the necessity of maintaining our self-esteem and proceed through life blindly, choosing at random.

Building self-esteem and developing character (values) are connected. When we behave in ways that conflict with what we judge to be appropriate, we lose face in our own eyes and our self-esteem suffers. We feel less worthy. The higher our self-esteem, the more apt we are to strive to make principled choices. Doing this makes us feel more worthy, increasing our self-esteem. We cannot earn self-esteem without values, and we cannot act consistently on our values without being influenced by our self-esteem.

YMCAs can help youth and families develop self-esteem and values by providing participants with sustained relationships with adults, such as YMCA staff members. The YMCA and its staff must convey consistent messages about values, attitudes, beliefs, and behaviors. (Values are not situational; the same values apply in all situations.) To do this, staff behaviors must be consistent with the values, attitudes, and beliefs that they preach.

Lifeguards, like all YMCA staff, must be willing to meet the YMCA's character development challenge and lead by example. Not "walking the talk" is a big problem in teaching character development. Assess your personal ability to lead by example. Once you know where you are and what you want to work on in yourself, you can challenge yourself to improve.

THE YMCA LIFEGUARDING PROGRAM

The YMCA has developed a unique program to prepare skilled lifeguards for a demanding profession. A *lifeguard* by definition has a legal duty to protect the safety of people in an assigned area. Lifeguards have a moral and professional obligation to prevent potential accident situations by enforcing the rules and regulations of their aquatic setting and to react to any emergencies that occur. Lifeguards have a legal duty to respond only if they are on duty at their facility. Should a lifeguard be involved in an accident while off duty, he or she is covered by Good Samaritan laws (see p. 212). These laws can't prevent lawsuits, but they do ensure that the lifeguard's actions are compared to the actions expected of others in similar rescue situations with similar training and certification.

To be a proficient lifeguard, you must first know about personal safety and survival skills, which are reviewed in chapter 2. These and other skills necessary for success can be developed in a professional lifeguarding course, such as the YMCA lifeguard training program.

The YMCA lifeguard training program provides a comprehensive education centered on preventing accidents in aquatic environments. It focuses on the practical aspects of what lifeguards need to know and on lifeguard and patron safety. Lifeguard training enables you to learn and apply safety principles in your own life, develop leadership skills, learn how to maintain a healthy lifestyle, and improve your decision-making skills.

Besides being advanced-level swimmers, candidates to become YMCA lifeguards should be caring, strong, quick to respond, confident, fit, and intelligent, with good interpersonal skills. The YMCA strives to include all people in their programs, but the hazardous duty of a lifeguard may disqualify some candidates with certain physical or mental conditions from becoming certified. To become certified as a YMCA lifeguard, an individual must be able to accomplish these tasks:

- Remain alert, with no lapses in consciousness.
- Sit for extended periods, including in an elevated chair.
- Move to various locations, including in and around an elevated chair.
- Communicate verbally, including projecting the voice across distances, and communicate swiftly and effectively with emergency personnel over telephone and in person.
- Hear noises and distress signals in an aquatic environment, including in water, understanding that significant background noise exists in aquatic environments.
- Observe all assigned sections of the water area.
- Perform all needed rescues and survival skills.
- Think in the abstract, solve problems, make decisions, instruct, evaluate, supervise, and remember.
- Operate alone as a lifeguard, without other lifeguards for support.

To become a YMCA lifeguard, you must meet the following entrance requirements, complete the course as described, and fulfill all certification requirements. Medical clearance before participation may also be required.

Entrance Requirements

To participate in the lifeguard training program, you must meet the following prerequisites:

- Be at least 16 years old before the start of the course. Parental consent is required for those under 18.
- Have and maintain current cardiopulmonary resuscitation (CPR) and first aid certifications. CPR certification must include training for administering CPR to adults, children, and infants, as well as additional training in two-rescuer CPR, modified jaw thrust, and use of pocket-mask and bag-valve-mask resuscitators. First aid certification must include training in victim assessment; treatment for bleeding, shock, burns, specific body area injuries, bites, stings, poisoning, cold- and

heat-related conditions, and bone, muscle, and joint injuries; and handling medical emergencies and rescues. For YMCA of the USA courses which require CPR and/ or first aid certifications as a prerequisite, appropriate certifications from the following nationally recognized organizations will be accepted: American Heart Association (Health Care Provider course for BLS only), American Red Cross, and National Safety Council.

- Pass the following swimming test:
  a. Perform a long, shallow front dive, then swim 500 yards, including 100 yards each of sidestroke, front crawl, breaststroke, sidestroke kick with one arm forward, and inverted breaststroke kick with arms on the stomach.
  b. Tread water for at least 2 minutes with legs only.
  c. Surface-dive head-first and feet-first in 8 to 10 feet of water and swim underwater for 15 feet.

Course Content

The lifeguard training course includes at least 28 hours of classroom and pool sessions, plus a 2-hour practical experience, that cover these topics:

- The importance of aquatic safety
- Personal safety survival skills and swimming strokes
- Aquatic environments and aquatic science
- Aquatic rescues, including situation assessment, use of a rescue tube or buoy (required for rescue) and other rescue equipment, nonswimming assists, and swimming rescues
- How to handle special situations, such as spinal injuries, rescue breathing, scuba rescue, open water guarding and rescue, search and recovery operations, and first aid procedures specific to the aquatic environment
- Lifeguard responsibilities and administration, including duties, rules, legal responsibilities, emergency procedures, reports, and pool maintenance
- Lifeguarding techniques
- Personal health and safety of lifeguards
- Job searches and additional training opportunities

Certification Requirements

Lifeguard certification is conducted by a certified YMCA lifeguard instructor. To be certified you must complete the course, scoring 80% or better on each section of a written or oral knowledge test, and perform all skills in a practical skills test. Certification may also include your instructor's subjective judgment about the maturity, attitude, and classroom participation you demonstrated during the course.

Your certification is reported to YMCA of the USA Program Certifications, 101 N. Wacker Dr., Chicago, IL 60606. The certification, which is renewable every 2 years through your local YMCA, is valid only if you keep your certifications in CPR and first aid current. If you are interested in becoming a YMCA lifeguard instructor, consult your local YMCA staff or YMCA of the USA Program Development (1-800-USA-YMCA).

OTHER YMCA AQUATIC SAFETY PROGRAMS

The YMCA offers three additional aquatic safety programs: the Aquatic Safety Course, the Aquatic Personal Safety and Survival Course, and the Aquatic Safety Assistant Course.

Aquatic Safety Course

This introduction to water safety requires no previous training. It is designed to be adapted to the needs of individuals in different aquatic settings, from a corporate fitness program to family backyard pool safety. Nonswimmers are encouraged to enroll and participate, to the extent that they are able, so they can learn about basic water safety.

The Aquatic Safety Course consists of 4 to 6 hours of classroom and water sessions and includes discussions of these topics:

- History and philosophy of the YMCA aquatic safety and lifeguard training programs
- Personal aquatic safety information
- Accident prevention principles
- Basic first aid and rescue breathing
- Nonswimming rescues

Oral or written tests are administered by the local YMCA.

Aquatic Personal Safety and Survival Course

This 8-hour course trains participants in personal safety and survival skills in and around aquatic environments. Classroom and pool sessions address

- the history and philosophy of YMCA aquatic safety,
- accident prevention principles,
- general aquatic information,
- personal aquatic safety information,
- basic survival skills and principles,
- nonswimming rescues, and
- basic first aid and rescue breathing.

To take the course, candidates must meet the following prerequisites:

- Be at least 11 years old.
- Be able to complete the following swimming test:
  a. Swim 300 yards, including 50 yards each of front crawl, breaststroke, elementary backstroke, inverted breaststroke (legs only), sidestroke left, and sidestroke right.
  b. Tread water for 2 minutes.
  c. Perform head-first and feet-first surface dives.

To receive a certificate of course completion, participants must score at least 80% on a written or oral knowledge test and demonstrate all skills on a performance test. The certificate of successful completion or participation in the course is issued by the local YMCA.

YMCA Aquatic Safety Assistant Course

The purpose of the YMCA Aquatic Safety Assistant Course is to present the knowledge and skills an individual needs to recognize and prevent aquatic risks and to assist a lifeguard in responding to an emergency such as an accident or injury. This 16-hour course trains assistants, coaches, and instructor candidates to

- recognize potential accidents or incidents and prevent them while teaching a class or leading a program

- recognize potential hazards related to the program and facility and eliminate them or communicate to someone in authority about them
- use and care for equipment properly
- recognize and report suspected child abuse
- assist lifeguards in keeping aquatic activities safe and in following their Y's emergency action plan and procedures, including managing the scene of an accident
- recognize distressed swimmers and try to help them with basic rescue techniques using swimming assists
- communicate the need for assistance for themselves or others as necessary
- protect themselves from personal injury while teaching
- serve as a good role model of Christian values and safe behavior

This certification does *not* include training in lifeguarding, so having an aquatic safety assistant in a program or class does *not* meet the requirement of having a certified lifeguard on duty. The certification only allows the person to assist a lifeguard during an emergency. Certification as an aquatic safety assistant also does not include instruction in how to teach or lead swimming or exercise classes. Such instruction must come through YMCA aquatic specialist instructor courses, for which the Aquatic Safety Assistant Course is a prerequisite.

To take the Aquatic Safety Assistant Course, candidates must meet the following prerequisites:

- Be at least 14 years old.
- Be able to complete the following swimming test:
  a. Swim 100 yards, any stroke.
  b. Tread water for two minutes.
  c. Perform a head-first or feet-first surface dive in four to six feet of water or submerge and touch the hand on the bottom of the pool in five feet of water.
- Have and maintain current CPR and first aid certifications (same as lifeguard prerequisites).
- Have the strength and maturity to assist in backboarding procedures.

The YMCA Aquatic Safety Assistant Course is conducted by a certified YMCA lifeguard instructor. To become certified as an aquatic safety assistant, participants must complete the course, score 80% or better on a written or oral knowledge test, and successfully perform all the skills in a practical skills test. Certification may also depend on the instructor's subjective judgment about participants' maturity, attitude, and classroom participation as shown during the course.

To keep this certification current, individuals must renew it every two years and keep their CPR and first aid certifications current. To renew the Aquatic Safety Assistant certification, participants must take the written and practical skills tests from a currently certified YMCA lifeguard instructor.

Review Questions

1. List several types of incidents that lead to drowning deaths or aquatic injuries.
2. What makes YMCA aquatic safety programs different from those of other organizations?
3. List 5 characteristics of a good lifeguard.
4. What are the certification requirements for the YMCA lifeguard course?
5. What other certifications must be maintained to keep Y lifeguard certification valid?

CHAPTER 2

Aquatic Personal Safety and Survival Skills

Aquatic activities are popular forms of recreation, but they do carry a degree of danger. You should know how to take care of yourself in the water, because accidents can happen even to good swimmers.

IN THIS CHAPTER YOU'LL LEARN HOW TO

- use a variety of techniques to stay afloat,
- perform surface dives and survival strokes,
- perform off-duty rescues
- understand physical conditions that may endanger swimmers,
- handle physical discomfort or risk from aquatic activities,
- follow safe boating procedures,
- stay safe when rafting or tubing,
- escape from a submerged vehicle, and
- rescue yourself or others who have fallen through ice.

STAYING AFLOAT

All people who work or play on or in the water owe it to themselves and to their companions to know how to stay afloat in deep water for an extended period. Doing this requires some knowledge of buoyancy and training in how to perform the survival float and how to tread water.

Buoyancy

Buoyancy is the ability to float in water. Three concepts can help you understand how the body floats: Archimedes' principle and specific gravity, vital capacity, and center of mass/center of buoyancy.

Archimedes' principle. When an object is lowered into water, it pushes away, or *displaces*, the water that was in that space. Whether the object floats or sinks depends on which is heavier, the object or the water it displaced. This is called Archimedes' principle.

A cubic foot of fresh water weighs 62.4 pounds. Any object that weighs more than that per cubic foot sinks in fresh water; if it weighs less per cubic foot, it floats. If the weight is equal to water, the object remains suspended between the surface and the bottom.

To make such comparisons easy, we use the concept of *specific gravity*, which is the ratio of the weight of an object to the weight of fresh water the object would displace if completely submerged. Table 2.1 lists the specific gravities of fresh water, salt water, and the major components of the body: bone, muscle, and fat.

Table 2.1 Specific Gravities of Water and Body Components	
Element	Specific gravity
Fresh water	1.0
Salt water	1.025
Bone	1.9
Muscle	1.085
Fat	.78 to .98

Something with a specific gravity higher than fresh water (1.0) will sink in fresh water; an object with a specific gravity lower than 1.0 will float. The same concept applies to salt water, but because salt water has a higher specific gravity of 1.025 (it weighs more than fresh water), objects are slightly more buoyant in salt water.

Notice in Table 2.1 that the specific gravities of bone and muscle are higher than 1.0, so bone and muscle alone would not float in fresh water. If you placed a bone with no visible fat in a pan of water, it would sink to the bottom of the pan.

People, however, are not made of bone and muscle alone. They also have body fat, with the amount varying from person to person. With a specific gravity of .78 to .98, fat will float in fresh water. So the more fat people have, the lower their specific gravities are, and the more buoyant they are in water. Most people have enough fat to help them stay afloat—only 1 person in 20 is unable to float.

Vital capacity. Another factor that influences buoyancy is vital capacity, the amount of air that the lungs can hold. For most people, vital capacity plays an important part in floating. By taking a big breath, you expand the volume of your chest, which lowers your specific gravity and makes you more buoyant, because air is much lighter than water. You can demonstrate the value of vital capacity by taking a deep breath and floating. Observe your position in the water. Then breathe out as much air as possible and float. What happened? With less air in your lungs, you either floated lower in the water or sank below the surface.

What this means is that you should breathe frequently to maintain your buoyancy; don't hold your breath until you are gasping for air. With greater buoyancy you'll be able to float and swim more efficiently.

Center of mass/center of buoyancy. Center of mass is the point around which your body's weight is evenly balanced. In most people it is located a few inches below the navel. The center of buoyancy, the point around which your body's weight will float, generally is located at chest level in the lungs. By knowing where these centers are, you can learn to balance your buoyancy and your stability around them.

You can change your center of buoyancy by adjusting your center of mass. Floating on your back, experiment by slowly raising your arms above your head and bending your knees. (If you move too quickly, you'll create momentum that will cause your feet to sink.) If you find that your legs sink in your floating position, it may help to raise your hands out of the water, moving more weight toward your head. Or bend your legs to bring your feet under your buttocks. These actions cause your center of mass to move toward your shoulders and your center of buoyancy to move toward your hips. These changes make your hips float to the surface.

Resting Stroke

The resting stroke makes use of your body's natural buoyancy to allow you to stay afloat with little effort or use of energy. Since Fred Lanoue developed his program for teaching the survival float in 1936, many variations on the technique have been experimented with and found to be successful.

The resting stroke technique is recommended for situations when you are in warm water and not wearing a personal flotation device (PFD). The method recommended for floating for a long period while wearing a PFD is called the *HELP position*, which is described on page 22.

The resting stroke lets you float in a relaxed position almost endlessly, even without the use of your legs and arms. The most common procedure is illustrated in Figure 2.1.

Figure 2.1

Resting stroke.

Here's how to do it: After taking a breath, let your body submerge, with your arms and legs relaxed and hanging down. Your back should be near the surface. This position will be easy to assume because the air in your lungs will lift your back up.

Hold your breath only as long as you feel comfortable. There is no need to wait until you desperately need a breath. When you decide to breathe, bring your arms close to the surface, separate your legs as you do when starting a scissors kick, and start exhaling. Press down on the water with your hands, complete the scissors kick, and lift your head above the water to breathe. Only your face should come out of the water. Take a quick breath and return to your relaxed starting position.

Because your head is submerged in the floating position, you will lose body heat while doing the resting stroke. In cold water and cold air temperatures, this heat loss can lead to hypothermia (described on p. 122). Heat loss is less of a concern if the water and surrounding air are warm.

Treading Water

Treading water, shown in Figure 2.2, is an important survival skill that should be mastered by everyone. When you tread water, your arms move in a wide in-and-out motion with your palms turned down at a 30- to 35-degree angle. This movement keeps constant water pressure against your hands and lets your body maintain its position in the water.

Figure 2.2

Treading water.

Several types of kicks can be used in treading water. For the single scissors kick, the same leg always goes forward and the other leg always goes backward. As the legs are brought together, they provide a strong upward lift. The double scissors kick is the same, except that the legs alternate their positions forward and back. The breaststroke kick performed vertically and the eggbeater, or rotary, kick (see Figure 2.3) provide the most consistent support of all the kicks, although they may be the most difficult for some people to perform. To do the eggbeater kick, alternating legs, you pull one heel toward your seat, turn your toes to the outside, and kick your leg around and to the front. This kick is very similar to the breaststroke kick, but the legs work alternately rather than both at once.

Figure 2.3

Eggbeater, or rotary, kick.

STROKES FOR SURVIVAL SITUATIONS

Several strokes can enable you to swim to safety in a survival situation efficiently, conserving your energy. Because these strokes should be performed with your head out of the water to try to maintain body heat and your arms underwater to conserve energy, the way they are performed in a survival situation differs from the techniques you may have learned in a swimming class.

In a survival situation in which you would need to swim a long distance, first try to find something to help you float—a piece of wood or some other buoyant object. Then decide whether your chances of survival are better if you swim or if you stay in one place and try to conserve body heat (see p. 22 for flotation positions that conserve body heat). Water under 70 degrees Fahrenheit quickly cools the body, putting you in danger of hypothermia (see p. 122).

Elementary Backstroke

The elementary backstroke (illustrated in Figure 2.4) is a very comfortable stroke for most swimmers. Because this stroke requires the head to be in the water, it is recommended for only short distances.

To do the elementary backstroke, initiate the kick by bending your knees, pulling your heels toward your seat and turning your toes out. As you bend your knees, pull your arms up your sides with elbows down and palms toward the body. Stretch your arms outward slightly above your shoulders. Then kick by whipping the legs out and around, then together, while pulling your arms back to your sides. You might use the following cues to coordinate your stroke: up, out, together.

Breaststroke

The breaststroke, a useful survival stroke in either calm or choppy water, is initiated from a front glide position in which your arms and legs are both fully extended (see Figure 2.5). Keep your head out of the water and look forward. Keeping elbows high, press your hands outward and downward, moving in a motion that resembles half of a heart. At the end of the pull, press your elbows toward your sides, bring your hands together in front of your chest, and reach again to the front.

To kick in the breaststroke, pull your heels toward your seat and turn your toes out to the sides. Kick the legs together in a circular motion. The coordination of the stroke is pull, kick, and glide.

Figure 2.4
Elementary
backstroke.

Figure 2.5
Breaststroke.

Sidestroke

The sidestroke, illustrated in Figure 2.6, should also be done with most of your head out of the water in a survival situation. To begin, assume a glide position on your side, with

Figure 2.6

Sidestroke.

the bottom arm stretched above your head in the water and the top arm along your side. Lean your head to the side with your ear in the water.

For the stroke, pull your bottom arm down toward your chest, elbow bent, and then turn the arm so the hand is palm up and stretch the arm back to the front. At the same time that you pull with the bottom arm, the top arm recovers. Then bend the elbow, reach with the top hand toward the opposite shoulder, and push the water toward your feet. The arms work in opposition, that is, while one is stroking, the other is recovering.

The kick follows the top arm: As the arm recovers, the legs recover; as the arm strokes, the legs kick. To kick, pull your heels toward your seat. Stretch your top leg forward and your bottom leg backward, then kick both legs together.

SURFACE DIVES

To get below the surface or away from danger, you may need to use a surface dive. This can be either a feet-first dive or an arm-over-arm dive. The feet-first dive is best used when you are not sure of the water depth or the presence of debris; if you strike something, the feet-first dive is less likely to lead to spinal injury than a head-first (arm-over-arm) dive.

Feet-First Dive

Follow these procedures to execute a feet-first surface dive, illustrated in Figure 2.7:

1. Begin from a vertical position.
2. Stretch one leg forward and one back. With one large kick, snap your legs together and push down on the water as you bring your arms to your sides. This should bring you up out of the water, and gravity will then pull you downward. Keep your body streamlined.
3. Use a wide motion to lift your arms over your head with palms facing up.
4. If you need to go even deeper, slide your arms back to your sides and repeat the upward lift.

Figure 2.7

Feet-first surface dive.

Arm-Over-Arm Dive

The arm-over-arm surface dive allows you to perform a head-first dive in a continuous motion. Depending on your ability and strength, you can do this dive in either a tuck or a pike position. Both are illustrated in Figure 2.8. The tuck position requires less strength because it shortens the distance between hips and feet. The pike position allows the legs to go higher out of the water, which speeds the rate of descent. Follow these steps:

1. As your right arm recovers from a crawl stroke, leave your left hand next to your left leg.
2. Reach down toward the bottom with your right hand while simultaneously ducking your head.
3. Pull your right hand back toward your right thigh.
4. Turn your palms down and sweep both hands toward the bottom. This helps lift your legs out of the water. Your hands and arms will end up over your head. Pull

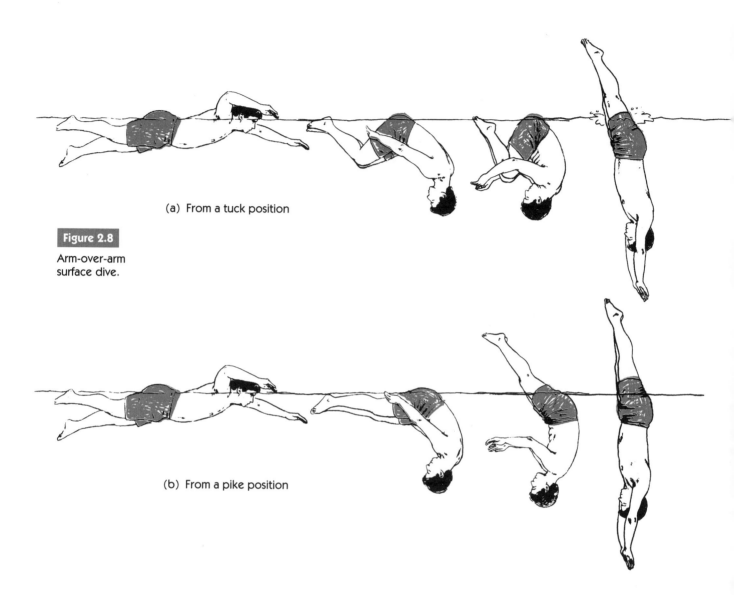

(a) From a tuck position

Figure 2.8

Arm-over-arm surface dive.

(b) From a pike position

both hands back to your thighs for a faster descent. Recover your hands above your head and pull to thighs again, if necessary.

SUBMERGE DEFENSE

A defense can be defined as any movement that lets you avoid being grabbed by a swimmer who is panicking. If you are on duty as a professional lifeguard, you take a piece of rescue equipment when you enter the water to assist a swimmer. But as a swimmer, you may be unaware of a trouble situation until the panicked swimmer grabs for you. Your ability to stay calm and react quickly will directly affect your safety.

Try to avoid being grabbed by a distressed swimmer by attempting rescue with a reaching or throwing assist (pp. 73 and 75). If you are in the water and a distressed swimmer grabs you, the best defense is to go limp and submerge. As the swimmer grabs onto someone to try to climb up for air, he or she will almost always immediately let go if you do this. However, if this is unsuccessful, take a quick breath, tuck your chin into your chest, push up on the swimmer's upper arm, and submerge. Push the swimmer away from you, and swim away (see Figure 2.9). Be sure not to surface too close to the person or you could find yourself in danger again.

Figure 2.9

Submerge defense.

OFF-DUTY RESCUES

Many YMCA lifeguards have asked the question "How can I rescue a distressed or near-drowning victim in situations in which I don't have equipment?" Such situations can occur during leisure time whenever a lifeguard is near water.

Of course, whenever possible, you should swim only in guarded areas. However, it's not always an option, especially during scuba, boating, surfing, water skiing, and other aquatic pursuits (unless they are conducted in a formal instruction program such as one that might be offered at a YMCA camp).

The simplest solution is to take a rescue tube or buoy and a pocket mask with you whenever you plan leisure activities around water. If space is limited in your car, boat, or other watercraft, consider taking an inflatable rescue tube. Currently two inexpensive models are available, one that can be inflated orally and one that uses a carbon dioxide cartridge for quick inflation.

You also can use the out-of-water and in-water nonswimming extension rescue procedures that you learn in this lifeguarding course, as well as wading and throwing assists (using a throw bag, ring buoy, or heaving line) for active victims (see chapter 6). Another possibility is a swimming extension rescue using a towel, canoe paddle, ring buoy, tree branch, spare tire, or other similar item.

Helping a passive victim is more difficult. If you should need to rescue a passive victim on the surface, remember that boaters, water skiers, and scuba divers may have some type of flotation device on them. If you have to rescue a victim who is not wearing a flotation device, take these steps:

- Swim around behind the victim, making sure to remain safely outside arm's reach.
- Check for spinal injury (see chapter 9). If the person does not seem to have a spinal injury, use a single or double armpit tow to bring the victim to a safe place where his or her airway, breathing, and circulation can be assessed and CPR begun if necessary.

Note: The YMCA conforms to the standards established by the Emergency Cardiac Care Committee of the American Medical Association, which specifies that rescue breathing should be started as soon as possible (here being as soon as the victim is contacted in deep water). However, if the rescuer doesn't have a rescue tube or buoy, assessment must wait until the victim is brought to pool side or into shallow water.

Victim assessment and rescue breathing can be accomplished in waist-deep water with the same technique used with a rescue tube in deep water and without a tube in shallow water.

PHYSICAL CONDITIONS THAT MAY ENDANGER SWIMMERS

As a swimmer you need to be aware of physical conditions that can cause you discomfort or put you at risk while swimming. Your ability to react correctly and calmly under these circumstances will greatly enhance your safety and enjoyment.

Panic

Panic is an emotional state in which someone is overcome by a sudden fear and loses the ability to help himself or herself. Panic usually occurs when a person is faced with a seemingly life-threatening emergency. For example, someone who gets a cramp while swimming and does not know what a cramp is or how to release it is likely to panic, which could lead to drowning. Panic is believed to be a major contributor to drowning accidents.

When you are in the water, practice the skills outlined in this chapter and throughout the book. Once they become second nature, you will have the tools to help yourself and others. In an emergency, take a deep breath, call on your knowledge of how to handle the situation, and move forward confidently. You can be in control of any situation.

Ear Squeeze

Ear squeeze is the pain you feel within your ear when you submerge in the water. The increased water pressure is greater in the outer ear than in the middle ear, which stretches the tympanic membrane (eardrum) inward, causing pain. To alleviate this problem, pinch off your nose, keep your mouth shut, and attempt to blow out through your nose gently. This action increases the pressure in the throat, which in turn opens the eustachian tube that connects the throat and middle ear, increasing the pressure in the middle ear. When the pressure on the outer ear and middle ear are equalized, the eardrum returns to its normal position and the pain stops.

Be sure to take time to equalize pressure in your ears when you descend in the water. The YMCA Scuba program recommends equalizing pressure at every 5 feet of descent or whenever necessary to relieve pain or discomfort. Failure to equalize could rupture the eardrum, causing potential hearing loss, loss of balance or orientation, and other complications. It is not safe to swim with such an injury until it is fully healed. It is also unwise to swim underwater when you have a cold or the flu. When your eustachian tubes are clogged, air cannot move through the tubes into the middle ear as you try to equalize and you could risk a serious ear injury.

Sinus Squeeze

The pressure associated with increasing water depth can cause pain in the sinus area as well as the ears. If you have a bad cold, your sinuses will already be swollen shut. This makes it difficult for your body to equalize the air pressure in your sinuses. Attempting to dive is not recommended when the sinuses are inflamed. Sometimes nose drops or decongestants can alleviate symptoms, but these remedies can wear off or cause drowsiness. It is best to stay on the surface when you have a severe cold, sinusitis, or any other inflammation of the sinuses.

Cramps

The actual process of how cramps occur is not fully understood. Cramps can be triggered by dehydration or by a lack of sodium (salt), calcium, potassium, or oxygen. The lack of oxygen is one of the most accepted theories for the occurrence of cramps in swimming.

Lactic acid builds up in the muscles as a result of the lack of oxygen and causes the muscle to contract beyond its normal range. When enough lactic acid accumulates, the muscle fibers contract and stop functioning, resulting in considerable pain. This condition is called *contracture*.

In the 1930s through the 1950s, cramps were blamed as the major cause of drownings, but they are not life-threatening if you remain calm. As in any situation, panic can cause a swimmer to drown. Most cramps occur in the calf, foot, or hand because they are the body parts most active in swimming. They are also the body parts farthest away from the heart, and as a result they receive oxygenated blood last, which increases the probability of a cramp.

If you experience a cramp, the first thing to remember is to stay calm. If you can, leave the water; it is much easier to release a cramp on land. If you must remain in the water, relax as much as possible.

To relieve the pain of a cramp, you first need to stretch the cramping muscle. The stretching should be slow and steady, not bouncy. Hold the stretch for as long as is comfortable. If the cramp is severe, the pain may initially get worse as you begin to stretch, but it will subside. Continue to stretch the muscle for the prescribed time. If the pain is still evident, continue stretching for an additional period.

After stretching the cramp, if you are still in the water, bend forward as if you were survival floating and massage the cramped muscle gently, massaging it toward the heart, not away from it. This will increase the blood flow to the area and bring more oxygen to the muscles, relieving the cramp.

Once you have released the cramp, don't go right back to swimming. Give the muscle time to recover. If you have been very active in warm weather, you may need to replace body fluids. If this is the case, stay out of the water to rest the cramping muscles, and drink plenty of water. Remember, returning to activity too soon will result in a speedy return of your cramp.

Stomach Discomfort

Most everyone has heard that you shouldn't go swimming for an hour after you eat or you'll get a stomach cramp. The time guideline may be common sense, but the warning is not particularly accurate. It appears that drownings that have occurred when people have gone swimming after a large meal have been the result not of cramping but of vomiting the meal and breathing in the vomit.

How soon you can go into the water after a meal depends on several factors:

- How much you ate
- What you ate
- Your physical condition
- How fatigued you are
- The water temperature
- How active you'll be in the water

After eating a large meal, most people don't feel like swimming or participating in any vigorous activity for an hour or more. This is nature's way of keeping the body quiet so that the digestive system can start the process of absorbing the food. Normally when you begin swimming, blood is diverted from your stomach to the muscles that need energy to maintain activity, which slows your digestive and absorption functions.

For young children it is usually wise to establish a minimum resting time between eating a meal and swimming. Older swimmers tend to regulate themselves well; if they feel uncomfortable, they get out of the water or slow their activity. All swimmers should recognize an uncomfortable feeling in the stomach as nature's warning and make appropriate decisions regarding their activity level.

BOATING SAFETY

Boating is a popular aquatic recreational activity, but it can be hazardous if you don't take some precautions and don't know what to do should you end up overboard. The following are some basics of safe boating.

Personal Flotation Devices

By federal law, a personal flotation device (PFD), such as a life jacket or vest, is required for each person on board any small craft or boat of open construction. The U.S. Coast Guard is the public agency that establishes minimum standards for PFDs.

Purchase only those personal flotation devices that bear the label "U.S. Coast Guard–approved." Other flotation devices on the market, designed to serve as teaching aids, are good for teaching situations and may be used as aids to assist swimmers, but they should not be relied on as lifesaving devices.

The Coast Guard approves five types of PFDs, as illustrated in Figure 2.10:

- Type I PFDs are used for off-shore vessels. Most commercial craft use these PFDs because they are the most buoyant, are good in rough waters, and can hold an unconscious person in an upright or slightly reclined position.
- Type II PFDs also turn unconscious people to safe positions. However, they are designed for use on inland waters where the water is calm and a speedy rescue is possible.
- Type III PFDs are classified as flotation aids. They do not right someone who is unconscious, but they are very comfortable for the wearer. Many water skiers use this type of vest.
- Type IV PFDs are throwable devices, such as boat cushions, ring buoys, and other devices designed to be held, not worn.

Type I

Type II

Type III

Figure 2.10

U.S. Coast Guard-approved PFDs.

Type IV

Type V

Child's Type II

- Type V PFDs are designed for special use. The label on the PFD will specify its approved uses. This category of PFD includes whitewater vests, board sailing or wind surfing vests, and work vests.

Heat Escape Lessening Posture

If you should fall out of a boat into the water far from land, your first concern should be keeping warm until help arrives. Immersion hypothermia, the cooling of the body from suspension in cold water, is dangerous and potentially life-threatening.

Don't remove your clothes in cold water to help you float. Your clothes serve as insulation against the cold water and help preserve your body heat. Your survival efforts will be aided by doing all you can to keep warm: keeping your head out of the water and protecting the front of your neck (near the carotid artery), your armpits, the front of your rib cage, and your groin. The heat escape lessening posture (HELP) was developed to assist you in protecting these four areas (see Figure 2.11). Wearing a PFD that is Coast Guard–approved will enable you to assume this position more easily and effectively than wearing an unapproved device.

The HELP position is accomplished in the following way. While wearing a PFD,

- float in a tuck position;
- squeeze your legs together, crossing them at the ankles;
- press your arms against your sides and hold the PFD across the chest; and
- keep your head above water.

Figure 2.11

HELP position.

When three or more people find themselves immersed in cold water, huddling in a group may help them survive longer (see Figure 2.12). Shared body heat and greater coverage of the heat loss areas, along with moral support, are the advantages of the huddle. The position, however, can be difficult to maintain.

Children are more susceptible to heat loss when immersed. Sandwiching the child between huddling adults will help conserve the child's body heat. The body heat generated by the group should cause the water in the area between them to be slightly warmer, thus prolonging the child's survival.

Rules for Boating

Safe boating in large part means using common sense, but it's easy when you're having fun to forget to follow some simple rules:

Figure 2.12

Huddle position.

- Be sure you know how to use your craft before you leave shore.
- Leave word with someone on shore as to when you are leaving, where you are going, and when you plan to return.
- Stay alert to weather conditions. Listen to a weather report before you leave and take a portable radio with you for periodic checks. If bad weather arises, quickly move to the nearest shore or safe harbor.
- Have everyone in the boat, including children, wear a Coast Guard–approved PFD.
- Don't stand up in a small boat.
- Don't allow rough play.
- Don't boat after dark.
- Don't overload your craft. Don't exceed the load limit on the boat's capacity plate, and be sure to distribute the load evenly.
- Anchor your boat only from the bow. A small boat can be swamped if the anchor is attached to the stern (rear).
- For any nonswimmer, have a swimmer also in the boat at all times.
- Return all equipment to the boathouse. Tell management if any equipment needs repair.
- Don't drink alcohol in or around boats.
- Attend a course on safe boating. Free courses are offered by volunteers from the Coast Guard Auxiliary, the Power Squadron, and the American Red Cross. To find the courses offered in your area, call the BOAT/U.S. Foundation CourseLine, 1-800-366-BOAT. Your local YMCA also may offer a safe boating course.

RAFTING AND TUBING

Rafting and tubing have become more and more popular as recreation in recent years. Lifeguards are rarely available for such activities, so you must take responsibility for your own safety. Keep the following guidelines in mind:

- Have each person wear a Coast Guard–approved PFD.
- Prepare before you go. Know the area you will be in—its dangers and its calm spots.
- Know and follow the local laws governing rafting and tubing. If you don't know them, contact the local conservation or park department.
- Be sure you have been trained to handle your raft or tube safely. If you have never rafted or tubed before, visit with an experienced person before starting your own expedition. Many park districts and outdoor or wilderness stores offer training or can suggest effective training programs.
- Check your equipment before entering the water.
- Be aware of other watercraft in the area.
- Carry bailers, sponges, extra paddles, a first aid kit, and other safety items.
- Avoid rafting or tubing after heavy rain.
- Avoid alcohol. You need your best judgment to remain safe.

If you end up in river rapids, walk through them if they aren't too strong by keeping your weight low in the water, with your legs apart to form a wide base of support. Don't stand up straight. If you find yourself in strong river rapids, remain calm. Roll onto your back and float downstream, feet-first to protect yourself from head injury. Once you have escaped the rapids, swim to shore. You might need to swim diagonally with the current, rather than directly against it.

AQUATIC SAFETY NEAR A DAM

Take special precautions when you swim or boat near a dam. There are several dangers:

- Shallow water below the dam can quickly become deep when the floodgates are opened. A wall of water is created as the water passes through the gates.
- Currents near hydroelectric power plants are strong enough to pull swimmers into and through the dam.
- Swimmers or boaters can be caught in debris or may be seriously injured by being pulled over a low-head dam and trapped in the current at its base (see Figure 2.13).

Figure 2.13

Current at the base of a low-head dam.

Illustrated by Ted Walke, Pennsylvania Fish and Boat Commission.

Cross section of lowhead dam

Backwash   Boil   Outwash

In water near a dam, look for instruction signs and obey them. If there are warning signals, act immediately. Stay away from floodgates or spillways, which should be marked with buoys and patrolled regularly. For your safety, make sure that you don't get too close to the dam.

EMERGENCY SITUATIONS

Few people know how to react if a vehicle goes underwater or if a person falls through ice. The following sections teach you what to do in both of these life-threatening situations.

Escaping From a Submerged Vehicle

Although it is not statistically likely that you will ever be involved in a submerged vehicle incident, knowing what action to take if you are is a key to survival. Remember that many drownings happen to people who never intended to go into the water.

Generally a vehicle that enters water from a height of 6 feet or less and lands on its wheels will float for an unpredictable time; but once the vehicle begins to sink, it will be underwater in less than a minute. Vehicles stay afloat longer if the windows are up, giving more time for escape or rescue. Once underwater, most vehicles sink at a steep angle, and they may come to rest on the roof.

Experts recommend that you not open a window as the vehicle descends until the pressure is equalized—when the car is completely submerged and filled with water—because water rushing into the car through the window will force you away from the escape route. You will not be able to get a door open until the pressure is equalized.

In any front-engine vehicle, an air pocket forms as the vehicle descends and is forced into the rear and possibly to the trunk area until the vehicle comes to rest. At that time, the air moves back into the passenger section. Usually the small size of the air pocket has no effect on the ability to open doors and windows.

Studies have shown that people wearing seat belts have a greater chance of surviving initial impact with water. However, after the impact you should unbuckle your belt. If the vehicle is floating in the water, wheels down, the best technique is to escape through an open window before the water rises to window level. If the vehicle sinks too quickly to escape, stay calm, move to the rear of the car to take advantage of the air pocket, and plan an escape by opening the nearest door or window once the pressure has equalized. If young children are in the car, prepare to push them out the opening before you exit.

Be aware that power windows do not operate once the car's engine stops. Car windows can be broken with a spring-loaded centering punch engaged at the bottom margin or with a hammer. If you drive in an area near water, you should keep one of these in the car at all times. The punch can be taped to the steering wheel column.

Before you attempt to rescue people in a submerged vehicle, call or have a bystander call for emergency assistance immediately. As you approach the vehicle, be aware that your clothes could get tangled on bent vehicle parts. If a vehicle has submerged with all the windows up, the best approach may be to break a side window and remove it from the frame. If you are trying to get someone out as the vehicle submerges, be aware of the force exerted by the water entering through the window.

Falling Through Ice

Although activities *in* the water become less enjoyable as the seasons change and the temperature cools, winter activities *on* the water draw many enthusiasts outdoors to enjoy skating, hockey, ice fishing, and the like. These activities can be fun and safe as long as participants know the areas they are using and are familiar with the conditions that will make each area safe. It is least risky to use monitored recreation areas where flags are used to signal the conditions of the ice (with red meaning "not safe" and green "safe").

Ponds, small lakes, and slow-moving streams are generally the safest for ice activities. The ice should be frozen to at least 4 inches before the area is used. Newly formed ice isn't as strong as older ice; however, in the spring, even the older ice begins to lose its consistent thickness with the spring thaw.

If you or someone with you breaks through the ice, follow these guidelines:

1. Stay calm; don't try to climb out immediately. Thrashing will make it more difficult to escape.
2. Kick behind you to keep your body near the surface in a horizontal position.
3. Extend yourself as far as you can on unbroken ice while keeping your lower body as close to horizontal as possible.
4. Work your way carefully onto the ice. If the ice breaks again, keep using this method until you reach stronger ice. Once you are out, stay low and distribute your weight over as much surface area of ice as possible as you move to safety (see Figure 2.14).

Figure 2.14

Kicking to avoid being pulled under the ice.

If you try to help someone who has fallen through the ice, be careful not to fall through yourself. Stay low and try to find something like a branch, rope, or a board to extend to the person in the water (see Figure 2.15). If no equipment is available, lie flat on the ice as far away from the hole as possible and grab the person's wrist. Encourage her or him to stay calm and kick to get into a horizontal position. Then you can pull the person up onto the ice. Remember to stay flat on the ice and slide to safety. Once the person is off of the ice, get to shelter immediately and treat for hypothermia (see p. 123).

Figure 2.15

Rescuing someone who has fallen through the ice.

Review Questions

1. What is Archimedes' principle and how does it relate to buoyancy?
2. Why is it easier to float in salt water than in fresh water?
3. What is vital capacity? How does it affect buoyancy?
4. Where is a person's center of buoyancy?
5. Name 2 skills that will allow you to stay afloat with minimum effort.
6. Name 3 strokes you can use to move safely with minimal use of energy.
7. Describe the submerge defense and when it is used.
8. What emotional state commonly leads to drowning?
9. What causes ear and sinus squeeze? How can you avoid them?
10. How do you relieve a leg cramp in the water?
11. How do you decide how long to wait after a large meal before swimming?
12. Describe the 5 types of PFDs.
13. If you are immersed in cold water, should you remove your clothes to improve your chance of survival?
14. Describe the HELP position and why it is so valuable.
15. List 5 safe boating rules.
16. List the 9 guidelines for safe rafting and tubing.
17. Why is it dangerous to swim near a dam?
18. When should you open a door or window to escape from a sinking vehicle?
19. After a vehicle sinks, where is the best place for passengers to position themselves?
20. What are the 4 guidelines to follow if you fall through ice?

CHAPTER 3

Lifeguarding Procedures

In the YMCA lifeguard training course you learn many skills to help you assist and protect swimmers in an aquatic environment. This chapter helps you understand the important responsibilities you accept as a lifeguard and provides valuable procedures for meeting those responsibilities.

IN THIS CHAPTER YOU'LL LEARN ABOUT

- ■ the characteristics of a successful lifeguard,
- ■ the responsibilities and role of a lifeguard,
- ■ the decision-making skills you'll use daily as a lifeguard, and
- ■ how to perform the duties of a lifeguard.

THE SUCCESSFUL LIFEGUARD

The best lifeguards are good at what they do because of particular personal characteristics. They are people-oriented professionals who share their aquatic abilities to enable others to safely enjoy water activities. A successful lifeguard

- cares about others,
- is strong and fit,
- is a good swimmer,
- is a responsible person,
- knows how and when to have fun, and
- wants to help others.

Are these characteristics true of you? If so, you are on your way toward becoming a lifeguard that other swimmers will look up to. If not, think carefully about whether the job of a professional lifeguard is one that you want to pursue.

Once you've learned lifeguarding skills, most of what will determine your success as a lifeguard is your attitude. In this section we'll look at the attitude a successful lifeguard presents, the physical conditioning necessary, the knowledge required, and the equipment the well-prepared guard brings to any work situation.

Attitude

You must have the right attitude to be a successful lifeguard. Do you really care about people? Are you ready to take on responsibility for the safety of others?

You give managers and patrons clues to your attitude and work ethic by the way you behave in both work and social situations. The image you present greatly influences how much respect observers have for you. Whatever your intentions are, the patrons of your facility will get their impression of your attitude from what they see and hear as you interact with them and with other patrons, peers, and staff. You will always be regarded as a leader, so lead others at your facility by your example:

- Look professional.
- Be well groomed.
- Be punctual.
- Follow the rules. (You can't expect others to follow them if you don't!)
- Be alert at all times.
- Avoid gossiping, joking around, or reading while you're on duty.
- Be courteous; avoid shouting or arguing.
- Direct questions for which you don't know the answer to a supervisor.
- Never report for your shift under the influence of alcohol or drugs.
- Do not abuse your authority.
- Maintain control of your assigned area.
- Cooperate with fellow lifeguards—you are a team.
- Be familiar with your area and its potential hazards.
- Try to prevent accidents before they occur.

Using plain common sense and courtesy will go a long way toward demonstrating that you want to serve patrons and that you are worthy of their respect and trust. It will make your lifeguarding service pleasant, satisfying, and rewarding.

Physical Conditioning and Wellness

By doing a good job, you will help prevent accidents that could require your rescue skills. But when you do need to use them, you need the strength and endurance to carry out the rescue. Regular exercise is vital to maintaining your physical conditioning. The best exercise for a lifeguard is swimming. Try lap swimming, stroke drills, and water games to help you build and maintain your strength, endurance, breath control, agility, and skill at the levels essential for effective lifeguarding.

Your attentiveness, vigilance, and fitness are crucial to the safety of those who use your facility. Your lifestyle will influence these areas of your preparation. Take some time to evaluate your lifestyle—your personal way of life. The lifestyle you choose affects your social, spiritual, intellectual, physical, and emotional wellness.

Lifestyle Assessment

Here are some questions to help you assess your lifestyle.

1. Do you have good personal relationships?
2. Do you balance your needs with the needs of others?
3. Do you have a purpose to your life—a goal?
4. Are you in good physical condition?
5. Do you regularly spend time doing some kind of physical fitness activity?
6. Do you eat healthy foods?
7. Do you get 7 or 8 hours of sleep every night?
8. Are you sensitive to the feelings of others?
9. Do you control your emotions effectively?
10. Are you overweight?
11. Are you underweight?
12. Do you smoke? Drink? Take drugs?

If you answered no to some of Items 1 through 9 and yes to some of Items 10, 11, and 12, you may want to consider some changes in your lifestyle. The changes you decide on could be important not only to the patrons of your facility but also to your personal development.

What changes would you like to make in your lifestyle?

Personal Equipment

As a lifeguard, you will need certain equipment to carry out your job and to be comfortable while on duty. Most of the equipment you will need is inexpensive. Some of it may be provided by your employer, but you must take the initiative to have the appropriate lifeguarding equipment with you at all times when you are on duty.

Checklist of Personal Equipment

Every Lifeguard

_____ Appropriate swimsuit

_____ Identifiable shirt

_____ Towel

_____ Whistle

_____ Rescue pack

_____ Rescue tube or buoy

_____ Aquatic shoes (optional)

Outdoor Facility Lifeguard

_____ Hat or visor

_____ Sunglasses

_____ Sunscreen or sunblock

_____ Water bottle

_____ Cold weather gear

_____ Rain gear

_____ Insect repellent

Open Water Lifeguard

_____ Binoculars

_____ Swim fins

_____ Mask and snorkel

_____ PFDs

You should always report for work properly attired in a *swimsuit* that is comfortable and practical. An *identifiable shirt* is important so that patrons can identify you as a lifeguard and to protect yourself from the sun if you are working outdoors.

The well-prepared guard also has a *towel* at the station. You may need this towel as a rescue aid. Or you may need to towel off after being in the water. (Your towel can also reduce the embarrassment of a patron who loses a suit after diving or going down the water slide!) And of course a towel helps pad the seat on your lifeguard stand.

Every lifeguard needs a *whistle*, preferably on a wrist strap to keep it close at hand. Your whistle is your prime communication tool; you may even want to have two or three whistles at your disposal. Test your whistle before you go on duty to make sure it's working. We recommend that you not use other guards' whistles; germs and viruses can be transmitted through such shared implements.

One thing you should *not* wear when lifeguarding is sharp or loose jewelry. This includes jewelry for pierced parts of the body. If you have to rescue someone, such jewelry can pose a danger to the victim or to you.

You need to always be prepared to begin emergency first aid. Your *rescue pack*, including protective equipment—a pocket mask (see pp. 116 and 149), surgical gloves, gown, and goggles—and minor first aid supplies, is essential. You need the protective equipment to protect yourself from the transmission of blood-borne diseases (see pp. 114-117). You may want to put these items in a fanny pack to keep them at your fingertips on land. During water rescues, be sure to bring your pocket mask.

Always have a *rescue tube* or *buoy* with you. This equipment is essential for any water rescue you might be called on to perform. Protect the extra line from the rescue tube by holding it in your hand, so it can't get tangled on the chair.

Many lifeguards work in *aquatic shoes*, which can be worn in or out of the water. On the deck, they help protect your feet from hot and irregular surfaces and from scrapes, cuts, and stones; they also provide additional traction on slippery surfaces. In the water, the shoes do not interfere with your ability to swim, and in open water they can protect your feet from unseen dangers.

If you are a lifeguard outdoors, you are exposed to the harmful effects of the sun. You'll want a wide-brimmed *hat* or *visor* to protect you from the sun's rays and from the glare of the sun off of the water. *Sunglasses* also help cut down on glare and reduce your blind spots; in addition, they protect your eyes from damage by ultraviolet rays. (Use them indoors as well when there's lots of glare.) When you choose sunglasses, look for a pair that filters out 99% to 100% of both UV-A and UV-B rays. Lens colors of gray, brown, or amber and polarized lenses can help reduce glare and eye fatigue.

Your sun protection will be complete if you add a *sunscreen* or *sunblock* to your equipment. The American Cancer Society recommends a sun protection factor (SPF) rating of at least 15. Remember, you are getting not only direct sun rays but also reflected sun. Reapply sun protection frequently during your shift, especially if you have been in the water.

Every day, especially on hot, sunny days, bring a filled *water bottle* to work with you, and drink water regularly to keep from becoming dehydrated. Other days will not be bright or sunny. Cool temperatures, wind, and rain can make you miserable if you aren't prepared. Have a *sweatshirt* and *sweatpants* available for cold days and *rain gear* (a coat, slicker, or rainsuit) for rainy days.

Insect repellent should also be a part of your equipment. You don't want anything to interfere with your ability to concentrate on monitoring the swimming area assigned to you. Using repellent may help you avoid the discomfort of multiple insect bites and swarming gnats or mosquitoes.

If you are lifeguarding on the open water—a river or lake or the ocean—you will need *binoculars* and *swim fins* because of the bigger area to be patrolled. With binoculars you can scan your area for trouble. If rescue is required, fins will cut down on the time it takes to reach a victim. (Fins also help speed underwater rescue in pools with diving wells.)

Other equipment needed for open water lifeguarding includes a *mask* and *snorkel* to make searching underwater for victims easier and *PFDs* if you are required to use a boat for patrolling or rescuing.

Get a special bag to carry your lifeguarding equipment. Having this equipment will make you well prepared for duty.

LIFEGUARD RESPONSIBILITIES

Your primary responsibility as a lifeguard is to protect the safety of all swimmers in your area: first by preventing accidents and second by responding to an emergency quickly and efficiently to minimize the danger to those involved. You meet this responsibility by

- having the skills in accident prevention, decision making, and rescuing to do your job,
- being in good enough physical condition to use your skills,
- knowing about your area of responsibility,
- being able to communicate that knowledge to your patrons, and
- enforcing the rules.

In addition to the skills and knowledge you must develop to be a good lifeguard, you must accept responsibility for your actions. As a professional lifeguard, you are part of a highly trained team, and your actions reflect on your whole organization, including your co-workers. Swimmers who come to your facility will notice your behavior whether you are on or off duty.

When you accept the responsibility of being a lifeguard, you also accept the legal and moral consequences of your actions and decisions. This is not a responsibility to be taken lightly. When you agree to protect the public's safety, you are accountable for your knowledge and your actions. (See chapter 12 for more on a lifeguard's legal obligations.)

As a professional lifeguard, you must make the following duties habit:

- Report to work on time as scheduled. Be in uniform and at your position when your shift begins.
- Have the appropriate equipment at your station (see p. 31).
- Check your area for hazardous conditions when you arrive at your station.
- Be professional, alert, courteous, and diplomatic.
- Stay alert to observe signals from other guards.
- Know and practice the proper emergency procedures for your area.
- Avoid socializing while on duty.
- Scan your area at all times.
- Enforce all facility rules. Be courteous but firm. Report a persistent problem to the head guard or manager.
- When enforcing a rule, briefly explain the reason behind the rule as well as the danger the rule infraction presents. Remember that your first responsibility remains protecting swimmers in your assigned area.
- Keep patrons from congregating on walk areas around lifeguard stands.
- Refer detailed inquiries to the head guard or manager.
- Safeguard the lives of your patrons first, but also ensure their comfort and pleasure. Don't tolerate recklessness or rough play.
- In outdoor facilities, clear all swimmers from the water during an electrical storm.
- Keep the swimming area clean and ready for inspection at all times.
- In open water areas, be alert for dangerous marine life.
- If you are working at open water, be familiar with bottom conditions and knowledgeable about the use of small craft for rescue.
- Know how to use all lifeguarding, rescue, and first aid equipment, and keep it ready and in good repair.
- Practice rescue skills regularly.
- Secure the area by locking all doors and gates when a lifeguard is not on duty.

CHILD ABUSE PREVENTION GUIDELINES

Child abuse, which includes nonaccidental physical injury, neglect, sexual molestation, and emotional abuse, has become a critical national concern. It is important that you, as an employee, never abuse children yourself or become involved in a situation in which you could be accused of abuse. To assure this, follow these commonsense suggestions:

- Don't ever be alone with a child unobserved by other staff.
- Don't socialize with or become involved in activities (babysitting, weekend trips) outside of your job with children who are patrons.
- Don't ever use physical punishment.
- Don't verbally or emotionally abuse children.
- Don't ever deny a child necessities, such as food or shelter.

Your employer should give you more training in guidelines for child abuse prevention and in procedures related to reporting signs of child abuse. Appendix A contains the "Child Abuse Identification and Prevention: Recommended Guidelines for YMCAs."

DECISION MAKING

For every decision you make, there is a consequence. For instance, say you are driving and see your gas gauge is near empty. You can decide either to fill up at the nearest gas station or to try to make it to your destination on the gas you have. If you fill up, it will cost you some money, but you won't have to worry about running out of gas on a deserted road. If you don't fill up, you could end up on foot!

The Decision-Making Model

As you make a decision, systematically follow some simple steps to ensure that you have considered the possible consequences. The *PACA* model may help you:

- **P:** What is the *problem* or situation?
- **A:** What are the *alternatives*?
- **C:** What are the *consequences* of each alternative, positive and negative?
- **A:** What is the *action* or decision?

Learn the acronym *PACA* to remember the steps. Now try this exercise to sharpen your decision-making skills.

Decision-Making Exercise

On a piece of paper, describe a situation in which you were faced with an important decision. Using that example, answer the following:

- Describe the problem or situation.
- List the ways you can resolve the problem or situation. Try to list at least three.
- List the advantages and disadvantages of each alternative.
- Make your decision and write a brief justification. Explain how you plan to follow through on your decision.

Preparation

Because each of us is responsible for the decisions we make, we need to think through what may happen as a result of our decisions. This is especially true when you take on the role of a lifeguard. Choosing to intervene and the action you take may mean the difference between someone's safety and a serious injury or death.

As a lifeguard you may have little time to make critical decisions. Often you'll have only seconds to respond. This fact makes it important to think through what to do in certain situations *before* you need to take action. The emergency drills and in-service training at your facility will help prepare you, but it is also important that you, personally, consider what to do in given situations. For example, how would you react if someone

- broke a minor rule that might endanger someone else's safety, like sitting on a ladder or running on the deck?
- looked frightened, unsure, or tired while swimming or diving?
- was reported missing?
- was breaking a major rule, perhaps pushing or dunking another patron?

When you think about what to do, it's not enough to tell yourself, "I'd just talk to him" or "I'd blow my whistle and ask her to get out of the pool." In the real-life situation, you might find you had forgotten to prepare for crucial actions. You need instead to know each step you would take and what you would say. Try this system of accident prevention to guide you in planning ahead.

Q-1-2 Accident Prevention System

As a lifeguard, you are always watching for potential problems in order to act on them before they become emergencies. But if you have to intervene over and over again, it becomes annoying to both you and the patrons. So how can you enforce the rules without blowing your whistle constantly?

One solution is to learn and use the Q-1-2 system, which works with children and adults alike. There are three advantages to using this system:

- It helps you be consistent and fair.
- It reduces the stress and emotion of enforcing rules.
- It allows you to remain focused on your assigned area.

Let's look at each step of this three-part system.

Q: Question. The process begins before someone actually violates a rule or does something potentially dangerous. You will frequently notice people who appear to be preparing to do something that might put them or someone else in danger, like one of these:

- A person walks very tentatively to the edge of the diving board or deep end.
- A swimmer starts across the pool but then returns, struggling and gasping for air.
- Someone floats a kickboard a few feet from the deck and appears to be preparing to jump onto or over it.
- A patron on the deck says to another, "Race you to the deep end."
- Someone is sneaking up behind another person.
- A person is walking faster than normal.

Although no one in these situations has violated a rule or done anything dangerous, the potential is clear. The first step, Q, is to ask the person a question. Ask him or her to come stand beside you, then ask your question without looking away from your assigned area or having to shout.

Questions are used not to accuse but to help make sure people have enough information about the situations they are in. The following questions might be useful in the scenarios just described:

- Have you ever jumped off the board before? Can you swim across the pool? Would you show me?
- Have you ever had swimming lessons? Can you stand up in that depth?
- Were you going to jump on the kickboard? Do you know what would happen if you landed on it?
- How are you going to race? In the water? On the deck?
- Were you going to push the person you were sneaking up on?
- Did you know we have a rule against running on the deck? Do you know why?

Sometimes the question itself gets the point across. However, be sure you listen to the answer. If it does not indicate that the person is aware of the potential problem, give more information or instructions:

- You need to be able to swim across the swimming pool before jumping off the diving board. Wait until the break and I'll let you try.
- Maybe you should swim in the shallow end for now.
- Do not jump on or over the kickboard.
- There seem to be too many people in the pool for you to race now.
- You cannot push (dunk, splash) another person, even if it's your friend and you are playing a game.
- The deck is wet. Please walk a little slower.

Q Step Key Points

- Watch for situations where you think someone is about to do something unsafe or against pool rules.
- Ask the person to come to where you are.
- Ask a question to determine if the person was about to do something unsafe or against the rules.
- Give more information or instruction.
- Watch your area of responsibility at all times.

1: Warning. The second step of the system is used when you see someone do something unsafe or against pool rules. First, call the person to your side so you do not have to shout or look away from the water. Next, tell the person what you saw. This may sound silly; what you saw might have been obvious. But people sometimes don't realize what they have just done. Also, you want to be certain the person knows what you are warning her or him about.

Because this will be the offender's one and only warning, use simple, direct statements using this format.

- I saw . . .
- That is . . .
- Please . . .

Here are some examples of how this would work:

- *I saw* you jump off the side of the diving board. *That is* dangerous because it is too near the deck. *Please* jump off the end of the board.
- *I saw* you running. *That is* unsafe because the deck is wet. *Please* walk.
- *I saw* you dive into shallow water. *That is* very dangerous because you may hit your head and injure your neck. *Please* dive only in the deep end.
- *I saw* you chewing gum in the pool. *That is* unsafe because you may choke. *Please* get rid of the gum.
- *I saw* you enter the pool without taking a shower. *That is* against our pool rules because it makes the water dirty. *Please* shower before entering the pool.

Always make simple, direct statements, without emotion. They are all statements of fact and do not need discussion. People will often want to argue in their defense, but try to avoid long discussions. You can listen, but maintain your focus on the water. Make it clear to the one being given the warning that if the undesirable behavior is repeated, you will have to ask the person to leave or to take a time-out (see next section).

---

1 Step Key Points

- State the warning using "I saw . . . ," "That is . . . ," and "Please . . ." statements.
- Don't argue with the patron.
- Watch your area of responsibility at all times.
- Make it clear that a repetition of the undesirable behavior is not acceptable and may mean the patron must leave or take a time-out.

2: Time-Out. If an adult repeats the behavior you have warned about, inform someone in management so he or she can ask the patron to leave the pool area (see below). With children, direct them to take a time-out from the pool instead. Giving a time-out means removing the child from the water and from the company of others to a chair for a short period. (Whether a teen is given time-out depends on your facility's guidelines and your own judgment.)

Again call the offender to your side. Then, without emotion, say, "I saw you run (push, jump off the side of the board) again. Please go to the time-out chair for 5 minutes. Then come back to see me."

The purpose of time-out is not public humiliation but to have the child think about proper behavior. The time-out chair should be away from the edge of the pool and out of the sun but in sight of a lifeguard or other staff member. It would be good to have the pool rules posted in the time-out area so the offender can think about what he or she should be doing more than what was done wrong.

Keeping track of the time should be the responsibility of the child, not the lifeguard. An easy way to assist in time-keeping is to give the youngster an inexpensive plastic stopwatch or kitchen timer. Start the watch or timer and hand it to the child with instructions to bring it back when it says 5:00 (or whatever time you choose).

When a child returns to you from the time-out chair, ask for a description of what to do in the future in the same situation. Ask why what you recommended is better. (Basically, you are asking for a repeat of the warning you gave.) If the person cannot answer appropriately, explain the warning and ask for it to be repeated to you.

---

2 Step Key Points

- Ask an adult to leave the pool area.
- Send a child to the time-out chair with a timer for a specified period.
- Ask a child following the time-out to tell you what he or she should do in the future in the same situation.

Asking a patron to leave. If an adult performs an undesirable behavior after a warning, or if a child does so after one or more time-outs, inform management so the head guard, manager, or assistant manager can meet with the patron and ask her or him to leave the premises voluntarily. If a minor is involved, the parent or guardian should be contacted. File an incident report afterward. To ensure consistency among lifeguards and the support of management, the issue of dismissing people from the facility should be discussed and procedures determined at staff meetings.

What if a child repeats the same behavior after a time-out? Every facility will have different rules, so be sure you know the steps your facility has established to enforce them consistently. However, unlike before, every repeated behavior need not be treated the same way. Not showering before swimming may earn a time-out; dangerous behavior may merit removal from the area.

Exceptions. The Q-1-2 system is designed to be fair and consistent, but exceptions will arise. The system is only a tool—you should use it, not allow it or swimmers to use you. Your judgment should always overrule the system when needed.

For example, a swimmer may do several different things that merit warnings but never repeat the same behavior to earn a time-out. Explain to the child that you have seen the several offenses and you want the child to take a time-out. After the child returns from time-out, ask for a list of the things that have gotten warnings.

A regular young patron who receives a warning one day and repeats the behavior the next day should go to time-out without a new warning. You may reasonably hold higher expectations for those who use a facility regularly.

Remember, regardless of what occurs, maintain a professional attitude. Treat patrons courteously and focus on the behavior to be corrected, not the individual. *Never* shout or use abusive language or physical violence.

HOW TO GUARD

The quality of any facility is due in large part to the commitment management makes to its patrons and staff. Most facility managers are committed to providing a safe and fun environment for patrons, ensuring that

- there are enough lifeguards on duty to serve the patrons,
- the lifeguards are certified, and
- lifeguards are positioned to assist swimmers.

The capacity of the facility is important in determining the number of lifeguards needed on duty. Each facility should have a minimum of one certified lifeguard on duty when it is open. Beyond that, state and local ordinances prescribe supervision requirements, and many facilities set their own stricter standards. These standards should be based on the size and shape of the pool, the number of swimmers, the activity in the pool, glare from the sun, and the number of high-use or high-risk areas.

The management is also likely to divide the facility into zones for particular activities, such as diving, wading, and perhaps ball playing. These zones help both patrons and lifeguards know what behavior is appropriate for each area.

The management of your facility should also make a commitment to you and provide a safe working environment. They ought to have completed the planning necessary to ensure that emergency procedures are established, equipment is available and in good repair, and lifeguards are stationed in appropriate areas to reduce accidents. Such preventative steps help protect patrons from injury and the facility and lifeguard from liability in the case of an accident (see chapter 12 for your legal responsibilities as a lifeguard). The management must also ensure that its policies and procedures protect your safety. You, then, must meet your duty to provide professional lifeguard services.

Supervision Systems

It is important that you know what area of the facility you are responsible for at all times. If just one person on a large staff neglects his or her area, a serious accident may be the result.

A number of factors influence what is considered a proper supervision system:

- Size and shape of the facility
- Demographics of the population using the facility
- Number of people in the water

- Number of lifeguards available
- Aquatic experience of swimmers and guards
- Environmental conditions
- Types of activities
- Positioning of guards

The most common systems are entire-area coverage or zone coverage. An emergency coverage plan should also be formulated.

Entire-area coverage. In entire-area coverage, a single lifeguard supervises the entire swimming area. The system works best when the swimming area is small and there are few swimmers. Entire-area coverage has both advantages and disadvantages:

Advantages

Few lifeguards are required.

The lifeguards understand their responsibilities.

Disadvantages

Lifeguards may be responsible for a large area.

Lifeguards tend to concentrate on boundaries rather than entire swimming area.

Lifeguards get little change of pace.

Although entire-area coverage is suitable for small pool settings with no obstructions, it would be difficult to use in a large, complex facility. If it becomes necessary to cover a large swimming area in this manner, consider closing some sections of the facility and concentrating the swimmers in a manageable area. When a single guard is on duty, additional trained staff need to be available to assist in emergency situations.

Zone coverage. In zone coverage, the swimming area is broken into smaller units, or zones, with one lifeguard responsible for each. The zones overlap to assure complete coverage (see Figure 3.1 for an example).

Several factors should be considered in designating zones for a facility:

- Zones should not require a lifeguard to scan more than 180 degrees. Some state codes are more restrictive, limiting guards to scanning less than 90 degrees.

Figure 3.1

Example of zone coverage.

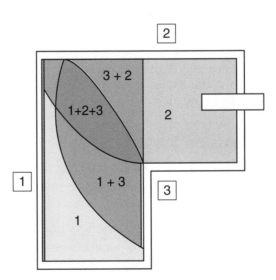

- Zones should minimize blind spots.
- High-risk areas should overlap into the areas of responsibility for two guard positions, ensuring double coverage.

Zone coverage is usually accompanied by a rotation system, discussed later in this section.

Zone coverage has its own advantages and disadvantages:

Advantages

Guards concentrate on limited areas.

There is double coverage in overlap areas.

Rotation keeps lifeguards refreshed.

Guards can interact with patrons more easily.

Disadvantages

More lifeguards are required.

Confusion about areas of responsibility may result in areas being unguarded.

This system allows the greatest flexibility for management and the greatest definition of area for lifeguards.

Emergency coverage.   Every facility needs an emergency coverage plan. Whenever there are two or more lifeguards and one must enter the water, the other lifeguards on duty must shift their responsibilities to cover larger areas. The guards remaining out of the water will probably have to move to new positions to cover the pool effectively and to perform emergency procedures. If your facility uses entire-area coverage, there must be assistance nearby so you can call for help in an emergency.

All lifeguards should know the procedures for emergency coverage. Management is responsible for seeing that all staff are aware of their responsibilities, and an emergency coverage diagram is to be posted. If you or other lifeguards are unsure of your responsibilities, ask. Your preparation could prevent an injury or accident.

Techniques for Guarding

Following a system when you guard ensures that you thoroughly check your assigned area. Here are several helpful techniques.

Guarding bottom to top.   This technique is an important tool for pool lifeguards. Guarding from the bottom to the top means being aware of the bottom of the pool each time you scan your area. It is tempting to look only at the people on top of the water, but it may be the people under the water who need your assistance. Each time you scan your area, visually check the bottom of the area you have been assigned.

Guarding the surface.   If you are lifeguarding in an open water area, do not use the bottom-to-top procedure. Because for the most part you'll be unable to see below the surface, concentrate your efforts strictly on the top.

Scanning.   Cover your assigned area by scanning it in a systematic, sweeping pattern. Observe the size, swimming proficiency, comfort, and facial expressions of swimmers in the water to determine what course of action would be effective in the event of an emergency (see chapter 5 for more on victim identification) or rule infraction (see chapter 4 for more on rules).

Your goal is to scan your entire area in 10 seconds and to strive to be able to respond to help a swimmer in distress in 10 seconds or less. This is called the *10 × 10 reaction*. To continue to scan in 10-second intervals, you must stay alert and attentive; even a brief distraction can cause you to miss important information that might prevent an accident or aid a victim.

In zone coverage, be sure to look at the lifeguard in the station next to yours at the beginning and end of each scanning sweep. This visual contact will help both of you feel confident that help is nearby. You will also be able to keep track of potential problems by communicating with that guard. Include the area beneath your lifeguard chairs in your scan; that high-risk area is sometimes difficult to monitor.

Using zones.   The key to using zone coverage successfully is each guard's knowing the area assigned to every lifeguard station in the facility. Management should post a diagram of the zone coverage system so you can learn the zones and any accompanying high-risk areas or blind spots. Pay extra attention to the high-risk areas (see pp. 52-59 for common high-risk areas); your vigilance will pay off. If you have a blind spot in your area, ask your supervisor if you may adjust your position to make that section more visible to you. If that is not possible, ask the manager about making additional coverage arrangements.

Guarding Guidelines

Follow these guidelines to ensure that you are covering the swimming area appropriately:

- Guard bottom to top in pools.
- Guard the surface in open water.
- Strive to achieve the 10 × 10 reaction.
- Scan your area continually.
- Start and end each scan with a visual check of the adjacent guard.
- Maintain vigilance.
- Know every lifeguard station area.
- Pay extra attention to high-risk areas.

Rotation Systems

When there are two or more lifeguards, it is a good idea to rotate periodically. Rotation relieves the boredom of watching the same area for an entire day, which keeps guards alert, and lets the management easily shift zone responsibilities when necessary. Rotation also distributes the most and least enjoyable areas among all guards.

Most rotation systems are set up on a time schedule. A lifeguard returning from break usually initiates the rotation, temporarily putting one extra guard on duty until the rotation is complete. Between rotation cycles, the guard who rotates off duty gets a short break. In some facilities the guard may be rotated not to a break but to another task, such as picking up trash or checking chemical levels.

Staff may also be rotated at a prearranged signal. This type of rotation is usually set in motion by a change in the number of swimmers in an area. The signal should be given only by the head lifeguard or another guard assigned to that duty by the management. An individual guard should not make such a rotation decision.

Rotation systems can be designed in different ways. Figure 3.2 illustrates a generic approach to rotation triggered by a guard returning from break.

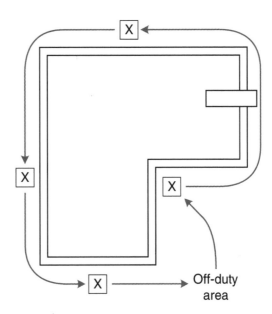

Figure 3.2

Example of a
rotation system.

If your facility uses elevated lifeguard stands, one guard replacing another on a stand must scan as the second guard climbs down. Once on the ground, that guard must scan the assigned area until the new guard is in position on the elevated stand.

If there are not enough lifeguards on duty to provide an extra guard for the rotation, guards should exchange positions in a prearranged order, watching the zones as they switch. One guard would move to replace another, and the guards would exchange any necessary information about the potential hazards. The relieved guard would then move to the next assigned position, and so on.

Whatever system is in operation at your facility, the following guidelines for rotation are important:

- Rotate regularly.
- Rotate systematically.
- Move the lifeguard from the most demanding position to either a break period or a less demanding spot.
- As you rotate, keep alert to potential problems and patron needs.

Lifeguarding Locations

Where you stand, sit, or rove is as important as determining the area that you supervise. The location of the sun and the placement of windows at an indoor facility have a definite effect on where lifeguards and lifeguard stands should be placed. Your location governs how well you can see your assigned area and how quickly you can react to an emergency.

Towers and elevated chairs. Both towers and elevated chairs give lifeguards a better vantage point than a station on the ground. People congregating at the lifeguard area can't obstruct your view if you are sitting above their heads. Elevated lifeguard stands are the best for supervising the swimming area, but be sure to scan the areas next to and beneath the chair, which are blind spots where accidents can happen.

The height of your lifeguard location requires some special consideration. In an emergency all of your equipment needs to be within easy reach. Rather than storing it on the ground, mount it on the tower or the elevated chair. A rescue tube or buoy should be on or next to you at all times. Protect the extra line from the rescue tube or buoy so it doesn't get tangled on either you or the chair.

In addition to having your equipment at the top of an elevated lifeguard station, you will need to practice getting down from the station. Depending on the height of the station, you may jump or climb down. When jumping from any height, look before you leap!

Check the area beneath you to avoid landing on a patron or injuring yourself. When you do jump, grasp any equipment you are taking with you tightly, being careful of lines that can get caught. You want to maintain control of your rescue equipment at all times. Finally, bend your knees when you land; landing with locked knees can be very painful and can cause serious injury to your knees and back. Practice getting down from the tower or chair until you can do it fluidly. Every second counts in an emergency.

If you intend to jump directly into the water, you must know that the water is deep enough for jumping safely. In traditional pools, that should be easy. In a wave pool, you must time your jump so you hit the water at the peak of the swell. In a river, the depth and speed of the water change with rainfall or drought. Know the conditions in your area before you jump from a tower or an elevated chair into the water.

Roving lifeguards.   Lifeguards who patrol the area by walking around the perimeter find it easier to handle public relations and courteously discipline patrons. These guards are also able to provide educational tips to patrons because they are more accessible. Many times roving guards are assigned to shallow water areas so they can carefully supervise the water and the surrounding deck or beach. Roving guards should carry a rescue tube or buoy so that it is ready for use. Roving guards may also serve as a communication link between lifeguard towers, particularly at beaches.

Guard Communication Systems

Communication is very important to your success as a lifeguard. Not only do you need to communicate well with the patrons of your facility, you must be able to do the same with the other members of your lifeguarding team. Several communication systems exist for lifeguards:

- Whistle signals
- Hand signals
- Rescue equipment signals
- Flags
- Radios

Your facility will select one or more of these systems, and you and all of the other lifeguards should be familiar with them.

Whistle signals.   Patterns of whistle blows can be used to signal particular situations. One common signal system is the following:

- One short blast—used to get swimmers' attention
- Two short blasts—used to get other lifeguards' attention
- One long blast—used to initiate emergency procedures

Hand signals.   Lifeguards frequently use hand signals to communicate with patrons and other lifeguards. Some examples are illustrated in Figure 3.3. These signals are frequently accompanied by whistle signals. Be sure to hold your signal a few seconds to be sure it has been seen.

Rescue equipment signals.   Some signals can be made using a rescue tube or buoy (see Figure 3.4). Rescue equipment held vertically and moved from side to side means

Figure 3.3

Common hand signals.

Used to give direction

Indicates lifeguard needs help

Used primarily at water slides to stop other staff from sending sliders into the water

Indicates activity can resume

Used to request that another guard watch your area temporarily

Figure 3.4

Rescue equipment signals.

Major Emergency
• Request additional help
• Urgent

• Request additional help
• Less urgent than first signal

Situation Under Control
• No additional help needed

assistance is needed. Rescue equipment held horizontally over the head means the situation is under control.

Flags. Flags are not used in most swimming pools, but they are used at some waterfront areas and are common at water slides and water parks. Waving a red flag means danger, or stop sending water sliders down the slide. Waving a green flag indicates that all is well.

Radios. Two-way and CB radios are most frequently used in large waterfront areas where visual contact is more difficult. These radios are for lifeguarding business only, not socializing.

Group Swimming Safety Check Systems

Most camps and youth organizations use one or more safety check systems to account for all individuals quickly. These systems keep lifeguards aware of the number and location of swimmers in the water; they are especially useful in lake or river environments where visibility is limited. Failure to enforce the system undermines its value.

Four of the most common safety check systems are the buddy system, the tag board (or roll call) system, the cap system, and the pool check. Each is useful for a different purpose. Although management will decide which system you'll use, you may be asked to give input. And for any system to work, swimmers must be informed of the procedures. You are likely to play a major role in that educational process.

Buddy system. In the buddy system, every swimmer is assigned a "buddy" of similar ability. If there is an uneven number of swimmers, one set of buddies may be a triad. Buddies are required to stay close to each other at all times. Then, if one buddy is having difficulty, the other buddy can signal for help.

At a predetermined signal, different from all other signals used by the staff, swimmers "buddy up"—they stop, join hands with their buddies, raise their arms high, and remain stationary. Such positioning lets staff members count groups and account for all swimmers. At a second sounding of the signal, buddies may drop hands and continue their activities.

It is important that you test this system frequently so that partners remain close together. If any buddies have strayed too far apart when you signal to "buddy up," warn the violators that another instance of being away from a buddy will result in time out of the water (see p. 38). Consistent enforcement of the system rules, along with other swimming rules, will make the buddy system work for you and your facility.

Tag board and roll call systems. The tag board and roll call systems work in the same way—swimmers are accounted for before they enter the water and after their swimming period is over. With the tag board system, each person gets a tag with his or her name on it. Swimmers hang their tags on a pegboard as they enter the water and remove them when they leave the water, both under the watchful eye of a lifeguard or camp staff member. A variation of this system uses color-coded tags with a different color on each side. One color indicates swimmers are in the water, the other that they are out. At the end of each swimming period, the group leader can easily check to see that all swimmers have left the water.

If a tag is unaccounted for, an immediate search is started. For the safety of all swimmers, the group leader must enforce the rule that each individual is responsible for her or his own tag. Spot-checking swimmers is a good way to test whether they are following the rules and placing their tags correctly on the board as they enter the water. Identify a swimmer and look to see that the tag is displayed appropriately. If it is not, summon the swimmer and discuss the rules.

The roll call system operates on the same principle of checking attendance before and after the swimming session, but no equipment is necessary. The group leader simply takes attendance by calling names aloud before the swimmers enter the water and immediately after they exit. If someone doesn't respond, a search is started immediately. One drawback of the roll call system is that the time between roll calls could be the time during which a swimmer becomes missing.

Cap system. This system allows lifeguards, staff, and swimmers to differentiate between different swimming skill levels by looking at what color bathing cap, headband, or wristband a swimmer is wearing. The system can be used with either of the other safety check systems. The following color coding is widely used.

- Nonswimmers and beginners wear red.
- Intermediate swimmers wear yellow.
- Advanced swimmers wear blue or green.
- Leaders and lifeguards wear white.

The advantage of this system is that a lifeguard can easily spot red or yellow in an area reserved for advanced swimmers and act quickly to move that person to a safer area.

Pool check. The widely used pool check system is designed for busy periods when lifeguards want to be sure that they can account for all swimmers. On a specified signal, all swimmers are asked to leave the water or sit on the edge of the pool. This system allows the lifeguards to periodically check that no one is on the pool bottom and provides the swimmers with a rest period.

Pool checks can be annoying to patrons if overused. However, if they are necessary to ensure safety, carry them out. To make checks less objectionable, consider coupling them with announcements for all patrons, brief swimming tips, or the beginning of special activities.

Special Guarding Situations

You will undoubtedly experience many different lifeguarding situations during the course of your service. Some are more common than others. Spend some time considering how you should react to each of the following situations. If you are likely to confront one of them, seek out any additional training you might need.

Classes. When you are assigned to lifeguard during a class, your role is simply to provide lifeguarding services. In any class situation, watch every swimmer, just as you would during a free swim period. Assess the comfort and skill level of each one, and use that information to guide your attention. Be sure to keep all class members grouped together (the instructor should help). They need to hear instructions and you need to know where they are and that they are practicing the skills for their class.

Day camps and day care. In day camp and day care situations, children should be given a skill test and divided into groups by skill level for swimming activity. If so, your job is made a little easier by your knowing that the swimmers are of similar abilities. If the group is not divided, it might be a perfect chance to institute one of the group-swimming safety check systems just described. Select the one that will let you keep track of swimmers most easily. Working with these young swimmers is an excellent opportunity to teach them water safety.

Review the rules frequently with children; repetition will help them learn and understand the rules. The camp or day care staff can assist you in teaching the rules and watching their groups. Be sure they have learned the rules and know your facility's emergency system.

Clear the water periodically. While the water is empty, scan the pool bottom. In a waterfront situation, check attendance carefully. These "out of the water" checks are good teaching opportunities and give swimmers a chance to rest.

In working with a group of only young children, you might find it useful to stand on the deck near them. You'll be closer should anyone become frightened or need help in the water, and you'll be close enough to begin teaching these young swimmers the rules. Be sure, however, to check with your facility manager before independently changing your position based on the group using your area.

Competitive events.   The most common activities a lifeguard at a competitive event will become involved in are assisting distressed swimmers or divers, controlling crowds, maintaining safety, and responding to potential spinal injuries. It is important that you establish communication with the meet director so that any incident is handled effectively.

Although you may feel that there is no possibility of needing to go into the water to assist a swimmer during a swim meet, you must be prepared. You should arrive at this assignment dressed as you would for a shift at a crowded pool. You'll still need rescue equipment available in the usual places. If an incident does occur, you want to be able to react efficiently and effectively. Stay alert and be ready to respond.

Rental groups.   Groups that rent a facility for a party need special attention. Some patrons assume that the rules are relaxed because they are the only ones at the facility.

The management of your facility should have a signed agreement with any rental group that clearly states the rules and enforcement policy and procedures. These rules should be enforced just as they are during a regular swim session. Be sure to review any special agreements the management might have made.

When the group arrives at your facility, learn who is in charge. That person will be your contact should any incidents occur. Next, review the rules with the group. Remind them that the rules are to ensure their safety. If the group doesn't follow the rules, they will be asked to leave and risk not being able to use the facility in the future.

Language barriers.   You may face a situation where a swimmer doesn't speak the same language as you. With our country becoming more ethnically diverse, there is probably another lifeguard or a patron who can translate. Get to know those around you who can help. If there is no one to translate, use common hand signals to communicate.

People with disabilities.   Under the Americans with Disabilities Act (ADA), people with disabilities must have access to all facilities and must receive equal opportunity to use them. Furthermore, they must be treated by the same standards you treat other patrons. Those with disabilities are people first! Aquatic facilities must determine how to work with each person with a disability.

Disabilities can be categorized in many ways. Perhaps the most common divisions are

- sensory disabilities (blindness, deafness),
- physical disabilities,
- developmental disabilities (may be either physical or mental), and
- mental disabilities.

People with sensory disabilities rely on their nondisabled senses to receive communication. For example, people who cannot see rely on their hearing, and those who cannot hear rely on sight. Practice giving instructions using just your hands and no words. Then use your voice and no hand signals. If your facility has deaf patrons, consider developing a vocabulary of sign language signals and having a board to write on available.

Swimming is a common therapeutic activity for people with physical and developmental disabilities. Some of these individuals may have difficulties communicating or moving that could place them in danger. So they can participate in aquatic activities safely, you need to learn how to handle emergencies involving people with disabilities.

People with physical disabilities may not have sufficient buoyancy, strength, flexibility, or agility to navigate certain areas of your facility safely. Give these individuals a little extra attention, especially if they are moving into areas requiring more skill.

People with developmental disabilities may have excellent physical skills. Your obligation with these patrons is to help them understand and follow the rules of the facility. People with communication deficits may have no trouble swimming or understanding the rules. They may have difficulty understanding what you are trying to communicate because of impaired senses, or they may have difficulty expressing their questions or concerns to you.

So what can you do to be effective in these situations? First, be alert enough to notice anyone with a disability who is at your facility. Talk with disabled patrons about the facility and about their needs. Most people with disabilities are happy to discuss their situations if you approach them in a supportive, professional manner. Be sure that people with a developmental or communication disability understand the rules and policies of the facility. Work with them and their companions to ensure that they understand. If one of them asks you a question, work hard to understand it and provide an answer that he or she can understand.

You can use the same rescue techniques that you will learn in chapter 6 to provide assistance to people with disabilities. But be flexible. You may need to be somewhat inventive. If someone does not have a right arm for you to grab, you'll have to do the rescue using the left arm. Or a swimmer may not be able to see the equipment you are extending—how can you get her or him to grab it? Once you know about a patron with a specific disability, think through how you will assist him or her should the need arise. Plan ahead, and use whatever works!

Review Questions

1. Describe a healthy lifestyle.
2. List the personal equipment a well-prepared lifeguard has on-site.
3. Why is it important to use sun protection?
4. List the lifeguard duties that should become habits.
5. Name some precautions you can take to ensure you are not involved in or accused of child abuse.
6. List the 4 steps to making good decisions.
7. Define the parts of the Q-1-2 system and give an example of each part.
8. What is the difference between entire-area coverage and zone coverage? List two advantages and disadvantages of each.
9. List and define the 4 techniques for guarding.
10. Describe a typical rotation system.
11. Why is rotation important?
12. List the advantages and disadvantages of towers and elevated chairs and roving lifeguards.
13. What are the 5 communication systems for lifeguards?
14. Name 2 signals that you can use with your rescue tube to communicate to other lifeguards.
15. List and describe 4 group-swimming safety check systems.
16. Describe how you would guard differently in a class, at a day camp, and during a swim meet.
17. What options do you have for communicating with someone with a communication disability?
18. Briefly describe how you would handle lifeguarding where someone with a disability swims.

CHAPTER 4

Rules and Regulations

To prevent aquatic accidents you need to be familiar with your state's bathing code, your swimming facility, and the hazards within your facility. You also need to establish rules that minimize these dangers and then consistently enforce them.

IN THIS CHAPTER YOU'LL LEARN ABOUT

- establishing and communicating rules in your facility,
- common rules for high-risk locations, and
- enforcing the rules.

ESTABLISHING AND COMMUNICATING RULES

In most facilities the management tries to keep the number of rules for patrons to a minimum to keep the atmosphere as enjoyable as possible. When additional rules are found to be needed, the management must consider both the safety and enjoyment of patrons. Any rules must be realistic, specific, and understandable.

Once the rules are established, the lifeguard must enforce them among patrons. The first step to enforcing the rules is communicating them. The most logical way to inform the users of a facility of the rules is to post them in the swimming area. Fences, lifeguard stands, and diving boards are all appropriate spots to mount signs. Copies of the rules can be handed out with pool passes or perhaps listed in a facility newsletter.

COMMON RULES FOR HIGH-RISK LOCATIONS

Certain areas of any aquatic environment can be more dangerous than others. Lifeguards must closely supervise the areas where accidents occur most frequently (see Figure 4.1). In the following section, each area's potential dangers are described along with some suggested safety rules.

Entrance

Wanting to get into the water as quickly as possible often leads swimmers to run at the entrance to the pool. A wet and slippery deck poses a high risk, and one swimmer can easily collide with another.

> *Suggested Rule:*
> Walk, don't run.

Pool Deck

Running and rough play are the primary concerns on the pool deck. Many falls are the result of runners' skidding or bumping into other patrons. Nonswimmers also can be knocked into the water by people running on the deck. Good-natured rough play often escalates, causing participants or bystanders to be pushed or knocked to the ground or into the water. This behavior detracts from the enjoyment of others at your facility.

> *Suggested Rule:*
> Pushing and rough play
> are prohibited.

Sunbathers on the Deck

Sunbathers lying too close to the pool's edge can cause swimmers walking around the pool to stumble or trip. Generally sunbathers should stay at least 6 feet from the edge to allow adequate room for swimmers to enter and exit the water. A 2- to 4-inch-wide safety stripe around the pool perimeter at this distance can help remind patrons to observe this rule. Breakable or metal items should not be permitted in the deck area.

Figure 4.1

High-risk areas in a swimming facility.

> *Suggested Rules:*
>
> Sunbathe at least 6 feet from the edge of the pool.
>
> Only plastic containers and toys are allowed
> in the pool, observation, and locker/shower areas.

Ladders

Ladders should be used only for getting into and out of the pool, and other uses can pose hazards. People who sit on the ladders to talk block access for tired swimmers. Other dangers include swimmers who use the ladders to pull themselves underwater and back to the surface; they risk getting caught in a rung, shoved off the ladder, or stepped on. Slippery ladders are dangerous when swimmers swing on them or dive from them. If swimmers swim between the ladder and the wall, they risk being caught, either on the surface or underwater.

> *Suggested Rules:*
>
> Use ladders only for getting into or out of the water.
>
> Only one swimmer on the ladder at a time.

Pool Gutters

Pool overflow gutters or troughs pose several potential dangers. Nonswimmers may use the gutters to travel from shallow to deep water, traveling along the side of the pool hand over hand when the guard is looking the other way. Danger can arise when the nonswimmer is pushed away from the wall or attempts to climb out of the water and traps a knee or elbow in the gutter. If you spot a nonswimmer moving along the gutter, have her or him climb out of the water on the nearest ladder and walk back to shallow water.

Prohibit patrons from standing on the gutters or climbing into them. Arms, hands, legs, or feet can get wedged into the gutter and cause an injury, particularly if the patron loses balance.

Small children also enjoy jumping into the water and turning to grab the gutter for support. Mis-timed turns result in many cut chins, so stop this activity immediately.

> *Suggested Rules:*
>
> Nonswimmers must stay in shallow water.
>
> Use a ladder to get out of the pool.
>
> Jump into the pool well past the gutter.

Lifelines

Lifelines mark the break between shallow and deep water. The chief danger to watch for is small children or weak swimmers who edge into deep water by pulling themselves along the lifelines. If they are pushed or otherwise lose a grasp on the lines, nonswimmers may be in water over their heads and consequently in danger. Swimmers should not sit or hang on lifelines; a lifeline submerged under the weight of a chatting swimmer is much more difficult for the distressed swimmer to find. Be sure to keep the lifelines strung tightly enough to be visible and to support panicky swimmers.

> *Suggested Rules:*
> Nonswimmers must stay in shallow water.
> Keep off the lifelines.
> Use lifelines only for temporary support.

The Water

Any water area is potentially hazardous if swimmers are not careful. Flotation devices like inner tubes and plastic toys can be dangerous if a nonswimming user floats into deep water or the device deflates and traps the person in it. If someone tries to get out of a flotation device, she or he may experience difficulty. These swimming aids are even more dangerous on crowded days when swimmers may accidentally bump into them, causing the user to fall away from the flotation device. They also obstruct the lifeguard's view of the bottom of the pool.

Many parents buy swimming aids for their children and perhaps gain a false sense of security from them. Parents must supervise their children at all times, whether or not the children are using swimming aids. But keep in mind that parental vigilance doesn't mean that you don't have to keep watch on those children as well.

> *Suggested Rules:*
> Only Coast Guard-approved PFDs permitted.
> Adult supervision required for all children.

A second general concern in any aquatic facility is patrons who enter the water at an unsafe depth. Consider a nonswimmer going down a ladder unknowingly into deep water or a skilled swimmer diving at a steep angle into the shallow end of the pool. You can decrease the probability that someone will enter the water not knowing the depth by pointing out depth markers to patrons.

Depth markers should appear on every side of the pool and on the deck. In some pools a contour depth line shows all swimmers exactly how deep the water is in relation to their height. The contour line, generally on a fence or wall, provides a profile of the pool depths. Patrons can easily stand next to the contour line to determine the point in the pool where it is safe for them to enter.

Shallow Water

The primary dangers in shallow water are diving and dunking. Even an experienced diver may hit the bottom, causing injuries to the fingers, hands, head, neck, or back. Depths should be marked at regular intervals and at changes in water depth and contour to alert divers to the conditions. Standing front dives should be performed in no less than 9 feet of water. (See Appendix B for YMCA guidelines on diving and diving water depth.)

Dunking is also a common activity for playful children and adults. The unsuspecting swimmer may ingest water and become scared or be injured hitting the side or bottom of the pool.

> **Suggested Rules:**
> Diving allowed only in marked areas.
>
> No dunking or rough play.

Deep Water

The primary dangers in deep water are nonswimmers and underwater swimmers. The nonswimmers can be spotted moving to the deep water along the gutter, on the deck, or from the diving board. Before entering the water, they may look very apprehensive and usually have their arms folded or wrapped around themselves. Prevent nonswimmers from getting into the deep water. Patrons should take a swimming test before being allowed to swim in the deep water.

Underwater swimmers may be jumped on, possibly receiving back injuries. Another common problem for underwater swimmers is blacking out from hyperventilation. Swimmers may take a series of deep breaths before swimming across the pool under water. This decreases the amount of carbon dioxide in the blood, and because carbon dioxide tells the brain when to breathe, the reduction interferes with the breathing process. In effect, a swimmer can black out—and possibly drown—because he or she doesn't breathe when necessary. (For additional information on hyperventilation, see p. 127.) If you notice swimmers taking deep breaths before swimming, use Q-1-2 and talk to them about the dangers of hyperventilation.

Masks, fins, and snorkels also lure poor swimmers into deep water by providing false security. Keep a close watch on anyone using such equipment (if your facility allows it). Goggles, while safe in water up to 5 feet deep, should not be worn at greater depths. The pressure on the eyes may cause discomfort or injury.

> **Suggested Rules:**
> Nonswimmers must stay in shallow water.
>
> No underwater distance swimming.

Starting Blocks and Platforms

Starting blocks and platforms pose a significant hazard, especially to the inexperienced swimmer. No one should be allowed to dive from a starting block or platform except in a competitive program. Your management should check local and state bathing codes for guidelines on placement of the blocks and the water depth required. They also need to check with their insurance carrier regarding the regulations that carrier requires. The YMCA of the USA recommends that diving blocks be placed in the deep end, with a water depth of at least 5 feet.

If starting blocks or platforms cannot be removed during recreational swims, the YMCA suggests they be capped and that warning signs be posted to stop patrons from using them. (Also see "Competitive Swimming Starting Blocks," p. 136, and Appendix B.)

> **Suggested Rules:**
> No sitting, playing, jumping, or diving
> from starting blocks or platforms.
>
> Starting blocks are for competitive
> swimming program use only.

Slides

Slides, which continue to become more popular in swimming facilities and water parks, are another high-risk area. Pools with slides should have at least one lifeguard whose main responsibility is the slide area.

All sliders should enter the water feet-first in a sitting position to avoid head injuries. Watch carefully that each slider returns to the surface and clears the area before the next person begins. Insist that the area at the bottom of the slide be kept open to avoid injuries from swimmers being hit by the slider. Also be aware that outdoor slides can get hot enough to cause burns, particularly on hot days. All slides should have a water spray to keep sliders safe. See chapter 12 for more on slides and acquatic attractions.

Suggested Rules:

No swimming in the slide area.

Move away from the bottom of the slide immediately.

Use the ladder only to get onto the slide.

One person on the ladder at a time.

One person on the slide at a time.

Go down the slide feet-first in a sitting position.

Diving Areas

Diving off a 1-meter board may be done either in a separate well or in an area of the pool that is at least 11 feet, 6 inches deep. In either case, you need to give these diving areas special attention and consistently enforce the rules. Many accidents associated with diving can be prevented by an alert lifeguard. Some of the many causes for diving accidents include the condition and arrangement of the equipment and diving areas, the visibility into the water, numerous weather factors, and the depth and distance to the upslope of the pool bottom. Lifeguards must check diving boards regularly throughout the day. The fulcrum setting should be restricted to keep the board "stiff" for recreational use. Watch each diver return to the surface and exit the diving area before another diver approaches. Watch also for rough play on and around the boards. See Appendix B for more information on diving and risk management.

Suggested Rules:

Use the ladder to mount the diving board.

No hanging under the board.

Only one diver on the board at a time.

No sitting on the guardrails.

Wait for the previous diver to swim clear before diving.

Only one bounce allowed.

Dive off the front of the board only.

Hands must enter the water first in head-first dives.

(continued)

> *Suggested Rules* (continued)*:*
>
> Swim to the ladder immediately after diving.
>
> No swimmers in the diving area.
>
> No fancy dives.
>
> No diving off 3-meter boards, platforms, or towers
> during recreational swims.
>
> No deep diving starts.
>
> No diving from the deck
> into water less than 9 feet deep.
>
> No diving from a 1-meter board
> into water less than 11 feet, 6 inches deep.

Lifeguard Towers and Equipment

Lifeguard towers and stands present a hazard because they attract young swimmers, who often gather at the foot of a stand, potentially obscuring the lifeguard's view. Be sure to scan the water under and around towers in your range of vision. Older patrons may enjoy socializing with the lifeguards. Keep your conversations brief and continue to monitor your area.

Ring buoys and other safety devices may prove equally attractive and dangerous. A ring buoy, like any flotation device, could prove dangerous as a floating aid to a foolhardy nonswimmer. Such equipment is to be used only by trained personnel.

> *Suggested Rules:*
>
> No climbing on guard towers.
>
> No sitting below guard towers.
>
> Emergency equipment for lifeguard use only.

Wading Pools

The reason most facilities decide to add wading pools is to provide a safe haven for nonswimmers to enjoy the water. Parents often supervise their nonswimming children in these areas, but sometimes they become involved in conversation and don't notice that a child is experiencing difficulty. Do not be lulled into thinking that your responsibility is covered by parents' supervision of their children.

Wading pool accidents are typically the result of rough play by older siblings or nonswimmers who are old enough to be in the main pool. They run and splash, creating an environment in which wading pool occupants can be knocked under the water or onto the deck, and should be warned to stop.

Others who frequent the wading pool are nonswimming adults seeking a cool dip. On very hot days the wading pool may become congested, and wet decking together with crowded conditions makes slipping and falling in the wading pool or on the surrounding deck a real danger.

> *Suggested Rules:*
>
> No running or rough play.
>
> All nonswimming children
> must be accompanied by an adult.
>
> No diving.

Hot Tubs

Hot tubs are a relatively new addition to aquatic facilities. If your facility has one, you'll need to learn your state's codes for spas and add this area to your list of danger zones. The most common physical hazards of a spa area are drowning, falling, and electrocution. The drownings and falls are often attributed to medical conditions or to the use of alcohol in the spa area. Electrocutions result from the use of electrical devices in the spa area.

When someone who is overheated from vigorous exercise or using a sauna gets into the spa, the danger of heat-related illness increases greatly. A proper cool-down is needed after exercising before entering the spa, and vigorous exercise in the spa should not be allowed.

Hot tubs attract even people who know they should stay away. Be sure that you post the rules of the hot tub prominently and enforce them rigidly.

> *Suggested Rules:*
>
> Do not use the hot tub alone.
>
> Spa use is not recommended immediately
> after intense physical activity or after sauna use.
>
> No aerobic exercise in the spa.
>
> Enter and exit the spa slowly and cautiously.
>
> Pregnant women, patrons with cardiovascular
> or respiratory problems, and children under 5
> should avoid using the hot tub.
>
> Older children must be accompanied
> and supervised by a responsible adult.
>
> Limit use to 10 minutes.
>
> No diving or jumping.
>
> No underwater submersion.
>
> No food or drink in the spa area.
>
> No body lotions, oils, or suntan products.

For additional information about spa management, see chapter 13 and the Pool Operator on Location Manual.

Special Situations

Although every facility has rules of conduct, some patrons inevitably try to test those rules. As an employee of a recreational facility, you are responsible to ensure that one patron doesn't endanger the safety of others. This section is designed to help you handle those situations. Your management may also post contact phone numbers in the pool office should you need additional assistance.

Disturbances. Disturbances that occur at an aquatic facility must be handled carefully. It is best to refer them to the manager or assistant manager. If necessary, contact local authorities for assistance. Disturbances that originate outside your jurisdiction but affect patrons of the facility should be referred to the proper authorities immediately. Complete an incident report form after any disturbance.

Theft. The management of your facility will probably post conspicuous notices regarding responsibility for loss of personal property. However, you should be alert to any theft. If an incident is reported to you, notify the manager or assistant manager so he or she may contact law enforcement officials.

Do not accuse a person of theft. Present your evidence to the law enforcement authorities and let them make any charges. You could be charged with making a false accusation if you act hastily and have no proof of your claim. Make sure you fill out the appropriate incident report form and obtain statements from witnesses before they leave the scene.

Sexual activity. Do not permit inappropriate sexual behavior in your facility. Diplomatically control these situations from the start of the swimming season.

Indecent exposure. Exposing oneself in public is a crime in most areas. If someone indecently exposes himself or herself, suggest that the person cover up immediately. If your request is ignored or if the behavior is repeated, contact the management and police.

Disregard for lifeguard authority. Working at a facility that your friends frequent can put you and them in an awkward situation. You are duty-bound to enforce the rules of the facility, no matter who violates them. It may help to explain that to your friends if they are causing problems.

Anyone who disregards the lifeguard's authority is creating a risk, and you must not allow patrons to ignore your instructions. Summon the manager or assistant manager with a prearranged signal, such as a raised, clenched fist, to assist you in these instances. Repeated disregard of authority is grounds for banning offenders from the facility. If necessary, contact local authorities to escort a troublemaker from the scene.

Substance abuse. People who are abusing substances such as alcohol or other drugs should not be in or around aquatic areas; their lack of judgment and reduced physical abilities could easily endanger both them and other patrons. Be aware of signs or behavior patterns that are characteristic of substance abuse:

- Unusual tiredness
- The odor of alcohol, tobacco, or other drugs
- Unsteadiness and lack of coordination
- Unusual detachment from the group
- Unusual changes in mood or attitude
- Unexplained lack of interest in normal activities
- Unusual giddiness
- Preoccupation with drug-related clothing, signs, or other paraphernalia
- Obvious slurring of words
- Public use of alcohol, tobacco, or other drugs

If you suspect that a patron in your area is under the influence of alcohol or other drugs, watch her or him carefully and request that the manager or assistant manager join you. If the manager agrees that the patron is acting suspiciously, he or she should ask the patron to leave. Encourage the patron to have someone take him or her home and not drive. Your manager may authorize calling a taxi or providing other transportation assistance. If the person will not leave, contact the police. Once the person has left, document the behavior on an incident report form. The manager may inform the parents of youthful abusers.

Concern for younger patrons. If you think you see signs of child abuse or neglect or of drug abuse in children, notify your manager or the appropriate staff member and explain what you have observed. That staff person can then contact the child's parents and take whatever steps are deemed appropriate and necessary, including referrals to agencies and services. (See Appendix A for "Child Abuse Identification and Prevention: Recommended Guidelines for YMCAs.")

Problems unique to your facility. Although the section you have just read may provide some basis for your decision making, each facility has its own unique difficulties and its own rules. And to a large degree lifeguards must make their own decisions about what constitutes a potentially dangerous situation. Study the layout of your facility and the rules that have been made to govern it. If you see potential problem areas, bring them to the attention of the management. Then assist in the creative process of establishing rules that will preserve a safe and fun environment.

ENFORCING THE RULES

Rule enforcement is always difficult. No one likes to play watchdog, and no one likes to be corrected. But you must enforce the rules to meet your responsibility of providing a safe environment in which patrons can have enjoyable aquatic experiences.

Discipline is needed whenever someone's behavior

- could result in injury to self or others,
- could result in damage to property, or
- infringes on the comfort and enjoyment of others in the area.

A few guidelines will help you enforce the rules at your facility:

- Know all rules and the procedures for enforcing them.
- Use a short blast of your whistle to get patrons' attention.
- Be consistent, enforcing the same rule in the same way for everyone. Don't make exceptions for friends, fellow employees, or adults. Also, enforce the rules in the same way each and every day.
- React immediately. Blow your whistle as soon as you detect a rule being broken. The patron will know what behavior has drawn your attention.
- Be specific. If there is a question over what behavior is prohibited, be specific in describing your concern. For example, you may say, "I saw you running on the deck. As you know, that is against the rules because you may run into another swimmer and knock someone down." You have pointed out the incorrect behavior and indicated why it was a problem.
- Provide alternative behaviors if you can. You might encourage the runner on the deck to take a group to the grassy recreation area, where there is room for such activities.

By following these guidelines, you should be able to gain the respect and cooperation of those who use your swimming facility. And each time you enforce the rules, you gain experience in how to deal with people successfully.

Your primary responsibility is to guard your area. Enforcing rules is one part of that duty. You must never stop scanning the water. If a rule enforcement discussion is lengthy or is taking your attention away from your assigned area, signal for assistance.

Review Questions

1. Why are rules needed in a facility?
2. How are rules communicated to patrons?
3. List the high-risk locations at a pool.
4. What are the dangers of deep water?
5. How is the hazard related to starting blocks minimized?
6. Name 5 suggested rules related to diving areas.
7. How should you respond when someone disregards your authority as a lifeguard?
8. What 3 general types of situations require disciplinary action?
9. List 6 guidelines for effective enforcement of the rules.

5

Victim Recognition and Drowning

A major part of a lifeguard's job is to be alert in order to prevent accidents or incidents. To do this effectively, you must know who is potentially a victim and recognize victims when they do get into trouble.

It is also true that, despite your best efforts to stop problems before they begin, you may at some time be faced with a situation in which a patron is at serious risk of drowning. For such a situation, it's essential that you understand what drowning is and how it works.

IN THIS CHAPTER YOU'LL LEARN

■ how to recognize potential and actual victims, and

■ the stages and types of drowning.

VICTIM RECOGNITION

The first step in executing an effective rescue is to detect the need for action. As a trained professional, you can reduce the anxiety of identification by learning to look for potential victims and by analyzing options before potential accidents occur. By doing this, you can determine what option is best for you. Identifying potential victims early is the key to your success as a lifeguard.

Types of Victims

You are likely to see several different types of victims in your service as a lifeguard. Potential victims come in all shapes and sizes, but there are a few groups you should watch closely:

- People of age extremes—the very young and the very old
- People of weight extremes—very heavy or very thin
- Pale people—their pallor may signal a lack of exposure or experience in outdoor aquatic activities
- Parents holding children—their skills may not be strong enough to support both themselves and a child
- Unstable or intoxicated individuals—their movement and behavior patterns may be impaired
- People using flotation devices—use of such aids may signal lack of comfort in the water
- Physical impairment—disabilities may signal limited ability to maneuver in and around the water
- Improper dress or equipment—may mean they are unfamiliar with the situation

Signs of Trouble

Because you may be called at any time to make a decision about how to react to an aquatic emergency, learn to detect signs of trouble. Observe swimmers before they enter the water for clues about their abilities. Once swimmers are active, other signs will help you identify potential victims. There are two types of victims: those in distress (tired swimmers) and those who are drowning (usually nonswimmers).

Early warning signs. Swimmers likely to become victims often display a variety of warning signs:

- Weak stroke—head low in the water, little over arm recovery, or a weak kick demonstrate a lack of ability
- Hair in the eyes—swimmer may be too concerned with keeping the head out of the water to push hair out of the eyes
- Glassy, empty, anxious-looking eyes—the facial expression preceding exhaustion
- Two heads together—a possible double-drowning situation
- Hand-waving—a sign of needing help
- Swimmer moving toward rocks or a pier—may be caught in a current
- Erratic behavior—any activity out of the ordinary
- Clinging to objects for security—swimmer may be too tired to swim to safety
- Neutral to negative buoyancy—means little air remains in lungs; the person may sink in seconds

- Inability to respond verbally—may indicate struggling to stay afloat or swallowing water

Being able to identify potential victims is crucial for a lifeguard; however, not everyone displaying one or more of these signs will be involved in an accident. Taking such an extreme position could lead to unnecessary tension and an embarrassing situation following an overreaction. Stay relaxed; keep a vigilant watch over your area, but let your common sense keep your responsibility in perspective.

Distressed swimmers.   A distressed swimmer is generally a tired swimmer who can't swim to safety. Characteristics of distress include

- waving the arms,
- shouting for assistance, and
- kicking to maintain an upright position.

A distressed swimmer can assist in his or her own rescue by following instructions, grabbing extended rescue equipment, keeping afloat, and kicking.

Drowning victims.   Nonswimmers or exhausted swimmers are the usual drowning victims (you will learn more about the physical aspects of drowning in the next section). Unlike distressed swimmers, they are unable to call for help. They are expending all of their energy trying to keep their heads above water and breathe. Characteristics include

- the inability to call for help,
- head back and the body low in the water,
- arms alternately out to the sides and then overhead as they raise the body into the air and sink again, splashing a lot,
- little or no support from the kick, and
- an upright position facing the nearest source of assistance.

Drowning victims are more difficult to spot than distressed victims because they cannot call attention to themselves. But it is critical to identify a drowning victim quickly—it takes as little as 20 seconds to slip below the surface. This situation requires immediate action. The victim will be unable to assist in the rescue.

Drowning victims may be passive or active. A passive victim is unconscious and displays no active movements. Such victims are usually found facedown or submerged in the water. An active victim, thrashing or showing signs of panic and fear, is more dangerous to rescue without risking harm to yourself. It is important to know that active victims can become passive victims easily if they are allowed to thrash around for a long time.

DROWNING

Drowning is asphyxiation (cutting off of the air supply) due to blockage or reflex spasm of the trachea (commonly called the windpipe), usually caused by water, which stops breathing. A potential drowning may arise for any number of reasons. Whatever the initial reason, most situations lead to panic and then progress through four defined stages of drowning. Panic is an uncontrolled and incapacitating fear that strikes when someone thinks she or he has lost control. Severe panic destroys all sense of logic and reason. Self-preservation becomes the top priority, even at the expense of friends and loved ones.

The behavioral pattern of a drowning victim takes the following form:

- Struggle for air
- Cessation of movement accompanied by limited exhalation and frequent swallowing of water

- Violent struggle for survival
- Uncontrolled efforts to take in air accompanied by convulsions and disappearance of reflex actions
- Death

The Stages of Drowning

The drowning process has been divided into four stages. Although the names given to the stages differ, the concept of each stage is basically the same.

Before examining the specific stages of drowning, let's take a brief look at the body structures involved. In the normal throat (see Figure 5.1), the glottis is the top edge of the beginning of the trachea that connects to the lower part of the throat. The glottis is covered by the epiglottis, a flap of skin that acts as a barrier to prevent foreign material from entering the trachea, which carries air from the throat into the lungs. The esophagus, which is next to the trachea, carries food and liquids from the throat to the stomach.

Figure 5.1

Anatomy of the throat.

Tongue

Epiglottis

Glottis

Trachea

Esophagus

What is called the reflex closure of the glottis is the involuntary (automatic), controlled process of swallowing. As water enters the mouth, the tongue blocks the back of the throat. The glottis then closes, blocking the airway, the tongue drops, and the water passes the trachea into the esophagus and to the stomach. During the drowning process, this reflex is disrupted.

Stage 1: Initial apnea.   Apnea means the absence of breathing. In drowning, the glottis closes by a reflex action, but unlike during eating or drinking where the air supply is resumed immediately once the food or drink passes the glottis, the water stays in the mouth and throat, cutting off all air to the lungs. No water yet enters the lungs, however.

During this step, the victim's panic increases. Struggling to get air, he or she may not call for help!

The time span of the first stage varies significantly, from seconds to minutes. Physiologically, the following occurs:

1. The blood pressure rises and the adrenalin flow increases due to panic and the self-preservation instinct.
2. The victim begins to struggle in an attempt to keep the head above the water.
3. The victim swallows water into the stomach, filling some of the available air space in the body and diminishing buoyancy.
4. The victim gradually sinks. Each attempt to raise the head above water is less successful because of fatigue and the extra water in the stomach.
5. The brain begins to degenerate because it does not get enough oxygen to function properly (a condition called hypoxia).
6. The lack of oxygen causes an excess of waste chemicals in the blood, making the blood more acidic (acidosis) and causing muscles to fatigue and stop functioning.

Stage 2: Dyspnea. Dyspnea refers to difficulty in breathing and occurs when the glottis begins to relax partially. Air and water begin to enter the trachea. Because the victim has swallowed water into the stomach and is growing weaker from struggling, the head will be lower in the water and more water will be swallowed. This time water flows down the trachea into the lungs. If rescued during this stage, the victim would suffer from a condition called aspiration pneumonia resulting from the breathing in of water into the lungs.

On the surface of every air sac (alveolus) in the lungs is a chemical known as surfactant that reduces the strength of the alveolus's membrane, allowing for the easy exchange of oxygen to and carbon dioxide away from the blood (Figure 5.2). In drowning, the water ingested into the lungs washes away the surfactant, making the exchange of gases more difficult and creating another complication to resuscitation. Because there are over 700 million alveoli in the lungs, many survive the wash-away to help exchange gases as long as they are exposed to the air. The mixture of water and surfactant causes a pink froth at the mouth of some victims. Resuscitation of victims in this stage may be quite difficult because of the decreased exchange of oxygen and carbon dioxide.

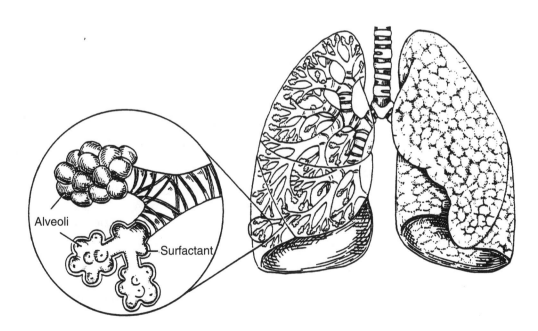

Figure 5.2

Alveoli in the lungs.

During dyspnea the victim experiences the following:

1. The failure of the swallow reflex causes the aspiration of water into the lungs. Although no one normally can intentionally take water into the lungs, by this stage the protective mechanism of the body has failed.
2. The influx of water into the stomach and lungs may cause vomiting.
3. Frothing may occur at the mouth because of the mixture of surfactant and water in the lungs.
4. Brain hypoxia continues, and very little rationality remains.
5. Acidosis continues to cause a severe chemical imbalance in the blood.

Stage 3: Terminal apnea.   As soon as the victim becomes unconscious and stops breathing, he or she has entered the third stage. Terminal apnea is respiratory arrest, in which breathing ceases. Water will be present in the lungs, making air exchange during resuscitation efforts very difficult.

During this stage the following occurs:

1. Brain hypoxia continues.
2. Acidosis continues.
3. In some cases, lack of oxygen to the brain causes convulsions in which the entire body becomes rigid and the victim jerks violently and involuntarily.
4. In some cases, the sphincter muscles may relax, in which case the victim will urinate or defecate, or both.

Stage 4: Cardiac arrest.   Cardiac arrest occurs when the heart ceases to function and pump blood. Depending on the circumstances, the third and fourth stages of drowning may occur simultaneously, with the heart and lungs stopping together. But because the heart can continue to beat up to 5 minutes after the lungs have stopped, rescue breathing alone can revive victims who have been underwater for a short time. Once the pulse has stopped, CPR must be used to revive the victim.

Drowning victims experience two types of death: clinical death and biological death. *Clinical death* occurs first; it is defined as the point at which both breathing and pulse have stopped and the body is in respiratory and cardiac arrest. Clinical death is generally considered to last about 4 minutes from the time the heart stops beating. The lack of oxygen causes the pupils of the eyes to dilate (widen) and the skin to become cyanotic (blue). This blue color is especially noticeable in the lips and the beds of the fingernails. If you begin CPR within the first 4 minutes, there is a good chance that no brain damage will occur.

Biological death is the point at which irreversible brain damage begins and the most sensitive parts of the brain start to die. Without oxygen, brain cells begin to die within 4 to 6 minutes. Longer periods of oxygen deprivation result in loss of more and more brain cells. Dead brain cells cannot regenerate like skin and bone; once dead, they are gone.

You can see why it is critical to reach a drowning victim and begin CPR as soon as possible. CPR maintains minimal circulation and respiration in order to sustain life until advanced medical care can begin.

In cold water, bodily functions are slowed significantly. As a result, less oxygen is needed to maintain the body, and a good portion of the oxygen available is used by the brain. Because of the slowed depletion of oxygen, cold-water drowning and near-drowning victims experience a delayed onset of biological death.

Types of Drowning

Not all drownings happen in the same way. Various situations and environmental conditions can cause different results.

Wet and dry drownings. Between 80% and 90% of all drownings are wet drownings—the glottis opens at the second stage (dyspnea) and allows water to enter the lungs, making the lungs wet. The remaining drownings are dry drownings, in which the glottis stays shut from the first stage (initial apnea) and allows no water to enter the lungs.

Silent drowning. A silent drowning includes no surface struggling because the victim is rendered unconscious, incapacitated, or dead. Lifeguards are given no warning of silent drownings, which is one of the reasons they must keep alert.

Various situations and physical conditions can result in a silent drowning:

- Heart attack
- Head injury
- Cardiac arrest
- Shallow-water blackout (due to hyperventilation)
- Stroke
- Epilepsy
- Alcohol abuse
- Drug overdose

Laryngeal drowning. There are two forms of laryngeal drowning. In the first the swimmer may aspirate vomit into the lungs, choke, and drown. This has been found to be a possible cause in some drowning accidents in which the victim had eaten a big meal immediately before swimming (supporting the idea of waiting an appropriate time after eating before swimming). The second type of laryngeal drowning, called a secondary drowning, occurs after the victim has been pulled out of the water. The epiglottis and the larynx have a reflex spasm, causing the victim to be unable to breathe. This can occur up to 24 hours after a near-drowning incident, so current EMS procedures recommend hospitalizing victims of near-drownings.

Saltwater and freshwater drowning. As far as the lifeguard is concerned, there is no significant difference in the method of reviving a victim of saltwater or freshwater drowning. When a victim drowns in salt water, the water in the blood diffuses through the membranes of the alveoli because the salt (sodium) content of the water is much higher than that of the water in the blood. Because sodium attracts water, the water in the blood is drawn into the lungs.

In an extreme case, the victim's blood volume can drop almost 40%. This drop is critical. As water is drawn from the blood, it gets thicker and the red blood cells cannot carry their full capacity of oxygen to the tissues.

In freshwater drowning, the imbalance of sodium is the opposite: Water enters the lungs and is drawn through the membranes of the alveoli into the blood because the sodium content of the blood is higher than that of fresh water. In an extreme case, where fresh water has very little sodium, water can be drawn in over several minutes so that the blood volume of a victim doubles. This blood dilution causes severe chemical imbalances, resulting in irregularities in body functions. Imbalances of sodium, potassium, chloride, magnesium, and other salt components in the blood are caused by the dilution, and these imbalances contribute to spasms of the heart muscle called ventricular fibrillation, a precursor to cardiac arrest, in 80% of freshwater drowning cases.

As red blood cells fill up with water in freshwater drowning, another problem arises. In some cases when the water content of the red blood cells becomes too great, the cells will explode (experience hemolysis) and no longer be able to carry oxygen. If enough red blood cells suffer hemolysis, oxygen transportation is significantly reduced.

Buoyancy of a Drowned Body

Whether a drowned body will float or sink depends on the victim's original buoyancy and on the amount of water taken into the lungs and stomach. Positively buoyant victims will float; negatively buoyant victims will sink. If the victim was borderline buoyant or nonbuoyant, the amount of air in the lungs—the vital capacity—may change the body's ability to float. As the body descends, the lungs are squeezed of their residual volume (the air that remains in the lungs). This causes the body to descend faster as it goes deeper. Air bubbles from the victim may appear on the surface for quite some time.

Most bodies will eventually surface if they are not held down in some way as the body decomposes and carbon dioxide and other gases are created. This process is slowed in cold water.

Review Questions

1. What signs can alert you to the potential for trouble before a swimmer enters the water? After a swimmer is in the water?
2. Describe the difference in how a distressed swimmer and a drowning victim behave. Why is this difference important?
3. What are the 4 stages of drowning?
4. What is the difference between clinical death and biological death? Why is the distinction important?
5. What is the difference between wet and dry drownings?
6. Define silent drowning and give at least 4 examples of causes of silent drowning.
7. What are the 2 forms of laryngeal drowning?
8. What factors determine the buoyancy of a drowned body?

CHAPTER 6

Rescue Skills

Lifeguards must be prepared to identify a trouble situation, determine what type of rescue or assist is needed, and execute the rescue. Your ability to identify the emergency, analyze the options, make a decision, and carry out the rescue will determine whether you are successful.

IN THIS CHAPTER YOU'LL LEARN ABOUT DETAILS OF PERFORMING RESCUES

- Rescue equipment
- Nonswimming assists
- Water entries
- Approaches
- Rescues using a rescue tube or buoy and in-water rescue breathing
- Multiple victim rescues
- Rescue towing
- Water exits

RESCUE EQUIPMENT

You will learn how to make a variety of rescues in your lifeguarding course. In each one you should use a piece of rescue equipment. The most common pieces of rescue equipment are pictured in Figure 6.1 and described here:

Figure 6.1

Rescue equipment.

• *Shepherd's crook and reaching pole.* The shepherd's crook and reaching pole are lightweight wood, aluminum, or fiberglass rods 10 to 15 feet long. The shepherd's crook has a blunt hook on one end that is large enough to place around an unconscious victim. Both the shepherd's crook and pole can be used to assist a conscious victim.

• *Ring buoy.* The buoyant ring buoy usually weighs no more than 2-1/2 pounds and is used primarily on lakefronts and in pools. The ring buoy is attached to a 40- to 50-foot line for use in throwing assists. The ring buoy is generally effective only with a distressed swimmer.

• *Rescue bag.* Used most frequently in moving water, the rescue bag is a self-contained throwing device with a 75-foot rope coiled inside a bag. The weight of the rope and the bag as they are thrown is sufficient to enable rescuers to be accurate in their throws. The rescue bag does not provide flotation and should be used with distressed swimmers.

- *Rescue tube.* A rescue tube is one of the most versatile pieces of equipment used by lifeguards. It can be used for reaching to a struggling victim, towing a passive victim, or supporting the rescuer. Although sizes and shapes vary, a typical rescue tube is made of buoyant molded foam, 3-1/2 inches by 5-1/2 inches by 40 to 54 inches. Many have a line with a loop attached to one end (the *tail*). The line may vary in length depending on the depth of the water in which it will be used.

- *Rescue buoy.* The rescue buoy is made of a lightweight, hard plastic and is buoyant. It has molded handles along the sides and end and, like the rescue tube, a tow rope attached to one end. The buoy can also be used in a reaching assist or as a buoyancy aid for victims. You cannot, however, use it to support an unconscious victim without maintaining contact with the buoy and victim. The buoy is used predominantly in surf rescues.

Remember, using rescue equipment reduces the risk of harm to you and to the victim. The equipment provides support for both of you, conserves your energy, and makes it easier to tow the victim to safety.

NONSWIMMING ASSISTS

A safe way to perform a rescue is using one of several assists from a stable position. These include reaching, extension, and throwing assists from the pool deck or pier and wading assists in water no higher than chest deep.

Reaching and Extension Assists

Reaching assists, although limited to rescues only a few feet from the side of the pool or dock, play an important role in lifeguarding. These rescues are recommended only for distressed swimmers and in situations in which your safety as the responding lifeguard is endangered. To perform a reaching assist out of the water, lie on the pool deck or dock to establish a stable position. Spread your legs apart to increase stability, keeping your center of mass centered over a wide base. Extend *one arm only* over the water. Your goal is to grasp the victim's wrist or upper arm. Proper positioning is illustrated in Figure 6.2.

Figure 6.2

Reaching assist out of the water.

Reaching rescues can also be made in the water. Maintaining eye contact and distance from the victim, slip into the water. Establish a firm grasp on a ladder, the side of the pool, or a dock support. Then extend your other arm or a leg to the victim, as shown in Figure 6.3. When extending the arm, be sure you grab the victim before she or he grabs you. If you are caught off guard, you may be pulled away from your anchor and become a victim yourself.

Figure 6.3

Reaching assist in the water.

If a victim is too far away to use a reaching assist, consider an extension assist. Traditional lifeguard equipment or a towel, clothing, or a piece of lumber can be used for a quick extension rescue. Remember to establish a firm base of support with your legs spread and your weight low and away from the victim (see Figure 6.4) so you aren't pulled into the water. Distressed victims can grab the extended equipment (although they may not do so). Be prepared for a sharp tug at the object.

Figure 6.4

Extension assist.

As you learned in chapter 5, a drowning victim will probably not grasp the extended object unassisted. In this instance, keep the object within reach of the victim, slide it under the victim's armpit, or press it against the victim's side. This will generally cause the victim to grab the object. Do not try to jab the victim with the object; it may cause additional injury.

Once the victim has a firm grasp of the object, maintain your position, with your weight shifted away from the victim; pull him or her in slowly, hand over hand. Communicate with and reassure the victim as you bring him or her to safety.

Throwing Assists

If the distance to a distressed victim is beyond the range of an extension assist, and if the necessary equipment is available, the next best option is the throwing assist. The key to success is throwing accuracy, and the key to accuracy is preparation and practice. A rescue bag, a ring buoy with a line, a heaving line (a line with a weighted knot on the end), or a heaving jug (a line tied to a plastic gallon jug with a small amount of water in it for weight) are all acceptable throwing devices.

To perform a throwing assist, as illustrated in Figure 6.5, follow these steps:

1. Hold the neatly coiled rope in an open hand with the throwing device in your throwing hand. Be sure the coils lie side by side to avoid any tangling. Secure the rope by standing on it, with a knot stopping the rope from slipping through. Step on the rope with your forward foot, which should be on the side opposite to the throwing arm.

2. Throw the rescue device underhand and let the rope feed freely from your open hand. Throw the device past the victim's head, then pull it to her or him. If you are on a river, throw upstream from your victim and allow the current to carry the device back to the victim. If the wind is strong, compensate for it in aiming your throw.

3. If your throw is unsuccessful and the device moves away from the victim, plant your feet and pull in the rope, letting it drop on the ground in front of you. Do not recoil the line; it wastes precious time. Simply throw the device again as soon as possible. Always be careful to avoid rocks, branches, or anything else that could tangle the line.

If you are using a rescue bag, remove the knotted end and leave the rest of the rope coiled inside the bag. Do not stand on the rope. Rather, hold onto the knot with your nonthrowing hand. Be sure to leave 4 to 6 feet of slack. The rest of the throwing procedures are the same. If your first throw is inaccurate, do not restuff the bag. The water gathered

Figure 6.5

Throwing assist.

in the bag as you tow it back to shore will provide the necessary weight to guide your second toss.

Wading Assists

A wading assist is more dangerous than the other nonswimming assists because you must enter the water. A wading assist should be used when the victim is too far away for a reaching or extension assist, is too close to warrant a throwing assist, and is in water that allows you to go no further than chest-high water. Safe wading assists follow these steps (see Figure 6.6):

1. As you enter the water, take a rescue tube or buoy to extend toward the victim.
2. Move into water no deeper than your chest.
3. Assume a stable position with one foot forward and one foot back and your weight shifted away from the victim.
4. Extend the nose end of the rescue device to the victim.
5. After the victim has grabbed the device, slowly walk to safety, holding on to the tail end (*not* the rope). Talk to the victim as you bring him or her to safety.

Figure 6.6

Wading assist with rescue buoy.

Nonswimming Rescue Guidelines

In making any nonswimming rescue, let the following principles guide you:

1. React calmly and quickly, following your emergency plan (see chapter 7).
2. Maintain visual contact with the victim at all times.
3. Find a piece of rescue equipment appropriate for the situation. Almost any object can be used as an aid for reaching, extension, and wading assists.
4. Establish a firm base for your rescue. Keep your weight low and away from the victim to avoid being pulled into the water or the victim's grasp (if you are already in the water).
5. Establish communication with the victim. You may get the victim to assist in her or his own rescue, and you may reduce the victim's anxiety.
6. Bring the victim to safety. Ask whether there is any pain and, if so, where. Keeping possible injuries in mind, help the victim exit the water.
7. Provide any necessary first aid or call for assistance.
8. Complete the appropriate accident or incident reports.

If you keep these principles in mind, you'll find nonswimming assists safe and valuable tools.

WATER ENTRIES

When a nonswimming rescue isn't possible, you need to swim to the victim. Before you enter the water, plan your rescue and make sure the strap of your rescue tube or buoy is in place so you won't lose your equipment. Take a pocket mask with you in case in-water rescue breathing (p. 86) becomes necessary. Activate the EMS and use your communication system to call for backup help.

You have several choices for entering the water. In a given situation, you will need to determine which of the methods described here is most appropriate. Whatever method you use, always maintain eye contact and communicate with the victim.

Compact Jump

To enter water at least 5 feet deep from a height of 3 feet or more, use a compact jump (see Figure 6.7).

1. Hold the rescue tube or buoy horizontally under your arms and against your chest.
2. Jump into the water with both feet parallel to the water surface and knees bent.
3. As you hit the water, your knees should be bent slightly to absorb the shock. Allow your rescue tube or buoy to lift you to the surface.

Figure 6.7

Compact jump.

Keep in mind that you will lose sight of the victim when you go underwater. Remember where you last saw him or her so that you can go there if for some reason you can't locate the victim when you surface.

Stride Jump

In water over 7 feet deep and from a height not more than 3 feet, you can enter the water quickly and maintain eye contact using a stride jump (see Figure 6.8).

1. Hold your arms out to your sides with your hands slightly above your shoulders.
2. Lean forward and step out away from the edge.
3. As your body enters the water, force your legs together using a scissors kick, and bring your arms forward and down to slow the jump and keep your head above water.

Where you hold the rescue tube or buoy during the entry depends on rescue conditions. If the victim is a short distance away, hold the rescue equipment against the chest and under the arms. If the victim is farther away, drop it to the side and the rear. If many people are in the water where you enter, hold the rescue equipment at your side or against your chest. When you begin your approach stroke, your rescue equipment should be close to you but should not interfere with your stroke.

Figure 6.8

Stride jump.

Shallow Dive Entry

When time and speed are crucial, a shallow dive might be the most appropriate entry. In this entry you sacrifice visual contact momentarily for greater momentum. Before deciding to use the shallow dive entry, you should know the water depth to be sure that you will not be injured. The YMCA recommends a minimum depth of 9 feet for a diving entry from deck. Rescuers trained to do shallow dives may use this dive only if the water is at least 5 feet deep. Also check the water conditions before diving. Seaweed, floating debris, rocky terrain, and pollution may make a shallow dive dangerous and thus inappropriate.

Execute a long shallow dive (see Figure 6.9). As you enter the water, propel yourself to the surface by steering up with your arms and head. Reestablish visual contact with the victim as quickly as possible.

Figure 6.9

Shallow dive entry.

DEEP WATER

Bring your rescue tube or buoy with you to the victim. As with the stride jump, simply release the apparatus to the side and behind you before you enter the water.

Waveless Entry

When the victim is fairly close to your point of entry or when waves created by jumping or diving into the water could cause additional injury, you should select a waveless entry. This entry is for shallow water.

1. Move to a location close to the victim.
2. Sit on the side of the pool or dock. Put your rescue tube or buoy in the water next to where you will enter.
3. Support your weight on your hands and arms and slowly slide into the water, maintaining visual contact with the victim.
4. Retrieve your rescue tube or buoy.

Once you are in the water, slowly wade toward the victim to avoid creating waves. Figure 6.10 illustrates this waveless entry.

A waveless entry for deep water or as an alternative for shallow water calls for the following steps (see Figure 6.11):

1. Sit on the edge of the deck. Put your rescue tube or buoy on the deck or in the water.
2. Place one hand on the deck near your leg.
3. Reach across your body with the other hand and place it on the deck or on the lip of the pool gutter.
4. As you lower yourself into the water, you will be turning 180 degrees to face the side of the pool. Maintain visual contact with the victim as much as possible.
5. Grab your rescue tube or buoy.
6. Swim toward the victim using a waveless, underwater stroke, such as the breaststroke or sidestroke.

Surf Entry

From a sloping shoreline, run into the water using high-stepping strides. Begin swimming toward the victim as soon as possible. In a surf situation, a shallow dive (as shown in Figure 6.12) may be used to get through the breaking waves. Dive through the face of the

Figure 6.10

Waveless entry for shallow water.

(a) Preparing to enter water

(b) entering water

Figure 6.11

Waveless entry for deep water (or alternative for shallow water).

(a) Reaching across the body

(b) lowering into the water

wave in a position parallel to the bottom, not downward. In a heavy surf, it may take several dives to get through the breakers. Release your rescue tube or buoy to the side and behind you as you dive into the waves.

Figure 6.12

Surf entry.

(c) surfacing

(b) diving through the face of the wave

(a) Running into the water

Successful entries with equipment require additional practice. Be sure to develop your entry skills with your lifesaving equipment.

APPROACHES

After you enter the water, you have to get to the victim as soon as possible. The stroke you choose will be based on five factors:

- The distance to the victim
- The number of people in the swimming area
- The concentration of people between you and the victim
- The condition of the victim
- Your strength and condition

Approach Strokes

Your goal is to reach the victim as quickly as possible with an adequate reserve of energy to enable you to perform a safe rescue and tow the victim to safety. In all cases, you need to have your rescue equipment, usually a rescue tube or rescue buoy, on and ready to assist you.

If the victim is severely injured or not breathing, use the fastest possible stroke to reach him or her. If you suspect the victim has a spinal injury, use an approach that creates few waves.

If the victim is near once you've entered the water or if you need to weave between people separating you from the victim, turn the rescue tube on edge and place your hand at the center on top or grasp the rescue buoy on the long side handle. Point the nose of the tube or buoy in the direction you are swimming. Swim to the victim using a single arm pull breaststroke or a combined stroke using the breaststroke kick and a single arm crawl. This positioning will let you manipulate the apparatus and move relatively quickly. In any instance, keep the apparatus in front of you. Keep the line end of the apparatus (the tail) pointed toward your armpit.

For longer distances, unless there is a possibility that the rescue tube or buoy will become caught on something behind you, allow the line to trail behind while you approach the victim. The crawl stroke allows the quickest approach. If speed is essential, you may place your face in the water. Turn your head to the side to breathe; then rotate your head forward to look at the victim before putting your face in the water again. When you are about 15 feet from the victim, keep your head up and your eyes on the victim.

Quick Reverse

When you approach a victim, you must prepare for contact whether the victim is active or seemingly passive. The quick reverse moves you into a position of safety in which you can move away from the victim if necessary. When you are just out of the victim's arm range (about 6 feet away), execute a quick reverse (see Figure 6.13).

1. Lean backward and position one side toward the victim.
2. At the same time, bring your arms forcefully together and your legs to your chest to assist in the turn.
3. Angle your legs toward the victim and your shoulders away from the victim. Be sure the rescue tube or buoy is between you and the victim before you make contact.

If you dragged the rescue tube or buoy behind you during the approach, do a quick reverse approximately 9 feet from the victim and retrieve the rescue equipment by

Figure 6.13

Quick reverse.

(a) Turning

(b) angling legs toward victim

grabbing the line and pulling it toward you. During this process be sure to keep your eyes on the victim.

RESCUES USING RESCUE EQUIPMENT

Any time you enter the water you need to take a piece of rescue equipment, secured to you with a shoulder strap. Generally the rescue tube or buoy is the most helpful. Having one of these pieces of equipment with you provides an added measure of security. It serves as a flotation aid to assist you in performing the rescue and in positioning the victim for rescue breathing.

If you are right-handed, be sure to place the shoulder strap so it hangs from the shoulder of your left arm to the opposite hip. If you then hold the rescue equipment in your right hand, the line will not interfere during the rescue. (If you are left-handed, reverse the placement.)

This section describes rescues using rescue equipment under seven conditions:

- Front, active victim
- Rear, active victim
- Front, passive victim
- Rear, passive victim
- Active victim just below the surface
- Passive victim just below the surface
- Submerged victim

All instructions are written for right-handed individuals. If you are left-handed, reverse the instructions accordingly.

Front, Active Victim

For an active drowning victim approached from the front, perform a quick reverse about 6 feet away. While treading water, grab the rescue tube or buoy line and pull the apparatus to you as you continue to look at the victim. If you are using a rescue tube, bring it in front of you and turn it on edge. Hold the rescue tube with one hand at the nose of the tube and the other hand in the center (illustrated in Figure 6.14). If you are using a buoy, turn it on

Figure 6.14

Rescuing an active victim from the front.

edge and hold it with one hand on the top handle and the other on the nose. Keep the equipment between you and the victim at all times.

To extend the tube or buoy to the victim, move to one side of the victim and press the nose under one arm. Once the victim grabs the apparatus, continue to give reassurance. If the victim does not grab the equipment, trap his or her arm over it. You may even have to remind the victim to hold onto the equipment or hold the victim's arms around it yourself. Holding the victim's elbow and the equipment, use a rescue kick to move the victim to safety. Upon reaching shallow water, the side of the pool, the deck, or a boat, be sure to assess the victim's condition.

If the victim grabs you in a way that places you at risk, take a quick breath and submerge, pushing the rescue tube up and into the victim (Figure 6.15). Swim away underwater. When you surface, reassess the situation and make another approach if necessary.

Figure 6.15

Avoiding a distressed victim.

Rear, Active Victim

The approach from the rear to an actively drowning victim uses the same technique. About 6 feet from the victim perform a quick reverse. Then proceed with the rescue as described for the active victim from the front, pushing the nose of the tube or buoy underneath the victim's arm and towing her or him to safety.

Front, Passive Victim

In this situation the victim is not struggling, and you have determined that there are no signs of spinal injury. (With signs of spinal injury, follow the procedures described in chapter 9 instead of these.) The victim is facedown or submerged in the water. Quickly move to about 6 feet from the victim and do a quick reverse. Maintaining visual contact, bring the rescue equipment to your side.

To perform this approach with a rescue tube, take the following steps (see Figure 6.16):

1. Place the tube between you and the victim so that it crosses the front of your body.
2. Place your left hand on the center of the tube.
3. Reach over the tube with your right hand and submerge it slightly with your left hand. Reach your right hand to the underside of the victim's right wrist.
4. Grasp the victim's wrist with your thumb on top. Turn the victim faceup by pulling the arm down and then back up toward the surface (draw a *U*). Simultaneously,

with the opposite hand in the center of the tube, push down to submerge the tube while pulling the victim's wrist just past your ear and pulling him or her onto the tube.

5. Once the tube is under the victim's back, release your hold on the wrist. Place your right arm over the victim's upper arm and place your right hand on top of the tube to secure her or him in place. Pull your other hand from under the victim.

6. If you are in choppy water or far from safety, grab one end of the tube's fastener in each hand and secure the tube. If you are in calm water and close to safety, there is no need to secure the tube.

7. Move to the right side of the victim's head. Place your left hand on the victim's forehead and tilt it back to check the airway, breathing, and circulation (the ABCs).

(a) Reaching over tube for victim's wrist

Figure 6.16

Rescuing a passive victim from the front with a rescue tube.

(b) submerging tube under victim and positioning tube below victim's armpits

(c) checking victim for ABCs and applying pocket mask

To use a rescue buoy for this approach and rescue (see Figure 6.17), come to about 6 feet from the victim and do a quick reverse. After checking for and finding no signs of spinal injury, do the following:

1. With your right hand, bring the buoy nose end first to a position between you and the victim. Then place your left hand over the buoy, grasping the hand grip with fingers on the outside and the thumb inside.

(a) Grabbing victim's wrist

(b) submerging buoy under victim

Figure 6.17

Rescuing a passive victim from the front with a rescue buoy.

(c) positioning buoy below victim's armpits

(d) grabbing buoy to stabilize victim and check ABCs

2. Reach over the buoy and grab the underside of the victim's right wrist with your right hand. Turn him or her faceup with the technique described previously while simultaneously submerging the buoy and pulling the victim onto it.

3. When the buoy is under the victim, release the victim's wrist, move to the right side of the victim's head, and place your right hand over the victim's right arm. Grab the buoy with your right hand and stabilize the victim.

4. Tilt the victim's head back with your left hand and assess the ABCs.

To determine whether the victim is breathing, level the victim, then tread water hard enough so you can place your ear close to the victim's mouth to listen for breathing sounds and see if the chest is rising and falling. Do not submerge the victim's head or turn it toward you, but look, listen, and feel for breathing for 5 seconds.

If the victim is breathing, tow her or him to safety. If not, and conditions allow, follow these steps to provide rescue breathing for a victim with no signs of spinal injury (see chapter 9 for rescue breathing procedures for those suspected to have spinal injuries):

1. After the victim is level, use your left hand to turn the head. Pull the corner of the mouth down to let any water run out.

2. Release the corner of the victim's mouth and place the heel of the left hand on the victim's forehead. Tilt the head back to open the airway.

3. Take out your pocket mask and be sure the dome is pushed out and the one-way valve is attached to the valve. Rinse it in the water, and shake it to remove most of the water.

4. Position the pocket mask over the victim's nose and mouth (Figure 6.18), making sure you maintain a good seal at the edges so air and water do not leak. Seal your mouth over the pocket mask orifice. Provide rescue breathing as you learned it in your CPR first aid training.

5. You should be able to feel the air move into the victim's lungs. If not, reposition the victim's head and try again.

After giving the first two full breaths, check the victim's pulse at the neck (carotid pulse) for 5 to 10 seconds. If the victim has no pulse, tow him or her to shore or the deck and begin CPR. If the victim has a pulse, continue rescue breathing as you tow the victim.

If the distance is great or if conditions don't allow you to perform rescue breathing, move to shallow water or safety. Once in shallow water or on land, begin rescue breathing; if CPR is needed, remove the victim from the water as soon as possible and begin CPR. Continue until emergency personnel arrive on the scene to relieve you.

As you learn how to do rescue breathing, practice often. It is a difficult but important skill to master.

Note: The YMCA conforms to the standards established by the Emergency Cardiac Care Committee of the American Medical Association, which specifies that rescue breathing should be started as soon as possible (here being as soon as the victim is contacted in deep

Figure 6.18

Rescue breathing with a rescue buoy.

water). However, if the rescuer doesn't have a rescue tube or buoy, assessment must wait until the victim is brought to pool side or into shallow water.

Victim assessment and rescue breathing can be accomplished in waist-deep water with the same technique used with a rescue tube in deep water and without a tube in shallow water.

Rear, Passive Victim

In this approach you come up from behind a victim who is facedown in the water. Swim quickly to about 6 feet from the victim and do a quick reverse. Check for signs of spinal injury. If you see such signs, follow the procedures outlined in chapter 9. If signs of spinal injury are not present, follow these steps for use with a rescue tube (see Figure 6.19):

1. With the right hand, bring the tube into position crossing in front of your body so the tail of the tube is on your right side.

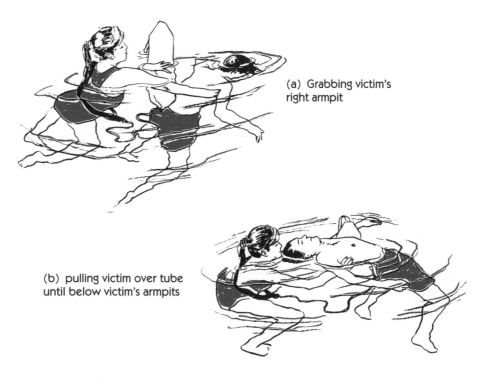

(a) Grabbing victim's right armpit

Figure 6.19

Rescuing a passive victim from the rear with a rescue tube.

(b) pulling victim over tube until below victim's armpits

(c) checking victim for ABCs

2. With your left hand on the center of the tube, submerge the tube as you reach across with your right hand and grab the victim's right armpit. Your fingers should be in the victim's armpit with your thumb toward the back.

3. Pull the victim over the tube until it reaches a position below the upper back. Then place your right arm over the victim's upper arm and place your right hand on top of the tube (if not clasped) to secure her or him in place. Pull your other hand from under the victim.

4. Evaluate the distance from safety. Grasp the ends of the tube and secure them together, if desired, to proceed to safety.

5. Move to the right side of the victim's head. Place your left hand on the victim's forehead to tilt the victim's head back to check the ABCs.

When using a rescue buoy for a rear, passive rescue, swim to about 6 feet from the victim and do a quick reverse. After checking for and finding no evidence of spinal injury, follow these steps (see Figure 6.20):

(a) Grabbing victim's right armpit

(b) pulling victim over buoy

Figure 6.20

Rescuing a passive victim from the rear with a rescue buoy.

(c) bringing right hand over victim's right upper arm and under the back and grasping the buoy handle

(d) checking victim for ABCs

1. With your right hand, bring the buoy nose end first to a position between you and the victim. Then place your left hand over the buoy, grasping the handgrip with fingers on the outside and the thumb inside.
2. Push the buoy underneath the victim with your left hand and pull him or her over the buoy toward you with your right hand.
3. Move to the right side of the victim's head.
4. Take your right hand and move it so it is over the victim's upper arm and under the back, gripping the buoy handle.
5. With the left hand on the victim's forehead, tilt the victim's head back and assess the ABCs.

Active Victim Just Below the Surface

For either a front or rear approach, perform a quick reverse about 6 feet from the victim. If you suspect the victim has a spinal injury, follow the procedures outlined in chapter 9; if not, then do the following:

1. Place the rescue tube or buoy so it is between you and the victim and move to one side of the victim. Reach over the tube or buoy and grab the victim's wrist or forearm. Pull that arm up, over, and around the top of the tube or buoy to keep the victim afloat on the surface.
2. Keep the rescue tube or buoy between you and the victim at all times.
3. Follow all other procedures for rescuing an active victim.

Passive Victim Just Below the Surface

A rear approach should be used when a victim just below the surface is passive. Perform a quick reverse about 6 feet from the victim. Again, if you suspect the victim has a spinal injury, follow the procedures in chapter 9; if not, then follow these steps:

1. Place the rescue tube or buoy between you and the victim and stay to the rear of the victim. Reach over the tube or buoy and grab the victim's armpit.
2. Pull the victim to the surface and onto the tube.
3. Follow all other procedures for rescuing a passive victim approaching from the rear.

Submerged Victim

Speed is crucial in rescuing a submerged victim. It may be a waste of time to perform the quick reverse; instead use a surface dive, either feet-first or arm-over-arm (described on p. 16).
Dive feet-first under the following conditions:

- The water is murky.
- You are not sure of underwater obstructions.
- You don't know the depth of the water.

Choose the faster and more accurate arm-over-arm surface dive when these conditions prevail:

- The water is clear.
- You know the area in which you are diving is safe for diving.
- You know the water is deep enough to safely dive head-first.

Swim quickly to the approximate place where the victim was last seen. Bubbles on the surface can be a clue to where the victim is submerged. If you suspect the victim has a spinal injury, use the rescue procedures described in chapter 9. Otherwise make a surface dive, leaving the rescue tube or buoy on the surface. If the victim is submerged too deeply for you to reach her or him with your rescue tube still attached to your shoulder, remove the strap. Approach from the rear and grasp the victim by the armpit. Bring him or her to the surface. Once on the surface, position the victim on the rescue equipment as described for the passive victim with an approach from the rear. Be sure to check the ABCs.

MULTIPLE VICTIM RESCUES

It's possible that you will encounter situations in which more than one person is in distress or near drowning. Multiple-victim near-drownings do occur, although two-victim incidents happen more often than those involving three or more people. Some of the situations in which one or more victims might grab nearby swimmers are the following:

- At a beach, victims might be knocked over by a wave, lose contact with the bottom due to waves or swells, lose an inflatable support, or step off into a hole or into deeper water.
- At a pool, victims might jump or be pushed into deep water, walk from shallow water into deep water in a pool that has no lifeline indicating the water depth, become tired while swimming across the pool width in deep water, or lose an inflatable support.

To rescue multiple victims, follow these principles:

- Have multiple lifeguards available to provide the best response. If only one is available, do extensive planning and rehearsal before and during the swimming season to ensure successful rescues under these conditions.
- Have an inflatable rescue tube available. A single rescuer can handle two victims, but a situation with three or four victims will require an inflatable tube.
- Have rescue tubes with clasps on the ends so the tube can be fastened around the first victim. He or she probably will not be able to stay afloat without this assistance.

Rescue techniques for multiple victims will vary depending on whether the victims are on the surface or on the bottom and on the number of lifeguards available and the number of victims.

Multiple Victim Rescues on the Surface

Here are procedures for multiple victim rescues with one or two lifeguards of two or more victims.

One lifeguard, two victims.   After assessing the situation, you may see victims who are face to face, one victim holding on to another one from behind, or one victim holding on to another from the side. Take the following action:

1. Blow your whistle, use an airhorn, or push the pool alarm button to indicate the beginning of a multiple victim rescue procedure. This should summon another lifeguard to cover your zone.
2. Enter the water and determine which victim is on top (this usually is the person who initiated the situation). Approach the top victim from behind. Place the rescue tube on edge. Grab the tube approximately 12 inches from the nose end with one hand (this gives you good control over the tube when submerging it).

3. With your free hand, grab the armpit of the top victim (right hand to right armpit or left hand to left armpit).

4. As you lift up on the victim's armpit push down on the tube. Thrust the tube between the two victims. Grasp both ends of the tube and clasp the tube around the top victim, providing flotation.

5. Swim around to the other victim and assist him/her in reaching the rescue tube or, approach victim two from behind, extend your hands under that victim's arms and grab hold of the rescue tube.

6. Tow or push both victims to the side of the pool, the dock, or the beach using a breaststroke or inverted breaststroke kick.

Two lifeguards, two victims. When a second lifeguard is available, perform the rescue of two victims this way:

1. Signal the start of the multiple victim/multiple rescuer procedure.
2. Enter the water and approach the victims.
3. If you are the first lifeguard to reach the victims, determine which victim is on top (the original victim), insert the tube between the two victims, and clasp the tube ends together behind the victim on top.
4. The second lifeguard to arrive should then approach the second victim and extend the tube while instructing the second victim to grab it.
5. If the second victim does not or cannot grab the rescue tube, the second lifeguard should follow the procedures for a front or rear active rescue, depending on which direction the second victim is facing.

One lifeguard, three or more victims. A situation with three or more victims requires both a primary and a secondary rescue tube. An inflatable tube would be a useful secondary tube. Two models are available, one that is inflated orally and one that uses a carbon dioxide cartridge to inflate. The one with the cartridge is probably the better one for these situations. It can be stored in a large fanny pack or attached with Velcro to the sash or rope on the primary tube.

Follow these procedures to rescue three or more victims:

1. Signal the start of the multiple victim rescue procedure.
2. Enter the water and approach the victims. Determine which two victims you can insert your primary tube between.
3. Clasp the ends of the tube together behind the victim whose back is nearest to you. Remove the sash from your neck so you can move to the other victims without getting tangled.
4. Retrieve the inflatable tube from your fanny pack or primary rescue tube, inflate it, and extend it to the third victim. Then tow the third victim on the inflatable to the fourth victim (if there is one), and allow these victims to be supported by the inflatable tube.

Two lifeguards, three or more victims. When two lifeguards are available, rescue three or more victims like this:

1. Signal the start of the multiple victim/multiple rescuer procedure.
2. Enter the water and approach the victims.
3. If you are the first lifeguard to reach the victims, attempt to determine which victim is on top (the original victim). Insert the tube between the first two victims, then clasp the ends together behind the victim on top.

4. The second lifeguard to arrive should follow the procedures for a front or rear active rescue for the third victim or, if the situation involves four active victims, attempt to insert the tube between the two remaining victims.

5. If the two remaining victims become separated, use the appropriate approach (front or rear active or passive) to the third victim, then tow the third victim and tube close to where the fourth victim can grab hold of and be supported by the tube.

6. If the second lifeguard has an inflatable tube, he or she can use it to rescue the fourth victim.

Multiple Victim Rescues of Submerged Victims

If it becomes necessary to rescue more than one submerged victim from the bottom, you will need the help of either another lifeguard or of individuals who are certified in CPR.

Follow these steps to recover multiple victims from the bottom:

1. Signal the start of the multiple victim/multiple rescuer procedure.

2. Enter the water with another lifeguard as soon as possible. Approach the victims on the surface to the point where they are directly beneath you, then surface dive to the bottom. If your tube line isn't long enough to reach the bottom, remove the rescue tube sash from your neck before diving.

3. Each of you should place your victim in a single or double armpit tow, then swim the victim to the surface.

4. Assess the ABCs and provide rescue breathing if needed. If the distance to the pool deck or the beach is short, continue towing the victim to safety. A one- or two-person lift or drag can be used to remove the victim from the water. If the distance is long, you should try to retrieve your rescue tube and attach it around the victim for additional support.

5. As the victims were on the bottom, they probably need CPR. Begin the procedure with a pocket mask immediately upon getting them out of the water.

If a second lifeguard isn't available, but one or more people with CPR certification are, you may have to rescue and tow the victims to safety one at a time. Those who have CPR certification can then care for them while you rescue the others.

RESCUE TOWING

Two techniques can be used to tow the victim to safety: the rescue stroke and the armpit tows.

Rescue Stroke

This is the stroke used to tow a victim. It consists of a one-arm pull with a scissors, breaststroke, or rotary kick.

Armpit Tows

If a victim is breathing, is truly passive, and has no evidence of a spinal injury, you can tow her or him to shore using a single or double (Figure 6.21) armpit tow. If you have clasped the rescue tube around the victim, tow by grasping either the tube or the victim's armpit. Grab the victim as close to the armpit as possible with your thumb on the outside of the arm, and keep the tube or buoy between you and the victim. For the single armpit tow,

Figure 6.21

Armpit tow.

use any rescue stroke that allows you to keep visual contact with the victim and swim to safety quickly. For the double armpit tow, grab both of the victim's armpits and kick to safety.

WATER EXITS

Once you have brought a victim to safety, you have to get him or her out of the water as quickly as possible to start emergency first aid. The type of exit you use is influenced by conditions such as terrain, proximity to medical assistance, your own size and strength, the assistance available, and the victim's size, condition, and injuries.

Supporting Assist

If a victim is conscious but very weak, assist him or her to safety. Stand next to the victim, pull the near arm across your shoulder, and secure it by grabbing the wrist with your far hand. Your free arm should support the victim's waist. You should be able to walk the victim to safety (see Figure 6.22).

Figure 6.22

Supporting assist.

One-Person Drag

The one-person drag is probably one of the quickest and most efficient ways to carry an unconscious person from an open body of water. After you have ruled out the possibility of a spinal injury, reach around from behind the victim under the armpits and grab your wrist with the other hand to lock your grip. Walk backward, dragging the victim's feet. Be careful to lift the victim primarily using your legs and arms to avoid injuring your back.

If you are smaller than the victim, you may have difficulty reaching all the way around and grasping your wrist. If you cannot easily maintain a tight grip, you may find it more secure to grasp the victim's opposite wrists, as shown in Figure 6.23.

If you are the second rescuer on the scene, you can assist the first rescuer who is performing a one-person drag. Simply lift the victim's legs from the knees, with one leg on each side of your body. From this position, called a *two-person carry*, you can move the victim to safety much more quickly. Again, lift primarily using your legs and arms.

Figure 6.23

One-person drag if victim is heavy.

(a) Reaching around the victim

(b) grabbing the victim's wrists with opposite hands

(c) dragging the victim

One-Person Lift

The one-person lift is used primarily in deep water (see Figure 6.24). If the victim is not breathing, provide rescue breathing while holding onto the side of the pool or deck (see pp. 86-87). Position a breathing victim next to the side of the pool or deck facing the wall or deck. Position yourself to the rear of the victim.

Reach under the victim's arm and grab the side of the pool to support the victim. You can also support the victim on your knee. Lift the victim's hands onto the deck, one on top of the other. If the distance between the deck and the water level is too great for you to lift yourself out of the water while maintaining control of the victim's hands and keeping her or his head out of the water, call for additional help.

After you have positioned yourself on the deck, grab the victim's wrists and lower the victim before lifting to gain momentum and make the lift easier. Do not submerge the victim's face. Keep in mind that the victim's head may be leaning forward. Take care to lift the victim straight up to protect the head from possible injury. Lift with your legs, not your back, to protect yourself.

As the victim's hips clear the deck level, step back and lower the victim slowly to the deck. Place your foot under the victim's face to prevent it from hitting the deck. Roll the victim onto his or her back to begin emergency procedures.

(a) Placing victim's hands on the deck and exiting the water

(b) lowering, then lifting the victim straight up

Figure 6.24

One person lift.

(c) lowering the victim onto the deck

(d) rolling the victim over

If the victim is too heavy for one rescuer to lift, a second rescuer may assist. Each rescuer takes one of the victim's wrists, and with coordinated movements the rescuers lift the victim onto the deck and continue with the procedures described for a single rescuer. For a large victim one or two assistants may be needed in the water to push the victim up while those on the deck lift.

Finishing an Exit

When you carry a victim to safety, remember to lower him or her carefully to the ground to reduce the chance of additional injury. Provide cushioning whenever possible.

Review Questions

1. Name and describe 6 pieces of rescue equipment.
2. List 3 things in your aquatic environment that could be used in an extension assist.
3. Why is it important to keep your weight shifted away from the victim in a reaching, extension, or wading assist?
4. Where should you aim in a throwing assist?
5. List and describe the 5 entries. When would you use each?
6. Why is it important to perform a quick reverse upon reaching a victim?
7. Why must you use rescue equipment in each rescue?
8. Describe the following rescues: active victim from the front, active victim from the rear, passive victim from the front, and passive victim from the rear.
9. Describe how to position a victim for rescue breathing using a rescue tube or buoy for additional support.
10. How do you rescue a partially submerged victim?
11. When should you perform a feet-first surface dive? An arm-over-arm surface dive?
12. How do you rescue a deeply submerged victim?
13. Describe how to tow a passive victim.
14. Describe the supporting assist and when to use it.
15. Describe the one-person drag and when to use it.
16. Describe the one-person lift and when to use it.
17. How do you prevent back injury to yourself when performing lifts and drags?
18. Describe how to rescue two victims with one and with two lifeguards and how to rescue three or more victims with one and with two lifeguards.
19. Describe how to rescue multiple victims who are submerged.

CHAPTER 7

Emergency Systems

It is likely that emergencies and potential emergencies will arise at your facility on occasion. Being prepared for common emergencies will help reduce the guesswork involved in reacting to them and the amount of stress you experience.

IN THIS CHAPTER YOU'LL LEARN HOW TO RESPOND TO EMERGENCIES BY EXAMINING

- types of emergencies,
- preparation for emergencies,
- steps for creating an emergency policy,
- emergency plans,
- how to complete accident and incident reports,
- how to use injury charts, and
- crisis control responsibilities.

TYPES OF EMERGENCIES

Seven specific groups of emergencies are presented in this section:

- Medical
- Water
- Missing persons
- Environmental
- Chemical
- Mechanical
- Facility

As you read this section and the rest of this chapter, consider how you and your facility would handle various emergency situations. Your facility should have an emergency plan for each category of emergency. If your facility does not have one for a particular type, suggest to management that they use the principles presented later in the chapter to preplan a course of action for that type.

Medical Emergencies

Medical emergencies can be divided into two general situations: life-threatening and potentially life-threatening. In life-threatening emergencies, death probably will occur if no action is taken. Such emergencies require immediate advanced first aid, such as CPR, and transportation to a medical facility. In potentially life-threatening emergencies death is less certain, but such conditions still require immediate action. Outside emergency medical assistance may still be needed, including transport to a medical facility. Here are some examples of life-threatening and potentially life-threatening emergencies:

Life-Threatening Emergencies

Cardiac arrest

Drowning/near-drowning

Uncontrolled bleeding

Poisoning

Cessation of breathing

Potentially Life-Threatening Emergencies

Seizure

Heart attack or angina

Spinal injury

Loss of consciousness

Fracture

Reaction to extreme heat or cold

Obstructed airway or respiratory emergency

Allergic reaction

Asthma attack

Diabetes or insulin shock

Cut or laceration

There are undoubtedly other medical emergencies that you could list. Staff should discuss how to handle such emergencies at your facility.

Water Emergencies

By the time you finish this lifeguarding course, you should have the skills to handle a wide variety of water emergencies. Through in-service training the staff at your facility should collaborate to develop the emergency procedures you need to react effectively and efficiently. Be sure you have plans to cover

- drownings and near-drownings,
- severe injury in the water and spinal injury in the water,
- cardiac or respiratory emergencies in the water, and
- missing persons.

Missing Persons

If a missing person is believed to be in the water, the situation is life-threatening. If she or he is believed to be out of the water, the situation is less critical. In any instance, you must assist in efforts to locate the missing person. See chapter 11 for a complete discussion of search and recovery techniques.

Environmental Emergencies

Chapter 10 provides some information concerning storms and signs of approaching bad weather. It is important that facility personnel know the policy and procedures for a variety of weather-related situations:

- Thunderstorms and lightning
- Hurricanes
- Tornadoes and high winds
- Heavy rain and hailstorms
- High and low temperatures
- Reduced visibility (due to fog, haze, dust, blowing debris, or other causes)
- Earth tremors or earthquakes

Chemical Emergencies

Pool operators should be very careful in handling the chemicals used to keep the water properly balanced for recreation. Unfortunately, accidents occur that can create potentially hazardous conditions. Each facility should have procedures for handling a variety of chemical emergencies:

- Liquid gas or chlorine leaks due to tank ruptures, leaks, or spills resulting in serious or fatal injuries
- Pool-acid spills resulting in caustic vapors and skin irritations
- Explosion of flammable chemicals (for example, chlorinated granulates or bromine)
- Imbalance in water chemistry (for example, cloudiness, or improper pH or chlorine level, irritating swimmers' skin or eyes)

For more information on pool chemistry, see chapter 13. Be sure you have read the material safety data sheets on chemicals, available from your manager.

Mechanical Emergencies

Various potential mechanical hazards exist depending on the type of facility you work at. Your facility should have procedures to handle

- structural failure,
- filtration system failure,
- lighting failure, and
- equipment malfunctions (slides, wave pool, diving boards).

Facility Emergencies

Not all emergency situations that affect your facility will occur within the pool area. Be sure you know your facility's provisions for handling a variety of emergency situations:

- Structural fire on the grounds
- Brushfire on the grounds
- Bomb threats
- Electrical outages
- Chemical explosion on the grounds or nearby, presenting danger from fire or fumes
- Fire nearby, presenting danger from fire or smoke

PREPARING FOR EMERGENCIES

The most successful emergency responses are a result of effective teamwork, which reduces the risks for both lifeguards and patrons. It also increases the speed and efficiency with which an emergency situation can be handled. All facilities should have plans and an in-service training program for handling a variety of emergencies. Evaluating staff performance after an emergency is useful in helping staff identify hazardous areas, refine their responses, and acknowledge their successes.

Your emergency team includes lifeguards, law enforcement officials, fire department personnel, emergency medical staff, civil defense officials, and the members of a variety of other local organizations. The involvement of each group makes your emergency plans more efficient and more effective.

Facility Layout

Another key to quick and successful emergency response is knowing the layout of your facility. That may sound simple enough, but knowing the easiest way for medical personnel to reach each area is vital in an emergency. Plan for emergency access—don't leave finding the best route for emergency personnel to chance! Determine ahead of time the shortest and safest routes for paramedics to reach all locations at your facility.

Consider the following factors:

- The length and width of the backboard (p. 145) and ambulance gurney
- Stairs
- Sharp corners and narrow hallways
- Locked doors or other obstacles

Once you have planned the shortest and safest access routes for emergency personnel, make sure that these routes are kept clear at all times. The excitement of an emergency situation may make clearing the routes difficult when it is most important.

Your facility should arrange in-service training sessions with outside emergency personnel to practice your procedures. During these practice sessions you can determine whether you have selected appropriate access routes. Those routes, along with the locations of fire alarms, fire extinguishers, telephones, first aid areas, and tornado areas, should be posted for all staff and patrons.

Equipment Assessment

Your equipment and supplies should be examined every day as part of your opening procedure. Every facility should have a variety of lifeguarding and emergency medical equipment, including an adequate supply of the following:

- Shepherd's crooks or reaching poles
- Ring buoys
- Rescue tubes or buoys
- Backboards and straps
- Head immobilizers and cervical collars (see p. 146)
- Telephones and posted emergency telephone numbers
- First aid kits (including pocket masks, protective glasses, rubber gloves, and gowns)
- Blankets

Every locale has different codes specifying the requirements for the equipment needs of recreational facilities. Contact your state, county, and local health departments for lists of the apparatus they require.

Safety equipment that is broken, in poor repair, or locked in a room is of little use in an emergency. And the equipment is valuable only if all staff members know where it is stored and how to use it. Most facilities should schedule regular staff in-service training sessions to ensure that lifeguards can react effectively to a variety of emergency situations.

Emergency Medical Procedures

All personnel should be aware of the needs and procedures of the emergency medical system (EMS) personnel who respond to emergencies. Ignorance or misunderstanding of these needs and procedures may cause increased danger for the injured individual and may expose the facility to increased legal liability.

EMERGENCY POLICY GUIDELINES

The YMCA encourages all facilities to document emergency procedures before any emergency occurs. Having trained, knowledgeable personnel can only enhance the quality and safety of your aquatic program. If you work for a facility that does not have these procedures documented, strongly encourage the management to take these steps:

- Specify an emergency team leader and define this leader's responsibilities and limitations.
- Specify the personnel who should be involved in an emergency response and assign specific duties.
- Specify a chain of command.
- Select one spokesperson for the facility and direct all questions to that person.
- Establish a sequence of emergency steps.
- List emergency phone numbers.

- Prepare a written script for calling in emergencies and post it by the phone.
- Define the procedures for moving and transporting victims.
- Instruct lifeguards in the importance of and procedures for completing accident and incident reports (described later in this chapter).
- Schedule regular emergency procedure training and practice sessions.

It is vital that the emergency procedures be practiced frequently and systematically. Only through practice will reactions be refined and procedures fully understood. Practice also makes the emergency situation less stressful as all team members become familiar with their responsibilities. The more comfortable team members are responding to their duties during an emergency, the more effective and efficient they will be. When you practice emergency action plans, evaluate your own performance and identify areas for improvement.

EMERGENCY PLANS

Emergency plans include six fundamental steps:

1. Initial reaction and assessment
2. Initiation of the primary response by the lifeguard, including calling EMS
3. Initiation of any necessary secondary response by other team members leading to resolution of the emergency (including providing first aid)
4. Notification of designated personnel (Staff should be instructed not to comment on the emergency situation to any witness, bystander, or reporter. Only those specified in the chain of command should be given information.)
5. Completion of the necessary incident or accident report
6. Investigation of the incident

The manner in which each of these steps is completed varies with the specific situation. Figures 7.1 and 7.2 are sample emergency plan flowcharts for single-guard emergency reaction and multiguard staff reaction, respectively.

The sample plans provided in this chapter, meant only as a guide, are for multiguard facilities. Each facility must determine which guards perform which duties. Single-guard facilities must establish a procedure for the lone guard to signal for immediate assistance. Responsibilities for the guard and assistant under those circumstances must be carefully defined.

Your facility should have written procedures for handling emergencies. Be sure you are familiar with the procedures and your responsibilities. Your in-service training and practice sessions will help you feel comfortable in responding.

Sample Pool Evacuation Plan

Each facility must have a plan for evacuating the pool area. In all emergencies, quick and organized action is important. This plan is appropriate for a weather emergency.

1. Signal other lifeguards to initiate the evacuation plan.
2. Signal swimmers to clear the pool.
3. Remain on post until all swimmers have left the water.
4. Assist other staff in directing patrons to a shelter or designated area.
5. Reassure patrons of their safety.
6. Report to management for further instruction or assignment.
7. Assist as necessary.
8. Assist in completion of the incident report form.

Figure 7.1

Single-guard
emergency plan
flowchart.

Based on a flowchart
prepared by the Klamath
County YMCA Pool
Administrators.

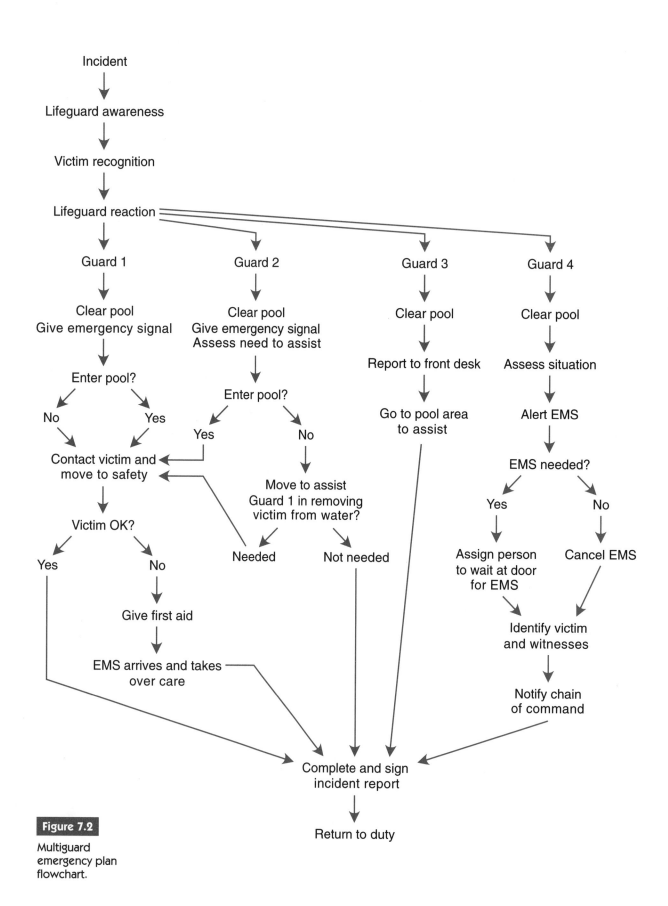

Figure 7.2

Multiguard
emergency plan
flowchart.

Sample Emergency Plan
for a Life-Threatening Medical Emergency

Follow this procedure for providing first aid for a heart attack victim requiring prompt attention:

1. Signal another guard to cover your area while you initiate first aid. If you are the only lifeguard, call for assistance using your preplanned emergency signal.
2. Assess the situation, call for EMS assistance, and provide the emergency first aid necessary.
3. Notify those in the chain of command.
4. Complete an accident report and file it with the appropriate person before returning to duty.
5. Review your actions with the manager.

Sample Emergency Plan for a Near-Drowning

The procedure for handling a water rescue situation at a multiguard facility is outlined here. Figure 7.2 illustrates one way that responsibilities can be divided.

1. Signal other guards to initiate emergency procedures. While you react, they will supervise your area, assist in the rescue or removal of the victim from the water, send for any first aid equipment or EMS assistance necessary, and control onlookers. If necessary, they will evacuate the pool.
2. Assess the situation and determine what rescue skills and equipment are necessary.
3. Carry out the rescue.
4. Begin any necessary first aid.
5. Calmly notify those on the chain of command of the accident; they in turn should notify emergency contacts (relatives or other designated individuals).
6. Complete and file an accident report.
7. Return to duty as soon as possible.

Sample Emergency Plan for a Missing Person

If a person is reported missing, having an emergency plan and practicing it is essential. A variety of different search and recovery techniques can be used for open water areas (see chapter 11).

For a missing person search at a pool, take the following steps:

1. Signal the other guards to initiate emergency procedures.
2. Signal an immediate pool check.
3. Clear the pool.
4. Get an accurate description of the missing person, including age, race, height, weight, color of hair, color of clothing, and where he or she was last seen. Keep the person giving this description in a designated area to be available whenever necessary.
5. Do a visual search as quickly as possible.
6. If the missing person has become a drowning victim, complete the rescue and begin emergency first aid immediately. Arrange for EMS assistance.

7. If it is determined that the missing person is not a drowning victim, swimmers may return to the water while the following steps are taken in order—
   a. Check all facilities, including washrooms, locker rooms, gymnasiums, and any related facility on the grounds.
   b. Check the missing person's home by phone.
   c. If the person is not found, notify those on the chain of command, who should in turn notify emergency contacts.
   d. Notify law enforcement officials. This is the duty of the manager or the head lifeguard.
8. Complete the necessary accident or incident report.
9. Return to duty as soon as possible.

ACCIDENT AND INCIDENT REPORTS

As a professional, you are responsible for your decisions. In the case of an emergency, completing accident and incident reports is often the only way to substantiate your procedures and actions if they are ever questioned. Complete the reports carefully as soon after the emergency as possible. Accurate detail is critical. An accident report is used any time first aid is required; an incident report is used for any other situation, usually one in which a lifeguard, staff member, or outside agency is called into action (such as discipline problems or theft).

In an accident that requires you to provide first aid, your responsibility does not end when the injured person is delivered to the appropriate medical care provider. You must follow your facility's procedures for reporting and recording the accident. Copies of this report should be made and sent to the appropriate authorities. Be sure to keep a copy for your own records.

A sample Accident Report Form is included in Appendix C. This sample should serve as a guide; amend it to meet the unique needs of your facility. From the form or other records, the following information should be provided:

- Names, titles, employment numbers, years of experience, locations of assignments, hours on duty, and lunch periods of employees involved
- Date, type, and amount of training for each involved employee
- Time, location, and nature of the accident
- Number of persons involved in the accident
- Weather and water conditions
- Number of people present at the pool or beach where the accident occurred
- General comments of importance in evaluating the situation
- Plan or sketch of the area showing any unusual conditions and assignment of personnel if deemed necessary (should be prepared by the supervisor and the lifeguard)
- Names, addresses, and phone numbers of witnesses to the accident

These questions should also be answered:

- How did the employee become aware of the accident?
- How soon did the employee respond to the emergency situation?
- What did the employee do in response to the emergency situation?
  - Did the guard have to enter the water to effect a rescue?
  - How far did the guard have to swim?
  - What action did the guard take to help the victim?

- What rescue equipment was used by the guard?
- What did the guard observe about the victim's condition?
- Did the guard observe signs of spinal injury? If so, what were they?
- Did the guard need assistance with the rescue?
- Did anything interfere with the rescue?
- Did the guard do everything possible to help revive the victim?
- Was the victim identified? By whom?
- What were the factors contributing to the accident?
  - What was the victim doing at the time of distress?
  - Could the victim swim?
  - Had the victim disregarded rules or orders given by the lifeguard?
- What first aid was administered?
- Was CPR necessary? Was effective circulation noted in carotid pulse or skin color?
- Were police, emergency squad, and ambulance called? At what time?
  - How soon did they respond?
  - What action did they take?
  - Was rescue breathing continued? By whom?
  - When did the EMS personnel or doctor take over?
  - When did the EMS personnel or doctor make a declaration of the victim's condition?
  - Was the victim removed from the beach or pool area? At what time?

Because some incidents require less emergency action, your facility may not have a form for reporting them. Minor incidents, such as a patron running on the deck, do not require a report. If you have asked a patron to leave the facility or if an outside agency has been contacted, it is wise to prepare a report describing the situation, those involved, and the actions taken. Your facility will define when you need to complete such forms.

INJURY CHART

One way to improve your facility's ability to prevent and react to injury situations is to determine what injuries occur and where. An injury chart can be an effective tool for gathering that information. The chart is a diagram of the supervised area, complete with all pieces of equipment, diving boards, ladders, lifelines, depth markings, lifeguard stations, fences, recreation areas, and auxiliary facilities. Each time an accident occurs, it is noted on the chart with a code.

Your facility may have a code system for listing all the types of injuries sustained. A letter, number, or symbol may be assigned to each injury. Figure 7.3 illustrates an injury chart in which the injury is signified by a number and the location on the body by a letter.

From this chart facility managers and staff can learn about the common accidents and injuries at the facility and where they are likely to occur. They can then plan the actions to be taken to prevent future accidents: establish new rules, repair equipment, install additional safety equipment, reposition lifeguards, add additional staff, or limit access to an area.

CRISIS CONTROL

Having emergency procedures in place is the first step to managing crises. However, it also helps to be prepared for handling people's reactions to those crises and to think about how to stay calm and reasonable during stressful situations.

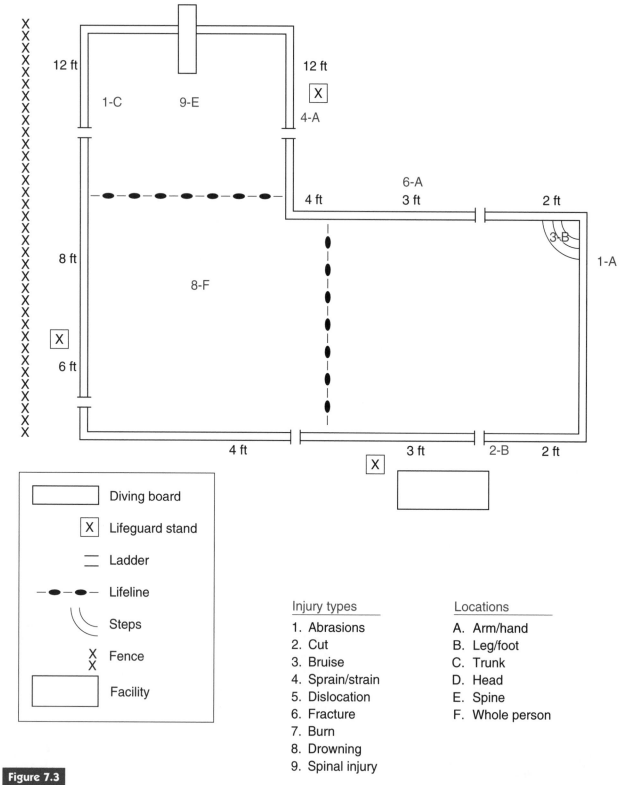

Checklist for Crisis Management

In handling any emergency situation, be sure you know the elements of crisis management shown in this checklist. Your facility may wish to post this checklist in the guard room and at the front desk.

Checklist for Crisis Management

Be prepared. Know your facility's emergency procedures, including how to fill out an incident report, and review them regularly. Make sure phone numbers are available for the following people or agencies—

Supervisor/manager:
Police/sheriff:
Fire:
Ambulance:
Poison control center:
Chemical accident hotline:
Health department:

Maintain order. Confusion and fear can make a bad situation worse. Stay calm and act with authority. Follow procedures as you have practiced them. Make sure that everyone present is in a safe place and unharmed before continuing with emergency plans.

Notify the chain of command. Report the incident to your supervisor or another designated manager as soon as possible. If necessary, call for emergency personnel or information.

Protect your facility. Make no statements to anyone about the incident; only the media spokesperson should discuss it publicly. File your incident report as soon as you can, using your facility's standard form. Include separate documentation of witnesses' statements.

Return to your post. Resume regular operations as soon as possible. This helps calm patrons and staff and reduces negative speculation about the event.

Learn from the experience. With other staff, review how the incident was handled. Discuss the event, determine the causes, evaluate your responses, and consider what other actions you could have taken. This lets you offer ideas for improving safety, express your emotions about the occurrence, and help improve emergency procedures.

Dealing With the Media

Be prepared for media involvement in any emergency involving a large facility or when an accident or incident has been reported to EMS personnel or the police. Your facility should have a crisis communications plan for handling the media. Although most reporters wish you and your facility no ill will, sensationalism sells news. So it is good practice to use care in making statements about emergencies.

Because public perception is very important to most facilities, it is important to convey appropriate information to all interested parties. Facility policy and legal responsibilities should outline what information is released.

The facility's crisis communications plan should designate a spokesperson to make all media contacts and public statements. All other staff should refrain from answering questions or making comments. Some patrons may ask seemingly innocent questions about events at the facility or about the situation itself. All too often the "patron" turns out to be a media or legal representative trying to obtain information that may or may not be relevant to the incident.

It may help to have a standard statement, such as this one: "The accident is under investigation, and a statement will be released by our spokesperson shortly. Thank you. Now I must return to my job." Once you have made the statement, move on and answer no more questions.

Staff Distress

Any time you are involved in a rescue, you are subject to great stress as a result of your duty to react to the emergency and the danger you face in doing so. Well-trained professionals generally can respond to emergencies without stress interfering with rescue efforts. It is vital that you remain calm while carrying out emergency procedures. That is why practice is so important. After the emergency is over, however, especially one in which a severe injury or death occurred, stress may overwhelm you. If you think you need help in dealing with it, seek professional services or support groups. In an extreme case, you might be able to make use of the critical-stress teams many communities have to help firefighters, police officers, and other rescue workers address their psychological trauma.

If such a team is not available to you, or if the accident was not severe, the following actions may help reduce the psychological effects of a rescue:

- Complete the accident or incident report. This is part of your responsibility.
- Think through your actions and emphasize the things you did well.
- Get some physical activity as soon as possible. It will remove you from the stressful situation and give you an opportunity to relax.
- Be aware that authorities are not trying to assess blame as they gather information about the accident; their questions are just part of the necessary "system." Be as objective as possible.
- Talk with supportive others to voice your feelings in a safe environment. Remember to be supportive of others if they are in a similar situation.
- Try to maintain a normal life schedule, including schoolwork, socializing, and lifeguarding.

An accident involving a death or serious injury may take considerable time to resolve. If you were prepared and acted according to your facility's emergency procedures, you performed your legal duty. Cooperate with the authorities and if you need to, seek help in managing your reaction to the trauma you have experienced.

Review Questions

1. What is the difference between a life-threatening and potentially life-threatening emergency?

2. What 7 major types of emergencies should any facility be prepared to handle?

3. Why is teamwork important in an emergency response?

4. Why is it important to work with your local EMS unit in preparing for emergencies?

5. List 3 issues you should consider in preparing for emergencies.

6. What 10 steps should be included in creating an emergency policy?

7. List the 6 steps common to any emergency plan.

8. What is the difference between an accident and an incident?

9. What is an accident report, and why is completing this report important?

10. What is an injury chart, and what important information does it contain?

11. Name the 6 points made in the checklist for crisis management.

12. How do you as a lifeguard respond to questions regarding a major accident at your facility?

13. Name 3 action steps you can take to control trauma or stress following an emergency.

CHAPTER 8

First Aid in Aquatic Environments

Because you must complete a first aid course before pursuing your lifeguard certification, this chapter does not provide guidelines for first aid treatment of all possible injuries in the aquatic environment. It focuses instead on handling both common and life-threatening situations.

YOU'LL LEARN ABOUT THE FOLLOWING ELEMENTS OF FIRST AID SPECIFIC TO LIFEGUARDING

- Medical alert tags and their value
- How to protect yourself against hepatitis and the human immunodeficiency virus (blood-borne pathogens)
- How to contact the emergency medical system
- How to recognize and provide first aid for

  - a heart attack
  - severe bleeding
  - three types of hyperthermia
  - hypothermia

  - an allergic reaction
  - an asthma attack
  - an epileptic seizure
  - hyperventilation

MEDICAL ALERT TAGS

Medical alert bracelets and tags, whether simple or flashy, serve a very important purpose. They provide you and the emergency medical team with medical information about the injured person. Speedy, accurate assessment is important to providing quality emergency care.

Most medical alert tags list details about the wearer's condition, allergies, and regular medications, covering areas like this:

Abnormal EKG	Glaucoma
Allergies (allergen is listed)	Hypertension
Alzheimer's/memory-impaired	Hypoglycemia
Angina	Medications (specific medications or
Asthma	categories of medications are listed)
Bleeding disorder	Pacemaker
Blood type	Seizure disorder
Diabetes (insulin-dependent or non-insulin-dependent)	Special needs (contact lenses, organ donor, living will)

Some tags provide a phone number to call for current medical information about the person. Look for these pieces of jewelry around the wrists, ankles, or necks of swimmers at your facility.

If you notice a patron with a medical alert tag, take some time to talk about it; most wearers are happy to discuss their special needs with you. They can help you prepare to assist them in an emergency.

PROTECTING YOURSELF FROM HEPATITIS AND THE HUMAN IMMUNODEFICIENCY VIRUS

You can contract many illnesses through direct contact with an injured, ill, or drowning individual's body fluids, such as blood or saliva. These illnesses are caused by *blood-borne pathogens*, microorganisms that live in human body fluids. Two of the most serious illnesses are the hepatitis B virus (HBV) and the human immunodeficiency virus (HIV), both of which can be life-threatening. The blood-borne pathogens can be transmitted to others through blood, saliva, nasal discharges, vomitus, tears, urine, or fecal matter in salt or fresh water (as in lakes or rivers) or improperly treated swimming pool water. That's why it is important that you understand what these illnesses are and how to protect yourself from exposure.

Hepatitis

Hepatitis is an infection or inflammation of the liver that is usually caused by a virus. The virus and resulting infection can take two forms. Type A, formerly called infectious hepatitis, is usually spread by fecal contamination of food, such as when an infected food preparer doesn't wash his or her hands after using the toilet. Type B, formerly called serum hepatitis, is spread by contact with blood or other body fluids. It is Type B that is of concern for you as a lifeguard.

The hepatitis B virus is carried in the blood and other body fluids of the infected person. Once contracted, the virus may be present for years, so any time you come in contact with another person's blood or body fluids, you risk contracting hepatitis B.

Hepatitis B infections are prevalent among intravenous drug users, prostitutes and others with multiple sexual partners, homosexuals, recipients of blood products (such as those with hemophilia or dialysis patients), and health care workers in contact with blood products and body fluids.

The symptoms of hepatitis B may include fatigue, nausea, vomiting, jaundice (a yellow coloration of the skin and eyes), dark yellow urine, and light-colored stools. The infection is generally severe and can lead to liver failure and death. A victim who survives the initial infection is likely to develop a long-term phase of the illness called *chronic hepatitis*.

During this long-term phase, the infected person is essentially free of symptoms but can still infect others with the virus. Anyone exposed to the blood or body fluids of a suspected high-risk individual should seek immediate medical advice and consider a preventive injection of hepatitis B immune globulin.

Anyone at high risk for exposure to hepatitis B should seek medical advice and consider the hepatitis B vaccine. The vaccine has been proven very successful in preventing people at high risk from contracting the disease.

Human Immunodeficiency Virus

Acquired Immune Deficiency Syndrome (AIDS) is a condition in which the elements of blood that control the immune system are damaged, leaving the body susceptible to opportunistic infections. AIDS is one of the manifestations of the human immunodeficiency virus (HIV). You can have this virus (be HIV-positive) without having the symptoms of AIDS.

Like hepatitis B, HIV is contracted through contact with blood and body fluids. Casual contact, coughing, and sneezing do not transmit the disease, nor can it be transmitted through the water in a swimming pool. HIV can be contracted through

- sexual contact,
- contact with contaminated blood or body fluids,
- use of contaminated needles (as is common among intravenous drug users), and
- the placenta and body fluids during pregnancy or birth.

Fortunately, outside the body the virus is not particularly hardy. As soon as the fluid has dried or been exposed to heat, the virus dies. A solution of 10% household bleach in water also kills the virus. As household bleach has a limited shelf life of 60 to 90 days, keep the supply fresh and replace it as needed.

AIDS has a variable incubation period (the time from infection to the appearance of symptoms), ranging from several months to over 7 years. There is currently no known cure for AIDS, so it is vital to protect yourself from contracting the virus. Become aware of the universal precautionary procedures (described next) and follow them every time you have the potential to come in contact with the blood or body fluids of another person.

Protecting Yourself

To protect yourself from contracting hepatitis or HIV through contact with contaminated blood or body fluids, follow the universal precautionary procedures developed by the Centers for Disease Control as a result of research into the transmission of blood-borne diseases. (See chart on next page.)

Take these additional precautions when rescuing a victim in the water:

- Approach a bleeding victim from upstream, on the wave side.

Universal Precautionary Procedures

1. *Use a barrier.* The use of gloves, masks, face shields, mouthpieces, gowns, and other barriers protects you from contact with the blood and body fluids of a victim. Assume all victims are infected.

2. *Wash your hands.* Good hygiene also reduces your risk. Wash your hands with soap and warm water after you come in contact with another person's blood or body fluids—even if you were wearing gloves.

3. *Clean up.* Clean surfaces that have been exposed to blood or body fluids with a mixture of household bleach and water. Combine 1 part of bleach with 10 equal parts of water. Wear protective gear during the clean-up procedure.

4. *Keep sharp objects separate.* It is unlikely that you will use any sharp objects, such as scalpels or hypodermic needles, with any victims you'll see, but sharp debris on the beach can pierce the skin and cause bleeding. Dispose separately of any sharp object with blood on it. Medical facilities have labeled red containers designed specifically for such hazardous material; some pool facilities have similar containers.

5. *Avoid contamination.* Don't allow swimmers to share towels contaminated with blood or body fluids. Instead place the soiled linen in a separate, plastic-lined laundry bin.

6. *Launder or dispose of soiled linen separately.* Bloody linens should be stored separately and double-bagged in plastic. Laundry personnel should handle the parcel as infected material and wash the linens in detergent with hot water.

7. *Cover wounds.* When someone receives a cut, scratch, or other open wound at your facility, require him or her to cover it. This procedure not only helps that person remain free of infection, it decreases the probability of other patrons coming in contact with that patron's blood.

8. *Provide CPR using a barrier.* There is a very low risk of contracting the AIDS virus through contact with saliva. However, the use of a breathing bag or pocket mask reduces your exposure to AIDS and other diseases by decreasing mouth-to-mouth contact. (Pocket masks for rescue breathing and CPR are described on p. 149.)

9. *Protect yourself.* If you have an open wound, avoid providing first aid to a victim with an open wound if at all possible. If you must provide first aid, wear gloves.

Note. Adapted from guidelines provided by the U.S. Public Health Service, Centers for Disease Control.

- If using a rescue tube or buoy, keep as much water as possible between you and a bleeding victim.
- Keep your head out of the water to prevent possible contamination through eye membranes, nose, and mouth.
- If rescue breathing is needed, use a pocket mask to avoid direct contact with the victim's mouth.
- Avoid contact with bleeding areas when removing a victim from the water. If accidental contact is made, wash the blood off immediately.

- After contact with a bleeding victim, always wash your entire body with disinfecting soap.

Your facility should give you additional training on blood-borne pathogens that includes the following elements:

- The OSHA standard for blood-borne pathogens
- The epidemiology and symptomatology of blood-borne diseases
- The modes of transmission of blood-borne pathogens
- An exposure plan (for employee training and facility precautions), including the points of the plan, the lines of responsibility, and how the plan will be implemented
- Procedures that might cause exposure to blood or other potentially infectious materials at your facility
- The use and limitations of control methods at the facility to control exposure to blood or other potentially infectious materials
- The use and limitations of personal protective equipment available at your facility and who should be contacted concerning the following:
  - Postexposure evaluation and follow-up
  - Signs and labels used at the facility
  - The hepatitis B vaccine program at the facility
  - Where to locate a copy of the OSHA standard

For more information, see Appendix F.

HOW TO CONTACT AND ACTIVATE THE EMERGENCY MEDICAL SYSTEM

In many areas of the country you can summon emergency medical assistance by dialing 911. Check to see if your community uses this system. If not, ask management to prominently post emergency phone numbers near all telephones at your facility.

If you do not make the call to the EMS yourself, be sure to delegate that task to another lifeguard or to a responsible adult. The caller has a crucial role in providing information to the medical team being dispatched. A script should be posted next to the phone with these guidelines for communicating with the EMS:

- Give your name, location, and telephone number to initiate the conversation.
- Explain what type of accident has occurred and what types of injuries have been sustained.
- Describe each victim's symptoms and what first aid has been provided.
- Answer honestly any questions asked of you. If you don't know an answer, say so. Do not guess! Someone's life is at stake.
- Wait for the EMS operator to tell you to hang up the phone, then wait until he or she has disconnected before you do hang up. This will ensure that the EMS has gotten all of the information needed from you before you are disconnected.
- Wait by the phone momentarily to see whether a follow-up call is made.

Never transport a victim yourself; wait for the EMS. If a victim's condition were to worsen while en route to the hospital in your car, you couldn't provide the necessary assistance, but paramedics could. You will also be protected from potential legal action regarding transportation by using emergency medical services rather than your vehicle. In a remote area, exceptions may be necessary depending on the type of emergency. Follow the emergency plan set up by your facility.

HEART ATTACKS

Heart attack is one of the leading causes of death in the United States. The American Heart Association estimates that each year a million and a half Americans will have heart attacks and almost a third of them will die as a result.

Heart attacks are caused by blood clots or blockages in the blood vessels that supply blood to the heart. You may hear heart attacks referred to by several names: coronary, cardiac, coronary occlusion, coronary artery thrombosis, or myocardial infarction. Each refers to the same life-threatening condition.

A person who is having a heart attack could lose consciousness or die immediately. More likely, he or she will exhibit several or all of the following symptoms:

- Shortness of breath
- Chest pains radiating into the neck and shoulders and down the arm
- Profuse sweating
- Pale, sweaty skin
- Squeezing pressure in the chest
- Indigestion

If any combination of these symptoms lasts longer than 1 or 2 minutes, encourage the person to seek immediate medical attention. It is not unusual for someone to refuse to see a physician or go to the hospital; if this occurs, document your recommendation and the refusal. It is still a good idea to contact the EMS. Most services do not charge for responding to such calls, and, once on the scene, EMS personnel may be able to convince the person to be transported to a medical facility. Any time you are unsure of what action to take, act in favor of the patron and request additional assistance.

You may be required to provide emergency first aid until medical assistance arrives at your facility. If the person is still breathing, take the following steps:

- Keep the person calm and as comfortable as possible.
- Assist the person in taking heart medication if she or he has such medication.
- Monitor the person's condition.
- Be prepared to begin cardiopulmonary resuscitation (CPR) if necessary.

SEVERE BLEEDING

Aquatic injuries can be accompanied by severe bleeding, which can be life-threatening if not controlled quickly. Blood coming from an open wound, or external bleeding, can be escaping from capillaries, veins, or arteries. Capillary bleeding is slow and oozing; it is the easiest to bring under control. Blood flow from veins is steadier but is still more easily stopped than flow from arteries. An artery, if completely severed, may seal itself off, but if it is only torn, it may bleed rapidly and spurt.

To control bleeding, take these steps, in this order:

1. Apply direct pressure to the wound using sterile gauze or, if it is not available, any clean cloth. Use latex or vinyl gloves or any other barrier material you can find to protect yourself from the victim's blood. If no barrier materials are available and the bleeding must be stopped quickly, apply pressure with your bare hands. In either case, be sure to wash your hands with soap and water afterward. Increase the amount of pressure if bleeding doesn't stop.

After applying pressure, cover the wound dressing if possible with a pressure bandage, such as a roller bandage that covers both the dressing and areas below and above the wound. Never remove a dressing; removal may restart the bleeding. If a dressing becomes blood-soaked, place another dressing on top of it.

2. If bleeding continues, keep applying pressure and elevate the limb above the heart. This will reduce blood pressure and slow the bleeding, which will aid blood clotting. Do *not* elevate a limb if it is broken.

3. If bleeding still has not stopped, try putting pressure on one of two pressure points (places where an artery is accessible for compression), the brachial point, which is located in the upper arm, and the femoral point, which is located in the groin. Try this only if you are trained to use pressure points, because it works only if you apply pressure to the exact location.

Once the bleeding is under control, the wound can be cleaned. Open wounds can become infected if not cleaned and treated properly. Table 8.1 lists the types of open wounds, their causes and symptoms, and first aid for each type.

Table 8.1   Open Wound First Aid

Type	Causes	Signs and symptoms	First aid
Abrasion (scrape)	Rubbing or scraping	Only skin surface is affected Little bleeding	Remove all debris Wash away from wound with soap and water
Incision (cut)	Sharp objects	Edges of wound are smooth Severe bleeding	Control bleeding Wash wound
Laceration (tearing)	Blunt object tearing skin	Veins and arteries can be affected Severe bleeding Danger of infection	Control bleeding Wash wound
Puncture (stab)	Sharp pointed object piercing skin	Wound is narrow and deep into veins and arteries Embedded objects Danger of infection	Do not remove impaled objects
Avulsion (torn off)	Machinery, explosives	Tissue torn off or left hanging Severe bleeding	Control bleeding Take avulsed part to medical facility

Note. From National Safety Council, *First Aid and CPR, Level 1,* © 1991 Jones and Bartlett Publishers, Boston. Reprinted by permission.

Internal bleeding cannot be seen from the outside, but it is accompanied by symptoms such as these:

- Blood coming from the mouth, rectum, or vagina (nonmenstrual blood) or seen in the urine
- Visible bruises or cuts
- A rapid pulse
- Sweaty, cool skin
- Pupil dilation
- Nausea and vomiting
- Abdominal pain or tenderness, rigidity, or bruising
- Chest bruising or rib fractures

If you suspect internal bleeding, call EMS immediately. Then give first aid for internal bleeding, following these steps:

1. Watch the person's breathing and pulse.
2. Be prepared for vomiting. Don't give the person any liquids; if vomiting occurs, place the person on his or her side for drainage.
3. Raise the legs 8 to 12 inches and keep the body warm.

HYPERTHERMIA

Heat cramps, heat exhaustion, and heatstroke are three progressively more severe forms of hyperthermia, or overheating. In each heat illness, environmental conditions cause the body's core temperature to increase, giving rise to a variety of symptoms. When the temperature and humidity are high, heat-related problems become more common. Figure 8.1 illustrates the combinations of heat and humidity that are the most dangerous.

Figure 8.1

Heat and humidity chart.

Relative humidity	Air temperature (°F) 70°	75°	80°	85°	90°	95°	100°	105°	110°	115°	120°
30%	67	73	78	84	90	96	104	113	123	135	148
40%	68	74	79	86	93	101	110	123	137	151	
50%	69	75	81	88	96	107	120	135	150		
60%	70	76	82	90	100	114	132	149			
70%	70	77	85	93	106	124	144				
80%	71	78	86	97	113	136					
90%	71	79	88	102	122						
100%	72	80	91	108							

☐ Risk of heat exhaustion

▨ Risk of heatstroke

☐ High risk of heatstroke

Note. Numbers within chart show equivalent temperatures. Shaded areas indicate when exertion may be dangerous. Reproduced with permission of The Walking Magazine, copyright © 1987, Raben Publishing Co., 711 Boylston St., Boston, MA 02116.

Heat Cramps

Heat cramps are extremely painful muscle cramps caused by the loss of electrolytes and salt in the body through sweat. These cramps are usually associated with exertion. A person suffering from heat cramps will generally exhibit some or all of the following symptoms:

- Muscle cramps (usually in the legs and abdomen)
- Sweaty skin
- Increased heart rate

- Exhaustion
- Dizziness

Heat cramps are not a life-threatening condition, but the person will want and need immediate attention. To care for someone experiencing heat cramps, take the following action:

- Get the person out of the heat.
- Provide water.
- Apply moist towels to the forehead and cramp to aid in cooling.
- Avoid massage—it will not help and may damage muscle tissue.

In most cases the cramp sufferer will not need to see a physician. However, if the person experiences faintness and recurring cramping, care by medical personnel is advisable.

Heat Exhaustion

The most common heat-related illness, heat exhaustion is also due to excessive electrolyte and water loss through perspiration. The symptoms of heat exhaustion include

- profuse sweating,
- cool and clammy skin,
- dilated pupils,
- pale coloring,
- increased heart rate,
- weakness,
- nausea,
- thirst,
- fainting, and
- anxiety or apathy.

Any bout with heat exhaustion requires medical attention because the condition can easily escalate to heatstroke. There are several things you can do to assist someone with heat exhaustion while awaiting medical assistance:

- Get the person out of the heat.
- Provide water (only if the person is conscious).
- Lay the person down.
- Loosen restrictive clothing.
- Cool the body with moist, cold towels.

There are several locations where cold towels will speed the cooling process. Figure 8.2 illustrates where towels should be placed to most effectively provide cooling.

Figure 8.2

Placement of moist, cold towels for efficient cooling.

Heatstroke

With extreme overexposure to the heat, a person may experience heatstroke. In this condition, the body's temperature regulation system essentially shuts down and the heat generated is recycled in the body, causing other body systems to malfunction. It is vital that you learn to recognize the symptoms of heatstroke and move quickly to assist anyone who develops it. Contact EMS immediately.

The symptoms of heatstroke vary some, depending on whether the person initially suffered heat exhaustion and how quickly you noticed the problem. The skin may be dry if the person was inactive or if the sweat has already dried. The skin may be sweaty if the person was active and you noticed the problem before the sweat dried. The key here is that the person with heatstroke will no longer be able to sweat. Many or all of the following symptoms are typical:

- Dry or sweaty skin
- Inability to sweat
- Increased then decreased heart rate
- Increased temperature
- Hot, red skin
- Rapid, shallow breathing that may then slow
- Constricted pupils
- Headache
- Confusion
- Disorientation
- Unconsciousness
- Seizure

If you notice a number of these symptoms, don't take any chances—summon medical assistance immediately. Heatstroke can be fatal!

Heatstroke is an extremely critical condition—almost 60% of those who develop it die, even under medical supervision. Your actions truly can mean the difference between life and death. While you are waiting for the EMS to arrive, provide the following first aid:

- Establish the ABCs.
- Do *not* give fluids.
- Get the person out of the heat.
- Lay the person down.
- Loosen any restrictive clothing.
- Cool the body immediately using ice packs or sheets soaked with ice water.
- Monitor body temperature and ABCs.
- Be prepared to handle convulsions if the body temperature drops very rapidly.

HYPOTHERMIA

Hypothermia is exactly the opposite of hyperthermia: The body temperature is decreased by environmental conditions. People can lose body heat in outdoor recreational pursuits, typically during the winter, but perhaps the most common cause of hypothermia is being in cold water for an extended period (immersion hypothermia). Because water cools the body 25 to 27 times faster than does air, hypothermia can occur even in warm weather. In water at 72 to 78 degrees Fahrenheit, unconsciousness can occur in 3 to 12 hours. In very cool water, the arms and legs will cool rapidly. It takes 10 to 15 minutes before the vital organs and brain begin to lose heat. Figure 8.3 illustrates the effects of cold water on the

Figure 8.3

Water temperature as a determinant for survival time.

Data from *Fishermen, Hunters, & Campers: Tips for Safe Boating* by United Safe Boating Institute.

length of time someone immersed can survive. The heat escape lessening posture (HELP) described on page 22 was developed to slow heat loss and increase survival time.

Watch children carefully; their smaller size makes them more susceptible to heat loss in immersion. The major arteries are closer to the skin, allowing quicker cooling of the blood.

Levels of Hypothermia

The symptoms of hypothermia vary greatly with the severity of the exposure and heat loss. The generalized symptoms of hypothermia include these:

- Initially intense shivering
- Rigid muscles
- Reduced coordination
- Slow and labored breathing
- Bluish tinge to skin, lips, and nailbeds
- Reduced blood flow to hands and feet
- Dilated pupils
- Loss of logic
- Difficulty speaking
- Disorientation
- Glassy stare
- Slow and irregular pulse
- Amnesia
- Eventual loss of consciousness

If you notice these symptoms, do not delay first aid; hypothermia can cause complications even after someone is out of the water. Table 8.2 compiles data on the severity of symptoms and the corresponding core body temperatures.

Emergency First Aid

Immediately upon identifying someone with hypothermia, contact EMS personnel. Then help the person remove any wet clothing; getting dried off is important so that the air does

Table 8.2 Levels of Hypothermia and Their Signs and Symptoms	
Level	**Signs and symptoms**
Normal (98.6° F)	No symptoms
Mild (94°-95° F)	Alert; hyperventilating; strong, uncontrolled shivering
Moderate (90°-93° F)	Conscious, but not thinking clearly; impaired speech; inability to grasp with hands; clumsy
Severe (86°-90° F)	May or may not be conscious; ability to think severely reduced; cold to the touch; rigid muscles; uneven pulse; skin may turn blue
Very severe (81°-85° F)	Usually unconscious; rigid muscles; slowed breathing and pulse
Critical (below 80° F)	Unconscious; no reflexes; shallow or no breathing; cardiac arrest due to cardiac arrhythmia

Note. Adapted from the U.S. Coast Guard (1977) and Canadian Red Cross (1983).

not continue cooling the body by evaporating the water. The rest of the first aid you will give centers on providing warmth. Take these steps:

- Move the person near a fire or heater if available.
- Cover the person with blankets, coats, newspapers—virtually any insulating material.
- If no insulating material is available, hug the victim to you to share your body warmth.
- Give a conscious person warm, nonalcoholic, decaffeinated drinks. (Alcohol and caffeine dilate the blood vessels, causing a continued loss of body heat.)

Watch for quick changes in body temperature. Rewarming can cause an after-drop syndrome (described in the next section).

Cold Water Drowning

Amazing stories of recovery from 30- to 45-minute exposures to cold water have appeared in media headlines since the early 1970s. The latest information available indicates that if a person drowns, even if all signs of life are absent, CPR must be initiated and continued until the victim reaches an emergency medical facility. Startling as it may seem, children who have been under the surface for up to 45 minutes have been revived, with little or no brain damage, after 4 to 5 hours of CPR and medical attention.

Such survival is possible because the body goes into a form of hibernation. The cold water causes constriction in the blood vessels of the arms and legs and a slowing or stoppage of metabolic activity in the body. Together, these changes partially eliminate the delivery of blood and oxygen to the limbs. This allows blood and oxygen to be diverted to the brain and vital organs.

As the temperature of the major body organs drops, the activity and oxygen utilization of the brain, heart, lungs, and kidneys are also reduced. With this reduction of oxygenation and the cool internal temperatures, the vital organs seem able to survive with the oxygen available in the organ, the surrounding tissues, and the blood.

To provide first aid, you must begin CPR as soon as the victim is removed from the water. Then call the EMS to transport the person to a medical facility. Immediate transportation is vital so that the rewarming and resuscitation processes can be continued and directed by a physician. *Do not* attempt to rewarm such a victim yourself. When the body is rewarmed, the cold blood from the limbs flows back to the internal core, causing the core temperature to drop. This syndrome, called the *after-drop syndrome*, can be minimized by keeping the victim still.

ALLERGIC REACTIONS (ANAPHYLACTIC SHOCK)

Many of us are allergic to something: a food, a certain insect bite, pollen, dust, or one of any number of other elements in our environment. Should a patron have a severe reaction to an allergen, you must know how to handle the situation.

There are several symptoms of extreme allergic reactions or anaphylactic shock:

- Difficulty in breathing
- Fainting or unconsciousness
- Swelling
- Itching or burning skin
- Hives
- Restlessness

If the person has medication for an allergy, help him or her take it. Regardless of how mild the reaction appears, always contact the EMS. You don't know how the body will react. While awaiting EMS personnel, treat the person as you would treat anyone experiencing shock.

- Ensure an open airway.
- Keep the person warm but not overheated.
- Monitor pulse and breathing.
- Do *not* give fluids or food.

ASTHMA

Asthma is a chronic condition that flares up periodically. During an asthma "attack" the person has difficulty getting fresh air into the lungs. The result is a wheezing or forcing of air in and out as the person struggles for air exchange. Attacks may be brought on by strenuous activity, exposure to an allergen, or emotional stress.

Symptoms of an asthma attack include the following:

- Wheezing
- Rapid pulse
- Hunched shoulders
- Pulling on the chest to assist in breathing
- Discoloration of skin, lips, or nailbeds (in severe cases)

Someone with asthma who has been active all day swimming and recreating at an aquatic facility may be susceptible to an attack. Should a patron experience difficulty, take the following steps:

- Position the person for ease of breathing—usually sitting upright.
- Help the person take any prescribed medication.
- Provide reassurance.
- If the episode does not subside quickly, contact EMS.
- Monitor pulse, breathing, and skin color.
- Keep the person warm but not overheated.

EPILEPTIC SEIZURES

Epilepsy is a chronic disorder of the nervous system; abnormal electrical activity in the brain causes a seizure, which may be accompanied by a loss of consciousness. Seizures can be triggered by various conditions or events, including hyperventilation, physical stress, nervous tension, poor regulation of body temperature, lack of sleep, low blood sugar, illness, hormonal changes, fluid and electrolyte imbalances, alcohol, and bright light. Many people with epilepsy can control their seizures through medication or behavioral prevention. Even so, a seizure may occur.

One type of seizure, the "absence" or "petit mal" seizure, is often not noticeable. The person loses awareness for only a few seconds, staring and perhaps fluttering the eyelids. Another type, the "tonic-clonic" or "grand mal" seizure, is more recognizable; the person may have a combination of these symptoms:

- Rigid muscles
- Jerky and convulsive movements
- Clenched teeth
- Drooling
- Loss of consciousness
- Loss of bowel and bladder control
- Biting of the tongue
- Period of apnea (not breathing)

Fortunately, before a grand mal seizure begins, many people with epilepsy will experience a warning in the form of an aura, often described as a bright light, a burst of color, or an odor. Upon recognizing a warning signal, the person can help you provide a safe environment for the seizure.

In a "psychomotor" or "partial complex" seizure, the individual may seem confused or dizzy. He or she may perform unusual motions such as twitching a hand or arm, walking aimlessly, picking at objects, or rubbing the hands together. The person also may speak in a repetitive or incoherent manner. People experiencing such a seizure are sometimes mistaken for drunks.

There is nothing that you can do to stop a seizure. Your role is to protect the person from any injury. If someone has a seizure out of the water, take the following steps:

- Provide an area with as much privacy as possible (many people with epilepsy prefer others not to view their behavior during a seizure).
- Lay the person down in an area where she or he cannot be injured by surrounding hazards.
- Protect the person's head as much as possible, placing a folded towel underneath it.
- Loosen any restrictive clothing.

Not every person about to have a seizure will be able to warn you of it. If an unexpected seizure begins, lay the person down in a location where he or she is not endangered by sharp objects or obstructions, loosen any restrictive clothing, and keep bystanders away from the scene. *Never* attempt to put anything in the person's mouth during a seizure.

If someone in the water has a seizure, you will need to get into the water and move the person away from hazards, such as the side of the pool. Stand behind the victim and grasp both sides of the head. This will help you keep the person's head above the water while the seizure runs its course. After the seizure, help the person out of the water; she or he will be sleepy.

Whether the seizure occurs in or out of the water, anyone who has had a seizure must see medical personnel; a number of complications could develop as much as an hour after the apparent recovery. Stay with the person until medical assistance arrives.

HYPERVENTILATION

Hyperventilation, or overventilation, is brought about by inhaling and exhaling deeply and rapidly. The goal of this practice is usually to stay underwater for a longer time. You will often see people hyperventilate and then try to swim across the pool underwater. Although such attempts may be fun, hyperventilating can be dangerous.

When you hyperventilate you lower the percentage of carbon dioxide in the air that always remains in your lungs. The carbon dioxide in the bloodstream is what triggers your medulla oblongata (the part of the brain that controls breathing) to initiate taking a breath. By decreasing the available carbon dioxide, you can remain underwater because you delay the point at which the brain signals the need to take a breath. The danger occurs when you delay the trigger point until after the lack of oxygen to the body is so severe that you become unconscious (black out).

You might think that you'd know when you were reaching the point that you would lose consciousness as a result of holding your breath. Unfortunately, research shows that the onset of unconsciousness is like falling asleep—a person really doesn't notice it. Some swimmers who have blacked out have felt beforehand as if they could stay underwater forever.

You may find it difficult to notice when a swimmer has blacked out underwater. Sometimes swimmers continue moving erratically even after losing consciousness. They may also continue kicking until they begin to surface.

You can normally identify people who are hyperventilating because they are taking rapid deep breaths. They may experience tingling in the arms and around the mouth, cramps in their fingers, or sharp chest pains. Prevent them from swimming underwater and explain why you are concerned.

Conscious hyperventilators who are breathing too fast, too slowly, noisily, or painfully may require EMS attention to restore appropriate levels of carbon dioxide in the blood. Even after treatment, you should continue to watch the hyperventilator for any complications that might arise.

If the person is unconscious, contact EMS and monitor breathing. Sometimes normal breathing resumes after the person loses consciousness; if breathing stops, provide rescue breathing.

Hyperventilation or black-outs brought on by deprivation of oxygen can also occur for other reasons, including overexertion—the most common cause of unintentional hyperventilation—and the pressure effect and the position effect, which are less common.

• *Overexertion.* During overexertion the body very quickly uses oxygen stored in the body, which hastens the lack of oxygen. Overexertion also decreases the body's ability to sense the trigger to breathe. Poorly conditioned or overtaxed swimmers are especially susceptible to overexertion black-outs.

• *Pressure effect.* When diving 20 feet or deeper, which is quite unusual for most lifeguards, the increased pressure of the deep water causes increased use of oxygen. Upon surfacing, the lifeguard may lack enough available oxygen and black out.

• *Position effect.* On an extended shallow underwater swim, the oxygen level drops. This drop is not significant enough to reduce the supply of oxygen to the brain, but when the swimmer stands up and the blood supply to the brain is reduced, there is a possibility of insufficient oxygen to the brain, causing a black-out.

FIRST AID QUICK REFERENCE

This chapter has presented important information about providing first aid. Table 8.3 provides a quick guide for you to consult when an emergency arises.

Table 8.3 First Aid Quick Reference Guide			
Condition	Symptoms	First aid	Necessary to call EMS?
Asthma	Wheezing Rapid pulse Hunched shoulders Pulling on chest Discoloration of skin, lips, or nailbeds	Position person for ease of breathing. Help take medication. Reassure. Monitor pulse, breathing, and skin color. Keep person warm.	Sometimes
Allergy (anaphylactic shock)	Difficulty breathing Fainting or unconsciousness Swelling Itching or burning skin Hives Restlessness	Ensure open airway. Keep person warm. Monitor pulse and breathing. Give no fluids or food.	Yes
Epileptic seizure (grand mal)	Rigid muscles Jerky, convulsive movements Clenched teeth Drooling Loss of consciousness Loss of bowel and bladder control Biting tongue May stop breathing for a period	Provide privacy. Provide safe environment. Lay victim down/protect head. Loosen restrictive clothing. Put nothing in mouth. Move away from pool side. Support head above water. Monitor until EMS arrives.	Yes
Heart attack	Shortness of breath Chest pains Profuse sweating Pale, sweaty skin Squeezing sensation in the chest Indigestion	Keep person calm. Make comfortable. Help take medication. Monitor condition. Be ready for CPR.	Yes
Heat cramps	Cramps Sweaty skin Increased heart rate Exhaustion Dizziness	Get out of heat. Give water. Apply moist towels. Do not massage.	Only in severe cases
Heat exhaustion	Profuse sweating Cool, clammy skin Dilated pupils Pale color Increased heart rate Weakness Nausea Thirst Fainting Anxiety or apathy	Get out of heat. Give water. Lay victim down. Loosen restrictive clothing. Cool with moist, cold towels.	Yes Warning: left unattended can escalate to heatstroke
Heatstroke	Dry or sweaty skin Inability to sweat Increased then decreased heart rate Increased temperature	Do not give fluids. Get out of heat. Lay person down. Loosen restrictive clothing.	Yes, immediately

(continued)

Table 8.3 *(continued)*			
Condition	Symptoms	First aid	Necessary to call EMS?
Heatstroke *(continued)*	Hot, red skin Rapid, shallow breathing that may then slow Constricted pupils Headache Confusion Disorientation Unconsciousness Seizure	Cool immediately using ice packs or ice water–soaked sheets. Monitor body temperature and ABCs. Be prepared for convulsions.	
Hypothermia	Initially intense shivering Rigid muscles Reduced coordination Slow, labored breathing Bluish color to skin, lips, and nailbeds Reduced blood flow to hands and feet Dilated pupils Loss of logic Difficulty speaking Disorientation Glassy stare Slow, irregular pulse Amnesia Loss of consciousness	Remove wet clothes. Dry victim. Provide warmth unless cold water drowning. Give warm liquids (nonalcoholic, noncaffeinated). If cold water drowning, begin CPR and do not rewarm.	Yes
Hyperventilation	Rapid, deep breathing Tingling arms and mouth Cramps in fingers Sharp chest pains Unconsciousness	Administer CO_2 from ambulance. Monitor for complications. Provide rescue breathing if breathing stops.	Yes, if breathing too fast, slowly, noisily, or painfully or if loss of consciousness
Severe bleeding	*External:* Bleeding from open wound *Internal:* Bleeding from mouth, rectum, vagina, or blood in urine Visible bruises or cuts Rapid pulse Sweaty, cool skin Dilated pupils Nausea, vomiting Abdominal pain, rigidity, or bruising Chest bruising or rib fractures	*For external bleeding:* First, apply pressure. Cover with bandage. Second, elevate limb. Don't elevate if broken. Third, apply pressure to pressure point. Care for the wound. Treat for shock by raising victim's legs 8-12 in. and keeping body warm. *For internal bleeding:* Call EMS. Monitor pulse and breathing. Prepare for vomiting. Treat for shock.	External, yes if extensive Internal, yes

Review Questions

1. What can you learn from a medical alert tag?
2. What is hepatitis?
3. What is AIDS?
4. List 4 ways HIV is transmitted.
5. List the 9 universal precautionary procedures you can use to prevent contact with body fluids.
6. What should you learn through workplace training regarding OSHA regulations and blood-borne pathogens?
7. List the 6 guidelines for contacting EMS.
8. List the symptoms and first aid for a heart attack.
9. What are the differences in bleeding from capillaries, veins, and arteries?
10. What are the 3 steps to control bleeding?
11. List the symptoms and first aid for internal bleeding.
12. What is hyperthermia?
13. List the symptoms and first aid for heat cramps, heat exhaustion, and heat-stroke.
14. What is hypothermia?
15. Why are children more susceptible than adults to immersion hypothermia?
16. List the symptoms of hypothermia.
17. What care can you give someone with hypothermia?
18. Why can people survive after being under water in cold water for a lengthy period?
19. What first aid should you provide a cold water drowning victim?
20. List the symptoms of anaphylactic shock. What first aid is necessary?
21. What can cause an asthma attack? What first aid should you provide?
22. List the symptoms of an epileptic seizure.
23. What assistance can you give to someone having a seizure on land? In the water?
24. Why do people sometimes black out when they hyperventilate?
25. What symptoms will someone have who has hyperventilated but not blacked out? What first aid should you give?
26. List and describe 3 other reasons people could black out in the water.

CHAPTER 9

Spinal Injury Management

Spinal injuries concern all who serve the public at aquatic facilities—and for good reason. According to a 1989 U.S. Consumer Safety Commission report, about 700 people sustain spinal cord injuries every year diving into swimming pools, lakes, and other bodies of water. Although the number may not seem overwhelming, the effect of the injuries can be devastating. All lifeguards must be skilled at handling injuries to the spinal cord. Your ability to handle the situation might make the difference between an unfortunate accident and lifelong paralysis.

IN THIS CHAPTER YOU WILL LEARN ABOUT

- those who experience spinal cord injuries,
- hazardous activities,
- open water diving hazards,
- pool design–related hazards,
- standards for safe diving, and
- No Diving signs.

YOU'LL ALSO LEARN HOW TO

- recognize a spinal injury,
- enter the water and approach a victim,
- perform spinal injury rescue techniques and provide in-line stabilization,
- handle different rescue situations,
- use a cervical collar and backboard to remove a victim from the water, and
- provide emergency first aid.

THE VICTIM

Most spinal cord injuries occur in a setting where there is no qualified lifeguard, instructor, or coach present to provide knowledgeable assistance. An overview of data indicates that the typical person who experiences a spinal cord injury has the following characteristics:

- An athletic male 18 to 31 years old
- 6 feet tall
- 175 pounds
- No formal training in diving
- First-time visitor to the location making a first dive there
- Not warned about dangers either verbally or through a sign

CAUSES OF AQUATIC SPINAL INJURIES

Spinal injuries can occur in both pools and the open water. Obviously, equipment and facility design play a larger role in a pool setting than a beach environment. Here are some of the main causes of aquatic spinal injuries.

Injuries in Swimming Pools

Most spinal cord injuries in swimming pools result from a dive into shallow water. This includes diving from

- a deck into an in-ground pool,
- a platform or rim of an above-ground pool,
- adjacent structures (roofs, trees, etc.) into an above-ground pool, and
- competitive starting blocks located in shallow water.

Dives or falls into deep water account for 20% to 25% of spinal injuries in pools. Injuries are caused by dives or falls onto the deck, dives in water 7 feet deep or less, or divers hitting the upslope of the pool bottom that was not far enough away. These dives or falls are from the following equipment:

- Springboards (26 inches or less above the water)
- 3-meter springboards
- 1-meter springboards
- Jump boards 4 to 6 feet long
- The deck into a hopper bottom pool (see p. 133)
- The 3-meter stand onto the deck

Water slides located in shallow water also account for spinal cord injuries. These injuries are due to

- sliding head-first,
- diving from the top of the slide, and
- falling onto the deck from the top of the slide.

Injuries in Open Water

Thousands of people enjoy swimming in open water; unfortunately, recreational fun sometimes ends in disaster. Spinal injuries in open water are a result of many factors.

Oceans and rivers. Currents and tides at ocean fronts and the flow of water in rivers can cause bottom contours to change very rapidly. Sunken logs, debris, and silt or sand build-up on the bottom are some causes of concern for the swimmer who is preparing to run and plunge. Any object underwater can create a danger for the unsuspecting swimmer.

A chief cause of spinal injury in an ocean environment is diving head-first into an oncoming wave. Every swimmer should take precautionary measures to ensure a safe entry into the water. Be sure to warn patrons by posting signs that read "No Diving" or "No Running Dives". In open water, an underwater obstruction could move into the area within minutes; lifeguards should conduct a bottom check each day before the facility opens to the public. Underwater obstructions should be removed or identified with a sign or buoy. Patrons should not run and plunge at any open water facility.

Diving from a dock into water shallower than 9 feet should also be prohibited. Signs that say "Danger—Shallow Water, No Diving" should be located on dock areas with water shallower than 9 feet.

Lakes and quarries. Although the water in lakes and quarries is not as active as in oceans and rivers, the bottom contour may still change and present hazards. Wind and wave action can carry submerged debris close to shore and deposit it on the bottom. Created lakes or reservoirs may have submerged tree stumps or logs close to shore. Large rocks or boulders may also be under water in lakes and especially in quarries.

The additional hazards of diving into quarries means it should be prohibited. Boulders, rock slabs, ledges, and even mechanical equipment left behind by former mining operations create hazards for swimmers.

DESIGN-RELATED SPINAL INJURY HAZARDS IN SWIMMING POOLS

Hazards associated with diving into deep water, especially in residential pools, often relate to the configuration of the bottom and sides of the pool and the placement of the diving board. Two specific pool designs present an increased risk for spinal injuries associated with diving from a diving board: hopper bottom and spoon-shaped pools.

Hopper Bottom Pools

The hopper bottom pool slopes on all four sides from the deepest point of the pool up to the break-point (see Figure 9.1). There is generally a very limited landing area for diving in the deepest part of the pool; in fact, diving into a hopper bottom pool is like diving into a funnel. The sides of the pool are all angled toward the deepest point, which may only be 2 feet by 2 feet. The depth markers on the deck and sides of the pool indicate the depth at the deepest point, but they don't give any indication of the side depths. The diver may think the depth is safe but find it shallower than expected because of the sloping sides. Diving from the diving board or from the side of the pool in the deep water area could result in striking the bottom or upslope of the pool in water that is shallower than the depth indicated by the markers.

Spoon-Shaped Pools

Another design that creates potential hazards is the spoon-shaped pool (see Figure 9.2). The bottom contour of this pool gives a false sense of depth and bottom surface area throughout the deep section of the pool. The distance from the end of the diving board to the upslope of the pool bottom is greatly reduced in spoon-shaped pools, as it is in hopper bottom pools. Striking the slope can cause serious neck and back injuries. The slopes are also found under the diving board and along the side.

Figure 9.1

Typical residential hopper bottom pool.

Courtesy of the American Red Cross.

No diving No diving

No diving

No diving

Shallow end

5
6
7
8

x

Deepest point 9 ft

No diving

No diving

No diving No diving

(a) Top view

(b) cross section view

Figure 9.2

Typical residential spoon-shaped pool.

Courtesy of the American Red Cross.

No diving No diving

No diving

No diving

Shallow end

5
6
7
8

x

Deepest point 9 ft

No diving

No diving

No diving No diving

(a) Top view

(b) cross section view

FACILITY AND EQUIPMENT HAZARDS IN SWIMMING POOLS

Many safety factors must be considered when a pool is being constructed. The width and depth of the diving area and the angle of the pool bottom are important for safe diving, as are the placement of diving boards and towers. Special features such as water slides, starting blocks, and underwater safety ledges should be built for safe use. Pool rules can be developed to help reduce any dangers inherent to the facility or equipment.

Residential Pools

Not all swimming pools are designed with diving in mind, especially in-ground residential pools. There are many sizes and shapes of in-ground residential pools; their length and depth can create hazards for owners and guests.

Most spinal cord injuries in residential pools result from diving into shallow water. Depths should be marked clearly on the deck near the edge of the pool and on the side of the pool coping itself. The depth on each side of the break-point distinguishing shallow water from deep water should be marked clearly. Signs saying "Danger—Shallow Water, No Diving" should be placed on the deck in shallow water and posted on fences or walls enclosing the swimming pool or on a stand at the entrance to the pool area. If you own a residential pool that is less than 11 feet, 6 inches deep and the distance from the tip of the diving board to the start of the upslope is less than 16 feet, 6 inches, remove the diving board.

Hazards associated with diving into deep water in residential pools primarily relate to the configuration of the bottom and sides of the pool, as previously discussed in "Design-Related Spinal Injury Hazards in Swimming Pools."

If you own a residential pool, do not let divers run on the diving board, attempt to dive for long distances through the air, or dive to the side if there is the slightest chance that they will

- strike the upslope of the pool that rises from the deepest section to the shallow section,
- strike a floating line marking the boundary of the diving area, or
- strike a swimmer inside the diving area.

Hotel/Motel and Apartment Swimming Pools

Many hotel/motel and apartment swimming pools present the same types of hazards as residential pools. Appropriate pool depths and construction are primary considerations for safe and injury-free diving. The lack of professional supervision at these facilities compounds their hazards. Lifeguards and swimmers should carefully assess the dimensions of the pool to assure minimum standards are met before diving is permitted. Catastrophic injuries can be avoided by eliminating diving in facilities that do not meet standards.

Public and Private Swimming Pools

Public and private swimming pools may present some of the hazards already discussed. Owners of these facilities need to be concerned with preventing diving into shallow water and with meeting minimum facility standards for safe springboard diving. Facilities also often maintain 1-meter, 3-meter, or tower diving facilities that must meet more stringent standards.

All swimming pools with diving equipment should display diving rules and regulations near the boards and towers such as those listed on pp. 57-58. These rules should be strictly enforced.

Water Slides Entering Shallow Water

Water slides, which vary in height, shape, and location, can provide safe fun providing proper precautions are met. Several factors need to be addressed regarding water slides. The speed of a swimmer entering the water from a slide depends on the height, friction, and design of the slide and the alignment of the swimmer. A swimmer entering water 3 feet deep at a near vertical angle from a slide 6 to 12 feet high achieves a head speed of 14.5 feet to 27 feet per second, fast enough to cause a spinal injury if the swimmer hits the bottom of the pool or another swimmer with the head.

The angle of entry from a slide most often is determined by the height of the lip of the slide over the surface of the water. The higher the lip, the greater the angle of entry. To reduce the possibility of spinal injuries, observe the following guidelines:

- Allow no head-first sliding.
- Have patrons cross their legs when sliding to prevent groin or internal injuries.
- Have the lifeguard signal when it is safe for one slider to begin when following another.
- Prohibit deliberate attempts at deep entries.
- Keep the landing area in front of the slide clear of swimmers.
- Provide a minimum water depth of 9 feet in the landing area.
- Anchor slides securely to the deck.
- Position the exit lip of the slide at deck or water height.

Competitive Swimming Starting Blocks

Starting blocks are used at the start of races in competitive pools. Competitive pools either have starting blocks permanently installed or have removable platforms. Competitive swimmers are trained in proper techniques for safely diving from platforms. Anyone who has not received training is at risk when diving from this equipment.

An improper dive could result in a spinal cord injury. To prevent injuries, starting blocks must be located in water at least 5 feet deep at the deep end of the pool. Use of the blocks must be restricted to trained swimmers during supervised competitive practices and events. Racing dives, such as the scoop, pike, and shoot start, cannot be allowed. At all other times, starting blocks must be removed or capped off. Safety warnings must be posted regarding starting block use, and access must be controlled by lifeguards. The blocks must be regularly inspected for stability, surface characteristics (traction), and any sign of wear.

Underwater Safety Ledges

Some swimming pools have underwater ledges (see Figure 9.3), sometimes called *safety ledges*, constructed so that swimmers could stand up in deep water when next to the side of the pool. These ledges present a hazard related to head and spinal injuries. If it is difficult to see the ledge, a swimmer can dive or jump into deep water and hit it unexpectedly. To reduce or eliminate this possibility, black stripes should be painted on the top side of the ledge with a black line on the border (see Figure 9.3) so swimmers can identify the width of the ledge.

NO-DIVING SIGNS

To ensure the safety of swimmers, any facility with water shallower than 9 feet should post warning signs indicating that diving is not allowed. Such signs may read "Danger—

Figure 9.3

Underwater ledge.

Shallow Water, No Diving". These signs should be posted on the deck near the edge of the pool and on walls adjacent to shallow water. They should be visible to anyone entering the pool and approaching shallow water.

Signs can be posted in a variety of ways:

- Universal No Diving sign painted on the deck
- Lettering painted on the deck
- Tiled lettering embedded in the deck
- Universal No Diving tile embedded in the deck
- Plastic signs mounted on walls, fences, or stands (see Figure 9.4)

Figure 9.4

No Diving sign.

Courtesy of Recreonics, Inc., Louisville, KY.

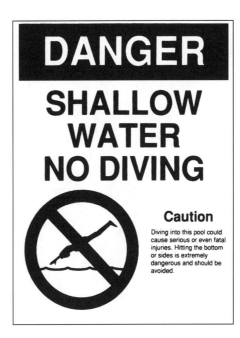

Because most spinal cord injuries occur the first time someone is at a facility, it is crucial to warn patrons of hazards. Multiple signs placed in strategic locations will help prevent injuries.

RECOGNIZING SPINAL INJURIES

Because most injuries to the head, neck, and back occur when swimmers are in shallow water, you should suspect a spinal injury any time someone

- is found unconscious (especially in shallow water),
- has been involved in a diving board or water slide accident,
- has fallen from a height, or
- has sustained a strong blow to the head or neck.

In any of these instances, a serious injury to the spinal cord may have occurred. To grasp the significance of such an injury, you must know the structure of the spine.

Understanding the Spine

The spine is a strong, flexible, bony structure that supports the head and trunk (see Figure 9.5). The bones of the spine, *vertebrae*, are somewhat circular in shape and are separated

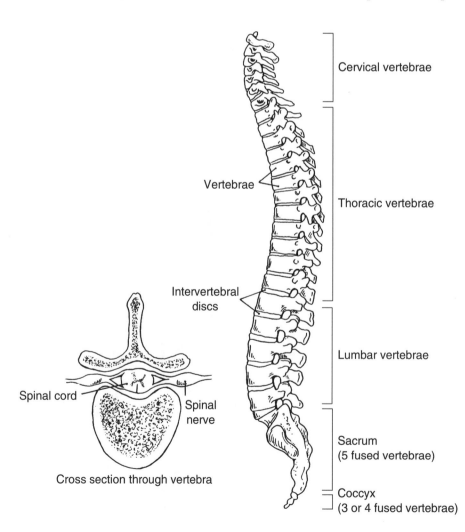

Figure 9.5

Anatomy of the spine.

Cervical vertebrae

Vertebrae

Thoracic vertebrae

Intervertebral discs

Spinal cord

Spinal nerve

Lumbar vertebrae

Cross section through vertebra

Sacrum (5 fused vertebrae)

Coccyx (3 or 4 fused vertebrae)

from each other by cushions of cartilage. This cartilage, called *intervertebral disks*, acts as a shock absorber when a person walks, runs, or jumps. The spinal cord, a bundle of nerves that distribute vital messages from the brain to different parts of the body, runs through the arches connected to the backs of the vertebrae. Nerve branches extend to the various parts of the body through openings on the sides of the vertebrae. So, the spine protects the nerve center of the body from damage.

The spine is further divided into five regions. The *cervical* spine, the area around the neck, is the most susceptible to injury when someone dives into shallow water. The *thoracic* spine is the middle back, and the *lumbar* spine is the lower back. The *sacrum* and *coccyx*, located at the base of the spinal column, complete the structure of the spine.

Signs of Spinal Injury

Injuries to the spine include fractures and dislocations of the vertebrae, sprained ligaments, and compressed or displaced intervertebral disks. Any of these injuries can cause damage to the spinal cord that may result in paralysis or death.

A victim of a spinal injury may exhibit any of the following signs:

- Pain at the site of the injury
- Loss of movement in the extremities
- Loss of movement below the site of the injury
- Tingling or loss of sensation in the extremities
- Disorientation
- Deformity in the neck or back
- Visible bruising over an area of the spinal column
- Difficulty in breathing
- Head injury
- Fluid or blood in the ears or nose
- Unconsciousness

If you notice *any* of these signs, handle the victim as if he or she has a spinal injury.

Be aware that someone who has sustained a spinal injury in the water may rise to the surface and move the head back and forth and minimally move the hands and arms before sinking to the pool bottom.

REACHING A SPINAL INJURY VICTIM

Just as for any rescue, speed is vital in assisting someone who may have injured the spinal cord. But you must take special precautions to avoid causing additional harm.

If an injury should occur on deck, do *not* move the victim. Call EMS, then make the victim as comfortable as possible until assistance arrives.

Entering the Water

You must go into the water slowly and carefully with a waveless entry, so that the movement of the water does not cause further injury. You can do a waveless entry in two ways. To enter shallow water, sit on the deck, place your hands on the deck at both sides of your legs, and lower yourself into the water. This entry is difficult to do in deep water without creating waves.

A waveless entry for deep water (or an alternative for shallow water) calls for the following steps:

Figure 9.6

Waveless entry
for deep water.

(a) Reaching across
the body

(b) lowering into
the water

1. Sit on the edge of the deck. Put your rescue tube or buoy at your side on deck.
2. Place one hand on the deck near your leg.
3. Reach across your body with the other hand and place it on the deck or on the lip of the pool gutter (Figure 9.6a).
4. Lower yourself into the water, turning 180 degrees to face the side of the pool (see Figure 9.6b). Maintain visual contact with the victim as much as possible.
5. Grab your rescue tube or buoy.

Approaching the Injured Swimmer

Whether you are in shallow or deep water, you must approach the victim slowly, carefully, and with as little water disturbance as possible. If you are in shallow water, walk toward the person slowly. If you are in deeper water, use the breaststroke or a modified crawl stroke with an underwater arm recovery.

Practice these approach techniques; they take some time to perfect. Remember, they must help you reach the victim quickly, without creating waves or disturbing the water.

SPINAL INJURY RESCUE TECHNIQUES

The YMCA recommends the head-splint rescue technique for victims with spinal injuries. Research has shown this method to be the most effective for stabilizing the head and neck during a rescue. It can be used if the victim is lying facedown in the water before turning her or him over or to stabilize a victim who is faceup in the water. *In-line stabilization* is accomplished by squeezing the victim's arms to trap the head between them.

This section describes how to use the head-splint technique during rescues in both shallow and deep water, on the surface and underwater. Remember that in all situations in which a spinal injury is suspected, EMS should be contacted immediately.

During all rescues, move the victim's extremities carefully and according to procedures to avoid causing additional injury. Practice rescue procedures regularly to ensure your ability to perform them correctly and quickly.

Shallow Water Surface Rescues

Shallow water surface rescues are the easiest type to execute; you should practice them first to master the head-splint technique. These rescues include rescuing a victim who is facedown and turning that victim over or rescuing a victim who is faceup.

Figure 9.7

Head-splint rescue in shallow water, victim facedown.

Victim facedown.   Follow these steps:

1. Approach the victim from the side, and stop while facing the head.
2. Grab the right arm just above the elbow with your right hand.
3. Grab the left arm just above the elbow with your left hand.
4. Move the arms sideways, toward the victim's head, to a position in which the upper arms cover the ears. This will center the head between the arms.
5. Squeeze the arms simultaneously against the head to trap it in position (stabilize it) (Figure 9.7).
6. Continue to apply pressure against the head during in-line stabilization.

Turning victim over.   When a victim is found lying facedown in the water, the head-splint turnover should be used to turn the victim faceup (see Figure 9.8). Take the following steps to turn a victim:

(a) Trapping victim's head and moving forward

(b) rolling victim toward you

(c) turning victim and lowering self to neck depth

Figure 9.8

Head-splint turnover.

1. After trapping the head between the arms, move the victim forward; the legs will rise. (Having the legs ride higher in the water will make it easier to do the turn.)
2. As you roll the victim toward you, turn to face the feet and legs.
3. At the same time, move your top arm (the arm that is over the victim) to a position beneath the shoulder. (You will notice at the end of the sequence illustrated in Figure 9.8 that the right arm, which was the top arm, now is under the right shoulder.) Your forearm should be in contact with the shoulder and upper arm.
4. As you turn the victim, lower yourself into the water to neck depth to avoid lifting him or her during in-line stabilization.

After you have turned the victim over, you should be in a position in which the arms are over your shoulder and close to your ear, cheek, or neck. You can stabilize the victim in a horizontal position by gently supporting the shoulder with your forearm, which is under the victim. Remember, the arm that is under the victim's shoulder was the arm that you originally reached over the victim to begin the head splint. The appropriate stabilization position is illustrated in Figure 9.9.

Figure 9.9

Stabilizing position in the head splint in shallow water.

Keys to the Head-Splint Turnover

1. Grab upper arms near the elbows, trap the head between the arms, and maintain pressure.
2. Move the victim forward.
3. Roll the victim toward you and turn to face the feet and legs. At the same time, move your top arm to beneath the victim's shoulder.
4. Lower yourself to neck depth as you turn the victim.
5. Finish the turn with the victim's arms over your shoulder, next to your ear, cheek, or neck.
6. Keep your forearm under the victim's shoulder for support.

Victim faceup.   Approach from behind; if the victim is conscious and floating on the surface, ask these questions:

- Are you OK?
- What happened?

- Do you feel pain anywhere?
- Can you move your fingers?
- Can you move your toes?

This will help you determine the victim's condition. Let the victim know that you are next going to provide in-line stabilization to protect the spine.

Explaining exactly what you are going to do, proceed with the following (see Figure 9.10):

1. Stand behind the victim.
2. Submerge so that the water level is at your neck.
3. Grab the victim's elbows in the same manner as previously learned.
4. Slowly and carefully move the arms sideways to a position that will allow you to trap the head between the arms. (You may have to reposition yourself while moving the victim's arms to trap the head.)
5. After the head is trapped, stabilize the victim for backboarding (see "Backboarding Procedures" later in this chapter).

Figure 9.10

Head-splint rescue in shallow water, victim faceup.

(a) Approaching from rear of victim

(b) moving victim's arms into position to trap the head

Shallow Water Bottom Rescues

If the victim is faceup on the bottom, place your hands in position to perform the head-splint rescue. The victim's position may require you to adjust the technique, but in any case, trap the head between the arms and carefully lift the victim by the arms with head trapped to the surface. You may have to exhale before you submerge to reduce your buoyancy and more effectively position yourself for the rescue.

If the victim is facedown, trap the head between the arms, lift the victim by the arms with head trapped to the surface, and then turn the victim over.

Deep Water Rescues

Although very few spinal injuries occur in deep water, you need to know how to respond if one does. Hitting the diving board, diving into another swimmer, or striking the head on the pool bottom or upslope are all ways a spine could be injured in deep water.

Stabilizing the neck in deep water is difficult. In shallow water you do not need to support yourself as you work, but in deep water you need a strong kick to keep yourself in position to perform an effective rescue. A pair of fins should be stored at all deep water lifeguard stations. With fins, it is far easier to maintain your position using a flutter kick. Without fins, a breaststroke, scissors, or rotary kick should be used. It is also possible to use a rescue tube for additional buoyancy during rescue. This procedure will be discussed later in the chapter.

Victim on the surface.   Put on fins and enter the water using a waveless entry. If fins are not available, place a rescue tube against your chest and under your armpits to provide buoyancy for you and the victim. In either instance, use an underwater arm recovery during your approach to avoid disturbing the water.

When you reach the victim, perform the head-splint rescue, including the turnover if necessary, as described previously; transport the victim to shallow water if possible, using a breaststroke, scissors, or rotary kick. If you use a rescue tube, put it against your chest and under your armpits during the turnover and transport. If you are at a pool or diving well with no shallow section, use a kick to transport the victim toward the side of the pool and perform the following sequence (see Figure 9.11):

1. An additional rescuer lies on the deck and talks you toward the side of the pool. Your goal is to position the victim perpendicular to the side of the pool.
2. As you approach the side of the pool, the rescuer on the deck takes the victim's upper arms and applies the head splint.
3. Once the on-deck rescuer has secured the arms and head, you release the victim's arms and grab the pool gutter. Your role now is to support the victim's hips if necessary and then slide a rescue tube under her or his knees.
4. The victim is now ready to be placed on a backboard. The backboarding procedure is discussed later in this chapter.

(a) Transporting victim in head-splint position to side of pool

Figure 9.11

Head-splint rescue in deep water on the surface.

(b) rescuer on deck grabbing victim's upper arms and maintaining head-splint position

(continued)

Figure 9.11

(continued)

(c) rescuer in water supporting victim's hips

Victim underwater. In most cases a person who is submerged will not be flat on his or her back on the bottom. You will not be able to use the rescue tube for buoyancy. Use fins or a strong kick to reach and transport the victim and to prepare for backboarding. Depending on the victim's position on the bottom, approach from above or behind. Trap the head using the head-splint technique and transport the victim to the surface with the face angled toward the bottom to avoid getting water up the nose and potentially into the stomach and lungs. Once you reach the surface, turn the victim faceup. Transport the victim either to shallow water, if possible, or to the side of the pool near a corner where you can get assistance.

PREPARING TO BACKBOARD

Before you learn the backboarding procedures, you need crucial background knowledge in three areas: how to select a backboard, how to apply a cervical collar, and how to administer rescue breathing and CPR to a spinal injury victim.

Selecting a Backboard

Some of the various backboards available are illustrated in Figure 9.12. Any of the pictured models is acceptable as long as it meets these requirements:

- It is made of marine plywood or lightweight resins.
- It is sturdy enough not to bend when used to lift a victim out of the water.
- There are slats or risers underneath the board or hand grips to help prevent rescuers from pinching their fingers when setting the board on the deck.
- It has holes on each side of the board for adjusting strap placement.
- Some form of head restraint is attached to the board for immediate use (sand bags or rolled towels should be used when a manufactured restraint is not available).
- The board is long and wide enough to allow rescue of people of varying sizes.
- At least six straps are connected to the board (one head strap, one chest strap, one waist strap, one thigh strap, one shin/ankle strap, and one foot strap; a wrist strap is optional).

For two-person backboard procedures, a marine plywood board is easiest to handle; plastic or resin boards are very buoyant, which makes them more difficult for the single guard who is in the water to handle.

Figure 9.12

Backboard styles.

Padding should be available to place under the victim's head if necessary. Generally there is a gap between the board and the head once the victim is positioned on the board. The padding prevents the head from dropping back onto the board or changing alignment.

Backboards should be kept on deck and ready for use at all times the facility is open. All straps should be connected to the board in a manner that duplicates how they will be connected once a victim is placed on the board.

Using a Cervical Collar

A cervical collar correctly applied stabilizes the head and neck very effectively. Various styles of collars are available; a few are illustrated in Figure 9.13. Each comes in several sizes for adults and youth.

Figure 9.13

Types of cervical collars.

(a) rigid emergency collar

(b) extrication collar

(c) Armstrong collar

Not all cervical collars are appropriate for use in an aquatic environment. Consider these factors:

- Collars must be rigid. (Foam collars are ineffective in the water.)
- Collars must be available in a variety of collar sizes, ranging from infant collars to adult long-neck collars.
- One-piece collars are easier to apply than two-piece collars in aquatic backboarding procedures.

Cervical collars should always be stored with backboards, either attached to a strap or in a bag that is attached to the board.

Before applying a cervical collar, always check the victim's breathing and pulse. If rescue breathing or CPR becomes necessary after the collar is on, you may have to loosen or remove it. *Never* apply a cervical collar to a victim whose head is angled sideways.

To use a cervical collar appropriately, you must first select a collar of the appropriate size, then apply it correctly.

Sizing the collar. Using an improperly sized cervical collar can cause further injury to the victim. For instance, a too-small collar can obstruct the victim's airway. That's why you need to select the correct size collar before applying it.

To some extent, the size will depend on the design of the collar being used. However, you can follow these two steps to determine the proper size:

1. Put your hand next to the victim's neck. Measure the distance from under the corner of the jawbone to the shoulder (in number of fingers) (see Figure 9.14a).
2. Choose a collar with the same measurement as the distance from the victim's jawbone to shoulder. Some collars have a black knob that fastens to the collar. Place your fingers beneath the knob and measure to the bottom of the plastic (not the bottom of the foam cushion). If the distance is the same as the measurement you made of the victim, the cervical collar is likely to be the correct size (see Figure 9.14b). If the collar doesn't have a black knob, measure the distance from the bottom of the chin cup to the bottom of the plastic. Also, if sizing instructions came with the collar, follow the manufacturer's directions.

If you find you don't have an appropriately sized collar, one that isn't too loose or too tight, use head restraints to immobilize the head instead.

Note that the rigid cervical collar is more of a reminder to the victim to not move the head than it is an actual immobilization device. Instruct the victim not to move his or her head and to answer questions verbally rather than by shaking or nodding the head.

Figure 9.14

Sizing a cervical collar.

(a) Hand on victim's neck

Black knob

(b) hand on collar

Applying the collar.   To apply the collar, begin by grasping it properly. Most cervical collars have an opening at the spot that fits in front of the larynx that makes it easier to apply the collar. Place your middle finger inside the opening, with all other fingers on the outside of the collar. Your thumb should be positioned on the opposite side from the fingers (see Figure 9.15). This lets you flex the collar to fit it under the chin.

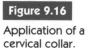

Figure 9.15

Hand position for applying cervical collar.

Some collars can be slipped under the neck and then bent to conform to the neck and chin. Others have preformed curves and need to be placed under the chin and then slid under the neck. Whatever style of collar you have, apply it carefully, following these steps:

1. Maintain manual stabilization, and avoid overextending the victim's chin when applying the collar.
2. Slide the back of the collar under the victim's neck without lifting or moving the head or neck (see Figure 9.16a).
3. Wrap the front of the device around the front of the victim's neck and carefully attach the Velcro strap so the collar fits snugly (see Figure 9.16b). In some situations you may have to place the chin cup beneath the victim's chin and carefully slide the chin cup into place. Use the method for holding the collar shown in Figure 9.16b for final placement of the collar.

Figure 9.16

Application of a cervical collar.

(a) applying collar

(b) Velcro on collar

See that the victim's chin rests easily in the collar, allowing the neck to remain in the neutral position. In this position, the victim's head should not be able to turn either side to side or up and down. Check to make sure that the collar doesn't obstruct the victim's airway.

If you discover the collar is the wrong size, remove it and try another size. Never try to force a collar into place!

If goggles are hanging around the victim's neck and interfere with placement of the collar, cut them off or remove them. The original rescuer should be the one to remove the goggles while a second rescuer maintains control of the head. The original rescuer carefully pulls the goggles over the victim's head and around the second rescuer's hands, then traps the head to the backboard as described in backboarding procedures. The second rescuer then carefully removes his or her hands from the victim's head (the goggle strap will be around the second rescuer's hands).

Applying a cervical collar correctly takes a good deal of practice. Use procedures that conform to your state and local codes, and be sure you become skilled at them before your season starts. The patrons depend on your ability to keep them safe. If local or state codes do not allow lifeguards to apply collars, do not do it.

Providing Rescue Breathing and CPR

There are situations in which the person who has sustained a spinal injury may require rescue breathing or CPR. Breathing may be weak and shallow due to drowning or paralysis of diaphragm and chest muscles. When the victim is first stabilized, the rescuer who trapped the victim's head should begin a check of the ABCs: airway, breathing, and circulation. Begin by checking the victim's breathing. Look for the chest to rise and fall, then listen for breathing. If the victim is breathing, he or she will have a pulse. If not, check for circulation after rescue breathing is initiated. When the head-splint rescue is being performed, it may be difficult to feel a pulse in the neck (carotid pulse). The wrist (radial) pulse should be checked instead. It may be possible to feel on the inside of the bicep (brachial) with your fingers while continuing to trap the head between the arms in the head split. If no pulse is found, the victim should be placed on a backboard immediately and lifted onto the deck so CPR can be initiated. Don't waste time strapping the victim to the backboard; CPR must begin immediately. The head-splint should be maintained as the victim is removed from the water on the board.

Protective equipment. Law requires that lifeguards be provided appropriate personal protective equipment (e.g., pocket or face masks, rubber gloves, gowns, and safety glasses) for performing first aid, rescue breathing, and CPR. If the victim is bleeding, the rescuer needs protection against blood-borne diseases. And because many victims vomit during rescue breathing, a pocket or face mask with a one-way valve is used to shield the rescuer from contact with the victim's body fluids (see Figure 9.17).

Figure 9.17

Pocket mask and case.

Modified jaw thrust.   If a spinal injury is suspected, the victim's head should not be tilted back for rescue breathing. This could cause further damage to the spinal column. In the modified jaw thrust, the rescuer performing rescue breathing places the thumbs on the cheekbones of the victim, as illustrated in Figure 9.18—the right thumb is on the right cheek, left thumb on the left cheek. The index and middle fingers of both hands should be positioned on the jawbone so that you can lift the jaw forward (you can feel the "corner" of the jawbone near the ear). This action moves the tongue away from the back of the throat without tilting the head back. Light pressure on the cheekbones will help to maintain the victim's head in a neutral position.

Figure 9.18

Modified jaw thrust.

Once you move the jaw forward, check for breathing. If the victim is not breathing, position the pocket mask over the victim's mouth and nose. Press down on the pocket mask with your thumbs while pulling the jaw forward to open the airway (see Figure 9.19).

Figure 9.19

Modified jaw thrust with pocket mask. (a) On deck; (b) in the water.

a   b

Provide two full breaths, then check the pulse. If there is a pulse but no breathing, continue rescue breathing. Give one slow, full breath every 5 seconds for an adult, and every 3 seconds for a child under 8. If you find no pulse, the victim must be placed on a backboard and removed from the water immediately.

If a cervical collar has been applied and the victim then stops breathing, carefully work your index and middle fingers down between the collar and the victim's jaw to pull the jaw forward. Provide two full breaths, then check the radial pulse or brachial pulse. If you cannot work your fingers into position for moving the jaw forward, loosen the cervical collar and do so (see Figure 9.20).

Figure 9.20

Modified jaw thrust after cervical collar applied.

Vomiting.   If the victim vomits during neck stabilization, rotate the victim to the side as a unit, maintaining in-line stabilization, and have an assistant clear the mouth. If the victim vomits while strapped to the board, use the following procedure, illustrated in Figure 9.21, in the water or on the deck:

1. One rescuer maintains in-line stabilization.
2. At least three assistants are positioned on one side of the victim, with the strongest at the victim's shoulders.

(a) preparing to turn victim

(b) turning victim

Figure 9.21

Turning the victim on a backboard to clear the mouth after vomiting.

3. Each assistant reaches across the victim and grabs the victim's far side (being sure to grab the victim, not the board; grabbing the board will result in pinched fingers). The arm that crosses should be pressed against the victim to trap him or her against the board.

4. The rescuer coordinates the tilt by counting "One, two, three, lift."

5. On the signal, the assistants lift up on the side of the backboard nearest to them until the victim is angled sideways.

6. An additional assistant, wearing rubber gloves, clears the victim's mouth of vomit, using a clean cloth to wipe it out.

7. The victim is lowered on signal to a flat position; breathing should continue to be monitored.

BACKBOARDING PROCEDURES

Putting a person with a spinal injury on a backboard is not a responsibility to be taken lightly. In some locales, paramedics request that you stabilize the injured person in the water and allow them to do the backboarding. Your facility's management needs to work with your local EMS to develop procedures for your facility. In any case, you need to be able to perform the procedures used in the event you are ever called on to remove someone with a spinal injury from the water.

This section addresses how to

- position a person on a backboard,
- strap a person to a backboard, and
- lift someone from the water.

Backboarding requires the involvement of several people. Rescuers who have had training in lifeguarding and spinal injury management and untrained assistants may both be needed. Any assistant should be supervised and act only on the instructions of a rescuer.

To prepare a backboard for use, disconnect the straps. Depending on their type, either remove the straps completely or disconnect one side from the board.

In a pool, gutter and deck construction and type of backboard may influence the procedures used. The rescuer on deck may have to adjust position to allow the most effective in-line stabilization. Deck-level gutter systems allow the rescuer in the water to approach the side of the pool perpendicularly or by angling into the corner. You may have to slightly alter the procedures that follow to make backboarding procedures effective at your facility. It is vital that you develop procedures that are useful for your facility. In-service training and rescue drills are effective means to establish and test those procedures.

If you should be in a situation where a backboard is not available, provide in-line stabilization in the water with the injured person until the EMS arrives. Do not remove the victim from the water unless CPR is needed.

Shallow Water Backboarding

Two different procedures will be introduced for shallow water. Some facilities may not have multiple rescuers to assist in backboarding procedures, so one set of procedures requires two rescuers and the other requires one rescuer and three assistants. In all of the descriptions, Rescuer 1 is the rescuer in the water with control of the victim's head at the beginning of the procedure.

Two-rescuer procedure. This backboarding procedure requires two rescuers, Rescuer 1 in the water and Rescuer 2 on the deck. While Rescuer 1 maintains in-line stabilization and moves to a position perpendicular to the side of the pool, Rescuer 2 moves into position to stabilize the victim from the deck.

Once Rescuer 1 is near the side of the pool, Rescuer 2 lies on the deck, grasping the victim's upper arms and applying pressure to trap the head (see Figure 9.22a). Rescuer 1 releases the victim and Rescuer 2 maintains him or her in a horizontal position. It may be necessary to place a rescue tube under the victim's knees to maintain the horizontal position (see Figure 9.22b). Rescuer 1 should then check the victim's airway, breathing, and circulation (ABCs). (If the victim is not breathing, Rescuer 1 should begin rescue breathing.)

After checking the victim's ABCs, Rescuer 1 climbs out of the water, gets the backboard and disconnects the straps, and positions it on edge next to the victim. The board should be placed so that it will glide under the victim and float up centered. (The closer the board is to the victim before it is submerged, the easier it is to glide the board beneath the victim.) Rescuer 1 then submerges the backboard (see Figure 9.22c), centers it under the victim, then allows it to float up (see Figure 9.22d). As long as Rescuer 2 provides in-line stabilization, Rescuer 1 can adjust the board as needed as it rises. Rescuer 1 then places one arm on the victim's sternum and cups the victim's chin, fingers on one side and thumb on the other side. Rescuer 1 places the other arm beneath the backboard and traps the victim to the board (see Figure 9.23). Rescuer 2 lowers the victim's arms to his or her sides and then lifts the edge of the backboard into the gutter (see Figure 9.24a). Rescuer 2 then applies the cervical collar (see Figure 9.24b and c). Rescuers 1 and 2 may need to alternate stabilizing the victim's head and neck during application of the cervical collar.

Figure 9.22

Two-rescuer backboarding procedure in shallow water.

(a) Rescuer 2 on deck, Rescuer 1 passing victim to 2

(b) rescue tube placed under victim's knees

(continued)

(c) Rescuer 1 angling board to submerge it under victim

Figure 9.22

(continued)

(d) Rescuer 1 centering the board as it floats up

Figure 9.23

Trapping the victim to the board with two rescuers in shallow water.

Figure 9.24

Applying a cervical collar with two rescuers in shallow water.

(a) Rescuer 2 lowering victim's arms to sides

(b) Rescuer 2 applying cervical collar as Rescuer 1 maintains head stabilization

(c) Rescuer 1 repositioning hand on victim's chin

Keys to Preparing for Backboarding in Shallow Water (Two Rescuers)

1. Rescuer 1 maintains in-line stabilization.
2. Rescuer 2 prepares to stabilize the victim from the deck while Rescuer 1 moves the victim into position perpendicular to the side of the pool.
3. Rescuer 2 lies on the deck and takes over in-line stabilization by grasping the victim's arms and applying pressure to the head.
4. Rescuer 1 releases the victim and may center a rescue tube horizontally under the victim's knees to maintain a horizontal position.
5. Rescuer 1 checks the victim's ABCs. (If the victim is not breathing, Rescuer 1 begins rescue breathing.)
6. Rescuer 1 climbs out of the water, gets the backboard and disconnects the straps, and positions it on edge next to the victim. The board should be placed so it glides under the victim and rises centered beneath him or her.
7. Rescuer 1 pushes the board under the victim and allows the board to float up. As long as Rescuer 2 provides in-line stabilization, Rescuer 1 can reposition the board if necessary.
8. Rescuer 1 traps the victim to the board.
9. Rescuer 2 moves the victim's arms to his or her sides and then lifts the top section of the backboard onto the lip of the gutter.
10. Rescuer 2 places the cervical collar on the victim.

To secure the victim to the backboard, take the following steps:

1. Rescuer 2 grabs the victim's armpits and traps the head between the rescuer's arms while Rescuer 1 straps the victim to the backboard. All straps are secured so they do not go underneath the backboard.

2. Rescuer 1 straps the victim's chest to the board directly under the armpits. This strap should be snug under the armpits and against the chest. (See Figure 9.25a.)

3. Rescuer 1 secures the waist strap, strapping the arms against the victim's sides with the waist strap or tying the wrists together with a separate strap. (See Figure 9.25b.)

4. Rescuer 1 removes the rescue tube from underneath the victim's knees and places it under the foot end of the board. To do this, Rescuer 1 moves to the foot end of the board and, grasping the tube with both hands, submerges the tube and pulls it toward the victim's feet. (See Figure 9.25c.) Rescuer 1 may give some support to the board by lifting one leg up against it.

5. Rescuer 1 secures the thigh strap, just above the knees if possible (placement of straps depends on the location of strap holes on the backboard). (See Figure 9.25d.)

6. Rescuer 1 secures the shin strap, just below the knees if possible. The placement of the thigh and shin straps helps keep the knees from buckling on an unconscious person or a person with paralysis in the lower extremities. (See Figure 9.25d.)

7. Rescuer 1 applies a strap figure 8 style to the victim's feet. It should be very snug against the bottom of the feet. (See Figure 9.25e.)

8. Rescuer 1 applies head restraints at each side of the victim's head, one restraint at a time. Rescuer 2 needs to move his or her arms from the side of the victim's head and reposition the arms on the outside of the restraints. Rescuer 2 should again apply gentle pressure toward the victim's head. (See Figure 9.25f.)

9. Rescuer 1 applies the head strap.

10. Rescuer 1 checks all straps to make sure they are snug.

11. Rescuer 2 grabs the head end of the backboard and Rescuer 1 grabs the foot end. (See Figure 9.25g.)

12. Both rescuers angle the board toward the pool bottom. Rescuer 2 pulls the board up while Rescuer 1 lifts up on the board. They should not slide the board against the pool edge during the lift if possible. The victim's weight and the rescuers' strength will determine if the board is against the pool edge or not. It is easier to lift a heavy victim by sliding the board. (See Figure 9.25 h and i.)

13. Both rescuers lift together on a count of "One, two, three, lift." They should lift until the backboard is about halfway onto the deck. (See Figure 9.25j.)

14. The rescuers rest the backboard against the edge of the pool and lay it down on the deck. (See Figure 9.25k.)

15. The rescuers lift (not slide) the board and move it completely onto the deck.

Be sure to lift primarily with your legs, not with your back alone. Incorrect lifting can cause serious back injury.

One rescuer and three assistants. In some situations one lifeguard will have to direct others to help in rescuing a person with a spinal injury. The lifeguard should maintain control of all aspects of the rescue; it is extremely important for the assistants to be directed by the lifeguard for all backboarding procedures.

In this rescue procedure the rescuer and all three assistants are in the water. After stabilizing the victim's head, Rescuer 1 checks the victim's ABCs. If the victim is not breathing, an assistant takes over in-line stabilization so Rescuer 1 can administer rescue breathing. If the victim is breathing, Rescuer 1 directs Assistants 1 and 2 to retrieve a

(a) Securing the chest strap

(b) securing the waist strap

(c) moving the rescue tube to the foot end of the board

Figure 9.25

Strapping the victim to the backboard.

(d) securing the thigh and shin straps

(e) figure 8-style foot strap

(continued)

(f) applying head restraints

(g) Rescuer 2 lifting the head end of the board to the deck

Figure 9.25

(continued)

(h) Rescuer 2 repositioning for the lift

(i) Rescuer 2 lifting with the legs

(continued)

(j) stopping the lift when the board is half out of the water

R2

R1

(k) laying the board down on the deck

R2

R1

Figure 9.25

(continued)

backboard. The three assistants disconnect the straps on the backboard and guide the backboard beneath the victim, as in two-person procedures. Now Rescuer 1 continues to apply pressure on the arms while repositioning so the backboard can be placed beneath the victim (see Figure 9.26a).

One assistant should then take over stabilizing Assistant 3's side of the board, allowing Assistant 3 to move away. Once the victim is centered properly and in contact with the board, Assistant 3 carefully slips her or his hands under the victim's arms and stabilizes the head (see Figure 9.26b). This allows Rescuer 1 to move the victim's arms down to his or her sides (see Figure 9.26c and d) and then apply the cervical collar. Rescuer 1 then continues by strapping the victim to the backboard.

Figure 9.26

Backboarding procedure for one rescuer and three assistants in shallow water.

(a) Rescuer 1 applies pressure to victim's arms while assistants position the backboard

(b) Assistant 3 stabilizes victim's head

(c) Rescuer 1 begins to move victim's arms down to side

(d) Rescuer 1 positions victim's arms to prepare for strapping

The following sequence should be used to secure a person to the backboard once he or she has been stabilized:

1. Rescuer 1 attaches all straps while Assistants 1 and 2 continue to stabilize the backboard and Assistant 3 stabilizes the head.
2. Follow the strapping sequence for two-rescuer procedures.

Figure 9.27 illustrates the victim appropriately strapped to the backboard (for all rescue procedures) and ready to be removed from the water. Rescuer 1 should check all straps

---

Keys to Backboarding in Shallow Water (One Rescuer and Three Assistants)

1. Rescuer 1 maintains in-line stabilization while Assistants 1 and 2 retrieve a backboard.
2. Assistants 1 and 2 submerge the backboard and center it under the victim. One assistant moves to the opposite side of the board and assists in stabilizing it. During this time Rescuer 1 continues to apply pressure on the arms while repositioning to allow placement of the backboard under the victim's head.
3. Assistant 3 slides hand under victim's arms and stabilizes the head.
4. Rescuer 1 moves victim's arms to the side and applies cervical collar and straps.

---

to see that they are secure. The straps should be snug but should not restrict breathing; test the tension by seeing if you can slide two fingers underneath. If you can, they are correctly tightened. If more fingers fit easily, the straps need to be tightened. If your fingers don't slide, the straps need to be loosened.

Removing victim from shallow water. Once the person is secured to the backboard, the next step is to remove him or her from the water. If available, additional assistance should be used for this procedure. The number of assistants needed depends on the strength of the assistants and on the victim's size and weight. Use common sense in deciding how many assistants are needed; there should be enough that the team can keep the backboard horizontal while lifting it from the water.

The strongest assistants should be positioned on either side of the backboard at the victim's chest. The others should be equally distributed on both sides of the backboard. The assistant stabilizing the victim's head should continue to do so throughout the procedure.

It is important to keep the backboard perpendicular to the pool wall to help the team perform a stable lift. Rescuer 1 coordinates the lift using verbal instructions such as, "One, two, three, lift" each time the board is to be lifted.

Figure 9.28, a-c, illustrate the procedure for removing the backboard from the water. On the first lift, the board should be moved to position the victim's shoulders over the deck. Be careful not to trap the victim's hair under the board, and be sure not to slide the board onto the deck; sliding may cause the straps to move on some boards.

After the top section of the board is on the deck, the two assistants at the victim's chest climb out of the water and continue to assist in lifting from the deck. Anyone lifting from the deck should be reminded to lift with the legs, not the back. During the second lift, try to position most of the board on the deck. Continue the lifting procedure until the backboard is resting securely on the deck.

(a) Preparing to lift

(b) first lift

(c) second lift

Figure 9.28

Removing someone on a backboard from shallow water.

Keys to the Shallow Water Backboard Lift

1. Use enough assistants to keep the board horizontal. The two strongest assistants are positioned at the victim's chest.
2. The rescuer at the victim's head continues to stabilize the head throughout the lifting process.
3. Lift simultaneously on a given signal.
4. On the first lift, move the board to position the victim's shoulders over the deck. Do not slide the board onto the deck.
5. The two assistants at the chest climb out of the water and onto the deck, where they assist with the second lift to position most of the board on the deck and with any subsequent lifts.

Deep Water Backboarding

Two methods for backboarding in deep water are presented in this section. One method uses two rescuers, the other uses two rescuers and two assistants. Your equipment, facility, skill, and number of rescuers will help you decide which method to use.

Again, in all descriptions, Rescuer 1 is the rescuer in the water with control of the victim's head at the beginning of the procedure.

Two-rescuer procedure. This can be performed in the same manner as the two-rescuer procedure for shallow water with some exceptions. Rescuer 1 may straddle a rescue tube, which will provide additional buoyancy for strapping the victim to the board. After Rescuer 2 grasps the victim's arms and Rescuer 1 has checked the victim's ABCs, Rescuer 1 slides the tube under the victim's knees. If the victim is not breathing, begin rescue breathing. If the victim is breathing, Rescuer 1 climbs out of the water, disconnects the straps on the backboard, and carries the board with him or her into the water. After strapping the victim to the board, Rescuer 2 positions the victim (on the board) vertically. Rescuer 1, in the water, grabs the pool edge and assists in lifting the victim out of the water. The rescuers should be careful not to slide the bottom of the backboard on the pool edge during the lift if possible.

During the lift from the water, the backboard will be more vertical than in shallow water procedures, and the rescuer in the water will need to hold the lip of the gutter to assist in the lift (see Figure 9.29).

Figure 9.29

Deep water lift of backboard.

(b) lifting

R2

(a) Preparing to lift

R2

R1

R1

This deep water procedure can be performed with two rescuers in most circumstances. If one rescuer cannot safely position the backboard under the victim, another rescuer or assistant may be needed in the water. Familiarity and practice with the equipment, facility, and procedures will help you identify whether two or three rescuers are necessary.

Two-rescuer, two-assistant procedure. When two rescuers and two assistants are available, Rescuer 1 performs the head-splint technique while Rescuer 2 lies on the deck in a corner of the pool. Rescuer 2 guides Rescuer 1 to the corner and grasps the victim's elbows to provide in-line stabilization. Rescuer 1 releases the arms and holds the gutter once Rescuer 2 has a firm grip on the victim. Rescuer 1 then provides support under the hips (see Figure 9.30a) and checks the victim's ABCs. If the victim is not breathing, Rescuer 1 begins rescue breathing. If the victim is breathing, two assistants retrieve a backboard, disconnect the straps, and re-enter the water with the backboard. They approach the victim from the side opposite Rescuer 1, place the board on edge, and center the backboard below the victim (see Figure 9.30b). After the board is centered under the victim, Rescuer 1 and one assistant on the opposite side grab the gutter and stabilize the board. The other assistant moves to the same side as Rescuer 1 and stabilizes the board. The two assistants continue to hold the gutter with one hand and stabilize the backboard with the other during the remaining procedures (see Figure 9.30c). Rescuer 1 straddles a rescue tube or straps the tube around his or her chest to provide flotation while strapping the victim to the board. Rescuer 1 traps the victim to the backboard in the same manner as described in the two-rescuer shallow water procedures. Rescuer 2 moves the victim's arms down to her or his sides and applies a cervical collar. After the cervical collar is attached, Rescuer 2 stabilizes the victim's head for the remainder of the strapping procedure by applying pressure to each side of the victim's head and cheeks. Rescuer 1 then straps the victim to the board in the same order described for shallow water procedures.

(a) Rescuer 2 grabbing victim's arms and applying pressure while Rescuer 1 grabs the gutter and supports victim's hips

Figure 9.30

Two-rescuer, two-assistant procedure in deep water.

(b) assistants turning the board on edge, and guiding the board under the victim

(c) assistants stabilizing backboard in corner

Keys to Backboarding in Deep Water
(Two Rescuers and Two Assistants)

1. Rescuer 1 maintains in-line stabilization and moves toward the pool corner.
2. Rescuer 2 lies on the deck with his or her shoulders over the water in a corner of the pool and guides Rescuer 1 to the corner.
3. Rescuer 2 grasps victim's arms and provides in-line stabilization.
4. Rescuer 1 releases arms, grasps the gutter, and supports under the victim's hips.
5. Assistants 1 and 2 approach the victim from opposite side of Rescuer 1 and center the backboard beneath the victim.
6. Assistants 1 and 2, on opposite sides, grab the pool gutter and continue to hold the board under the victim.
7. Rescuer 1 traps the victim's head to the backboard.
8. Rescuer 2 moves the victim's arms down to his or her sides and applies a cervical collar.
9. Rescuer 2 applies pressure to each side of the victim's head and stabilizes it for the remaining procedure.
10. Rescuer 1 straps the victim to the backboard.

Removing the victim from deep water.   Once the backboard is ready to be lifted onto the deck, at least six lifters (Rescuer 1 and five assistants) are needed in the water and one rescuer (Rescuer 2) on the deck. If the board is not already in the corner of the pool, the six angle the board into a corner. Rescuer 2 on deck continues to provide in-line stabilization. Three people are positioned in the water on either side of the board; each should have one hand on the lip of the pool gutter and one under the backboard (see Figure 9.31, a-d). Lifters must brace their feet against the side of the pool to get leverage for lifting. The strongest assistants should be at the victim's head.

Rescuer 1 directs the lift using a cue like "One, two, three, lift." From this point, the lift is performed just as in shallow water. Lifters must be careful not to trap the victim's hair under the board, and on-deck lifters should lift mainly using legs and arms, not just the back.

Figure 9.31

Removing someone on a backboard from deep water.

(a) preparing to lift

(continued)

(b) starting first lift

Figure 9.31

(continued)

(c) ending first lift

(d) second lift

Keys to the Deep Water Backboard Lift

1. Angle the board into a corner.
2. Have Rescuer 2 on deck continue in-line stabilization.
3. Position three lifters on either side of the backboard, with the strongest ones at the victim's upper body. Each lifter should have one hand on the lip of the pool gutter and one under the backboard.
4. With feet braced against the pool wall, lift simultaneously on a given signal from Rescuer 1.
5. Once the top of the backboard is on the deck, have two lifters move up on deck to lift from there.
6. On the count of "One, two, three, lift," pick the backboard up and move it farther onto the deck.

PREPARATION FOR SPINAL INJURY MANAGEMENT

Spinal injury management skills must be practiced regularly so you are ready to use them should the need arise. Proper management can make a critical difference in an injured person's future quality of life, it can even mean the difference between life and death.

All potential spinal injuries should be handled with the utmost care. Your training and practice relating to these skills are vital to the standard of care you provide the patrons of your facility. As you practice, follow the sequence of events shown in Figure 9.32.

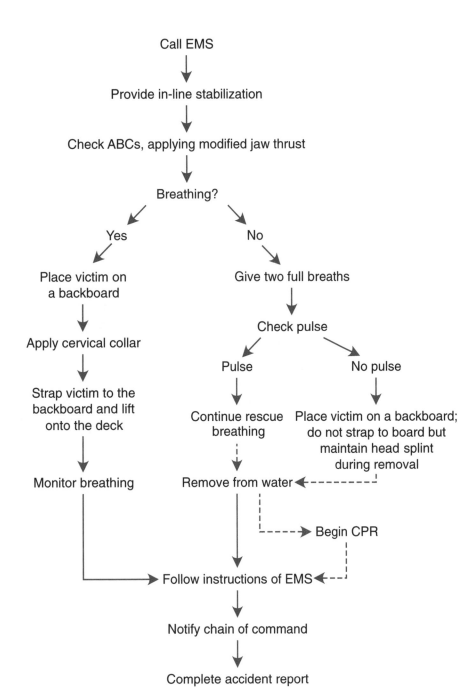

Figure 9.32

Sequence of events in a spinal injury emergency.

Review Questions

1. Describe the typical victim of a spinal cord injury. What is the usual situation leading up to the accident?
2. What hazards lead to spinal injuries in pools? In open water?
3. What swimming pool designs increase the risk of spinal injuries?
4. How deep should water be to allow diving from a diving board? From a starting block?
5. Why are No Diving signs so important?
6. List 4 conditions under which you should suspect spinal injuries.
7. Define the following: spine, vertebra, intervertebral disk.
8. List the 5 regions of the spine.
9. List 11 signs of a spinal injury.
10. Describe the technique used to enter the water when a spinal injury is suspected.
11. How can you reduce water disturbance as you approach a victim?
12. List the 5 steps in the head-splint rescue when a victim is facedown.
13. List the 4 steps required to turn a facedown victim over using the head splint technique.
14. How do you stabilize a faceup victim using the head splint?
15. How should you bring a victim to the surface in shallow water? In deep water?
16. List the qualities of a good backboard.
17. List 3 guidelines for cervical collars at aquatic facilities.
18. Describe how to apply a cervical collar.
19. Describe how to secure a victim to a backboard.
20. How should a backboard be lifted out of shallow water? Out of deep water?
21. When should you check for ABCs?
22. What should you do if a victim is not breathing?
23. What should you do if a victim has no pulse?
24. What protective equipment should be provided for your use during rescue breathing and CPR?
25. Describe the modified jaw thrust.
26. What should you do if a victim vomits?

CHAPTER *10*

Hazards of the Outdoor Environment

Lifeguarding outdoors, whether you're guarding a pool or open water, poses challenges beyond those of controlled environments like indoor pools. This chapter will help you understand the outdoor environment and your responsibilities for protecting patrons from its hazards.

IN THIS CHAPTER YOU'LL LEARN ABOUT

- weather conditions and
- open water conditions.

WEATHER CONDITIONS

Understanding weather conditions is important to providing a safe environment for swimmers in your area. Although you cannot control the weather, you can take necessary precautions to prepare for weather changes and to protect the safety of the swimmers you are guarding.

Storm Conditions

A local weather forecast may warn you that a front is expected to move through your area. Barometric changes and sudden shifts of wind direction and speed are sure signs of weather changes. As warm air meets cooler air, moisture in the form of rain or a thunderstorm usually results. The forecast should be your signal to be on the lookout for storm conditions.

Cloud formations will also alert you to potentially hazardous weather. Figure 10.1 shows three types of clouds you should be familiar with. Cumulonimbus clouds, often called "thunderheads," are dark and thick, seem to have great height, and often take on an anvil shape; they signify a storm. Stratocumulus clouds are continuous, connected globes of clouds that usually occur before and after a storm. Altocumulus clouds are high, white clouds that drift across the sky. As they become larger and darker, they signal a storm.

A squall line is another cloud formation that will help you determine when severe weather is on its way. A squall line usually appears as a gray bank of clouds accompanied by frothy white clouds on the horizon. It is, in fact, the approaching edge of the storm system.

Figure 10.1

Cloud formations.

Cumulonimbus

Stratocumulus

Altocumulus

Thunderclouds

As a storm approaches, you are likely to see clouds develop from stratocumulus into the classic anvil-shaped cumulonimbus thunder clouds. The height and darkness of these clouds can be signs of the severity of the associated storms.

Thunderclouds and the lightning that accompanies them are serious weather conditions. The body can act as a natural conductor of electrical current from lightning when someone is in the water or touching it, possibly resulting in death.

Don't take any chances when you see lightning. Follow your facility's procedures and clear the area before a storm hits. You can estimate how many miles away a storm is by counting the seconds between seeing lightning and hearing thunder, then dividing the number of seconds by 5. For example, if you count 10 seconds between lightning and thunder, the storm is about 2 miles away (sound travels 1 mile in about 5 seconds whereas light travels 1 mile almost instantly).

Guidelines for clearing swimmers from an outdoor area will depend on the type of facility, the management's policy, and the speed of the approaching storm. If there are no procedures for bad weather, encourage the staff and management to establish them, possibly patterned after similar facilities in your area. Once procedures are established, practice them. The safety of those in your area depends on it. Consider the following procedures for bad weather.

Bad Weather Procedures

- Clear and secure the area (put up equipment, lock up facility), making sure everyone is out of the water.
- Move to shelter, preferably in a building. Avoid standing in an open structure or under a tree.
- Stay away from metal objects, which might conduct electrical current.
- Get down from lifeguard stands; lightning is attracted to the highest objects.
- Don't use showers.
- Monitor forecasts by radio or weather radio.
- Don't allow swimmers to return to the water until at least 15 minutes (or more—some states require longer) after you see or hear the last evidence of the storm.

Indoor pools can be safe during storms. Current building codes call for all pools to be grounded, but check to see if your facility is totally grounded. If you have any doubt about the safety of your indoor pool during a storm, clear the pool.

High Winds

High winds often cause changes in water conditions that could present danger for swimmers in the water who are unaware of the change. Swimming pools are not likely to be as affected by the wind as is open water like lakes, rivers, and oceans. Wind can create or enhance the size of waves, influence currents, and reduce water visibility. In any open water area, management must set standards for safe wind levels for aquatic activities.

Tornadoes and Waterspouts

Whatever your aquatic environment, tornadoes and waterspouts pose grave dangers. Tornadoes occur in thunderstorms in which there is a cold downdraft. Before the cloud contacts earth or water, it is known as a funnel cloud. If it contacts land, it is upgraded to a tornado; if it contacts water, it is called a waterspout. These cloud formations are illustrated in Figure 10.2.

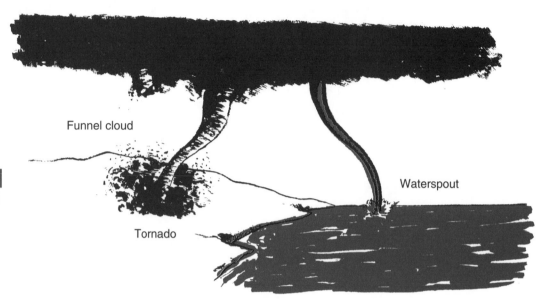

Figure 10.2

Funnel cloud formations.

Funnel cloud

Waterspout

Tornado

Tornadoes. Because tornadoes are associated with thunderstorms, they rarely arise without warning. If you are in an area that experiences tornadoes, your local civil defense should have warning systems. Typically there are three stages of tornado alert. The first is a watch, which means that conditions are right for tornadoes to develop, not that a tornado will occur. The second stage is a warning, which means that a funnel cloud has

Tornado Safety Procedures

- Clear the water and surrounding area.
- Move patrons to a designated shelter (an approved tornado shelter or a strong structure) immediately. Do not close all windows and doors tightly; the force of the storm may create a vacuum and increase the amount of damage.
- Avoid trailers and garage-type structures.
- Stay away from windows and doors. The safest locations are the center or lowest parts of the building or the corner closest to the storm's approach. Interior bathrooms and closets, basements, and spaces beneath stairs are good shelter choices.
- Hide under a strong table, if available, or huddle covered with towels on the floor.
- If no shelter is available, lie flat in a ditch or on a low section of ground. Where there are towers and other large objects, position yourself and others between the approaching storm and those objects. Do not seek refuge in vehicles.
- Monitor a weather station, weather radio, or civil defense frequency for progress reports on the tornado.
- Once you hear a siren warning of the tornado, remain in your safe location until you hear an all-clear signal. Such signals vary; make sure you know the one used in your community.

been sighted. Finally, in most areas, a siren means that a funnel cloud has been sighted in your immediate area.

Waterspouts. Waterspouts are tornadoes over water. They can be weak or strong, but either type is dangerous enough to warrant action.

Weak waterspouts form from one of a line of cumulus clouds when winds are very light. Showers, but not thunderstorms, are usually nearby. Weak waterspouts have winds around 40 knots and lose strength quickly if they come onshore. Most have no particular direction and usually dissipate in about 10 minutes. Despite their weakness and short life, these waterspouts can overturn objects or throw them around, so it's best to evacuate the water and have patrons move inland at least 100 yards. Because weak waterspouts move slowly, there's usually plenty of time to get everyone to safety.

Strong waterspouts are much more dangerous. They form from cumulonimbus clouds and are usually accompanied by lightning and thunder. Usually moving in the same direction as the thunderstorm, they may reach forward speeds of 50 knots or more. Strong waterspouts can spin at up to 200 knots and have been known to damage boats and structures on land and to kill people. If a strong waterspout should occur, quickly clear the water and have patrons move to a solidly constructed, permanent structure.

The National Weather Service issues a Special Marine Warning whenever a waterspout is spotted, whatever its strength. If you hear such an alert, follow your facility's procedures for getting patrons to safety.

Fog

Fog occurs when the ground or water surface is warm and the air is cool and moist. The resulting sensation of being inside a cloud can severely reduce visibility and the safety of those in your aquatic area. If the fog limits your ability to see swimmers or boaters in your area of responsibility, clear the water and close the facility until conditions improve.

Fair Weather

We don't often think of good weather as dangerous, but it holds some uncontrollable hazards for which you should be prepared. Hot summer days usually bring people to the water. Heatstroke, heat exhaustion, and sunburn are just some of the hazards you'll face. First aid for hyperthermia was discussed in chapter 8; it can also affect you and your ability to guard.

Sunburn is not just uncomfortable; it also can be dangerous. The primary cause of skin cancer is prolonged and repeated overexposure to sunlight. The American Cancer Society estimates that 500,000 Americans develop preventable and curable skin cancer each year. To avoid sunburn and to reduce your risk of developing skin cancer, take the following personal precautions.

Sunburn Precautions

- Wear a suitable sunscreen. The American Cancer Society recommends a sunscreen with a sun protection factor (SPF) of 15. Use a higher protection level for sensitive areas, like the face and the tops of the feet.
- No sunscreen is water-resistant; reapply after swimming.
- Wear a hat.
- Wear sunglasses with a good UV (ultraviolet ray) rating to reduce glare and exposure to ultraviolet sunlight.
- Wear a uniform shirt.

To further protect yourself from the dangers of skin cancers, examine your body regularly for lesions and for changes in moles, freckles, or pigmented areas. If you notice any changes, contact your doctor or a dermatologist.

OPEN WATER CONDITIONS

In contrast with pools, open water environments have particular characteristics and risks. One of the most significant differences is the constantly changing nature of open water environments. The ocean, for example, may be calm one moment and rough and dangerous the next as a squall moves landward. In any open water, currents may shift, debris may wash in or out, and sandbars may move as conditions change. As an open water lifeguard you need to be aware of the characteristics and dangers of the environment and know how to respond to them.

Water Temperature and Clarity

Water temperature and clarity are common issues of concern in any open water. In most open water areas water temperature varies greatly depending on the time of the swimming season. The water is generally colder both early and late in the season. As you learned in chapter 8, cold water can increase the risk of hypothermia for swimmers and lifeguards. Figure 8.3 on page 123 provides a graphic review of water temperature and survival time.

Usually water temperature is layered in *thermoclines*, with the warmer water on the top. Normally the warmer water stays at the surface, but a shift in the surface temperature can cause the warmer water to cool and drop. This could take a swimmer who is not used to cold water by surprise, and fatigue and hypothermia can set in more quickly in these conditions.

Shallow lakes or ponds generally turn over due to thermoclines twice each year, once in the spring and again in the fall. This thermocline activity adds to the seasonal water temperature extremes.

Water clarity should be monitored, particularly in an area with nearby industry. In the absence of water circulation, certain conditions could make the water excessively murky and unhealthy. Report factors such as discoloration, temperature changes, dead fish, or a putrid smell to local health officials. These conditions could pose health hazards in your area.

Ocean Environment

A combination of wind and bottom conditions contributes to the size of ocean surf. The stronger the wind and the sharper the dropoff, the larger and stronger the waves. Be familiar with the surf conditions in your area.

Winds. Depending on the wind conditions, waves can take many forms. The *fetch* is the distance of open water over which any wind blows to develop waves (see Figure 10.3). The longer the fetch, the greater the possibility of large waves. (So you expect to see larger waves in an ocean than in a lake.)

Two other wind-related terms are important for your awareness of potential dangers. An *onshore wind*, one that blows toward the shore, brings debris inland. Be alert for objects floating or suspended in the waves. An *offshore wind*, on the other hand, blows toward the water and can carry flotation devices and unsuspecting swimmers from shallow into deeper water. Be aware of these possibilities and act to prevent swimmers from getting into situations they can't handle.

Waves. Several terms are used to describe parts of waves (see Figure 10.3). The *peak* (or *crest*) is the highest point of the wave, at which it breaks either from right to left or left to right. When the wind forces the top of the wave into the trough, the wave is said to be *spilling*. *Foam* describes whitewater; air is trapped in the water, giving the wave a foamy appearance. The shallow area where waves break is known as the *surf zone*.

You should become familiar with several different types of waves (see Figure 10.3). Gently sloping waves generally found in deep water are called *spilling* or *rolling waves*; they are not particularly dangerous. *Plunging waves* occur either near shore or in shallow water over a sand bar or reef because the bottom slows the speeding water. The break can be quite strong and is caused by water being pushed over the crest of the wave. These waves can be dangerous, especially to inexperienced bathers, who may jump up to avoid the force of an oncoming wave instead of ducking under it. When lifeguarding, you may want to warn such bathers about this danger.

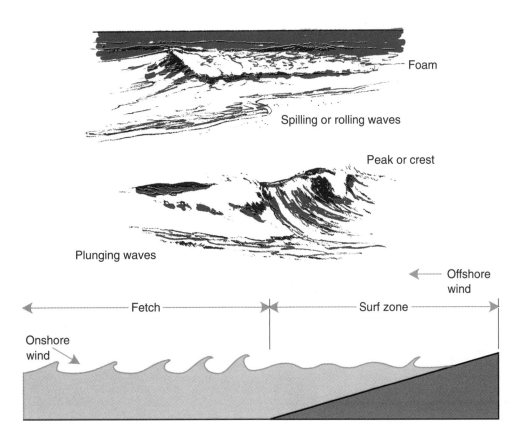

Figure 10.3

Terms relating to wind and waves.

Foam

Spilling or rolling waves

Peak or crest

Plunging waves

Offshore wind

Fetch

Surf zone

Onshore wind

Running and plunging into waves is dangerous; don't allow patrons in your areas to do so. The waves may contain debris that could cause serious injury.

Sets and lulls. A series of breaking waves is called a *set*, and the calm between sets is the *lull*. Any wave can be dangerous because it could knock an unsuspecting swimmer down. But lulls are dangerous too; they give swimmers a rest period in which they may become unprepared for the next series of waves or be swept further out to sea in a rip current.

Tides. Tides are created by the gravitational pull exerted by the sun and moon on the earth's water. Water is pulled away from the shore during low tide (ebb tide), becoming more shallow, and moves toward the shore during high tide (flood tide), making the water deeper. Tidal variations usually are greater on U.S. northern beaches than on southern beaches.

The primary danger associated with the change in tides is that swimmers may inaccurately estimate the depth of the water they are swimming in; a poor swimmer may panic upon trying to stand and finding that the water is too deep. A secondary danger created by tides is variation in prevailing currents. Lifeguards must be aware of these tidal variations in depth and current to protect swimmers in their areas from danger. Take time to learn about how the tides affect any area where you work or swim.

Parallel current.   A parallel current usually is caused by waves that break on the shore at an angle. Also known as a *longshore, lateral,* or *littoral current,* it means that swimmers can be swept along parallel to the shore. Swimmers or rescuers caught in a parallel current should not try to move straight in to the shore, even though it is the shortest distance. Rather, they should go with the current and gradually angle in; they will arrive on shore safely without having become fatigued from fighting the current.

Runback.   The return flow of water from waves that have rolled ashore is a *runback,* often called an *undertow,* or *backrush.* Contrary to popular belief, it does not pull objects out to sea. The strong runback instead moves under the approaching waves, pulling objects down into the water. The strength of the runback, which depends on the slope of the shoreline, usually lessens at a depth of 3 feet.

Rip currents.   *Rips,* or *runouts,* are currents created where there are sandbars or reefs just offshore or around structures such as piers or jetties. The runout is a backrush current of water moving out to sea created by the return of water through any break in the sandbar or other obstruction (see Figure 10.4). The current picks up speed as it moves through the channel and dissipates after passing through.

Figure 10.4

Rip current.

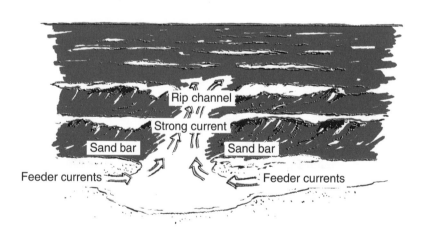

Rip currents are the most common surf condition for which beach lifeguards must be prepared. A rip current usually looks different from the surrounding surf and is easy to spot from an elevated position. Learn to spot these currents and keep swimmers away from them. Key characteristics include the following:

- The rip may be dark and appear to be deep water.
- The water may be rough and choppy because of waves and the opposing action of the current.

- The rip may appear muddy or brown from carrying dirt and sand stirred up from the bottom.
- The rip may contain floating debris moving seaward.
- Rips have stronger force after a wave set has hit the shore.
- People swimming in or near the rip will be drawn to the sea.
- A rip may have one to as many as three feeder currents.

Many beach areas have permanent rips. These areas should be a key point in your watch and should be indicated by posted warnings or warning flags, especially on rough or windy days. A permanent rip is caused when the ocean floor is deeper in one spot than in the surrounding area. Stationary objects projecting into the water, such as rocks or piers, may cause such a rip; they may be present for an extended period or may change from season to season. A flash rip is a temporary rip generated by a sudden wave buildup, generally resulting from unusual wind or water conditions changing quickly. Flow from rips continually changes the bottom conditions and causes hazards to those unfamiliar with the danger.

Because the rip current is pulling seaward, it is too tiring for swimmers to try to swim directly to shore to escape it. Instead, a swimmer caught in a rip should signal for help and move parallel to the shore or drift out with the current until the seaward pull decreases to a level that swimming toward shore is possible. The swimmer should then swim parallel to shore for a short distance to move away from the rip current and finally swim toward shore.

For a rescue, use the rip to your advantage to get to the victim quickly. Waves will seldom break in through a rip, which will make it easier for you to maintain eye contact with the victim as you approach.

Marine life. A final potentially hazardous ocean element is the marine life. Most aquatic creatures are as frightened of swimmers as swimmers are of them; in fact, most are quite passive unless threatened. Still, some injuries are likely to occur. Some aquatic animals, such as jellyfish (see Figure 10.5a) and the Portuguese man-of-war (Figure 10.5b), have long tentacles that inflict painful stings. Some shells and coral can inject venom or inflict sharp cuts. Reactions to these contacts can range from a mild stinging sensation to shock, nausea, and respiratory difficulty. If the reaction is severe, seek medical attention immediately.

First aid for most jellyfish, Portuguese man-of-war, or sea anemone stings is simple. Rinse the affected area with sea water (not fresh water), and soak the skin with vinegar

Figure 10.5

Stinging marine life. (a) Jellyfish; (b) Portuguese man-of-war.

a

b

or isopropyl alcohol. If vinegar or alcohol is not available, meat tenderizer, a baking soda paste, or ammonia diluted with 3 parts water will soothe the skin irritation. Do not use ice or rub the skin. Encourage the injured person to stay out of the water. Contact EMS if the victim doesn't know what stung him or her, if the sting is on the face or neck, or if the victim displays any allergic reaction or difficulty in breathing.

On surf beaches, predatory fish such as sharks, barracudas, and bluefish are threats, and you must be on the lookout for them. Most shark attacks occur near shore, most often between the first sandbar and the shore but sometimes between sandbars where sharks may be trapped at low tide or near steep dropoffs. On southeastern beaches, attacks occur most often in the winter and early spring.

Here is some advice you can give patrons for avoiding shark attack:

- Always swim in a group. A shark is less likely to attack a group of people than an isolated individual.
- Avoid swimming in darkness or at dawn or dusk, when light is limited and sharks have a competitive advantage.
- Do not enter the water if you are bleeding from an open wound or menstruating.
- Avoid wearing shiny objects, which approximate the sheen of light on fish scales.
- Do not enter the water if a shark is known to be present, and evacuate the water if a shark is seen.
- Do not wander too far from shore.
- Avoid water with known effluents.
- Avoid waters being used for commercial or sport fishing.
- Use extra caution when water is murky.
- Refrain from excessive splashing.
- Exercise caution when occupying the area between sandbars or near steep dropoffs.
- Do not provoke sharks.

As a lifeguard, you have the responsibility to alert patrons to the presence of all dangerous marine life. Learn about the types in your area so you know the proper precautions.

Rivers and Streams

In rivers and streams, as in the ocean, currents can be particularly dangerous because they change so frequently. As currents shift, unsuspecting swimmers can be caught in a current and carried away from shore. Watch for changes in the currents and be prepared to act.

Current strength is very deceptive. If you are caught in a river current, do not try to swim directly against it—you'll only tire yourself out. Swim diagonally across the current until you escape its strength (see Figure 10.6).

Figure 10.6

Swimming diagonally across a river current.

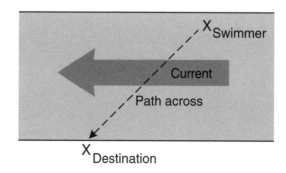

Never run and plunge into moving water. As in oceans, the current may carry debris, which in addition to being potentially hazardous may change the bottom contour. Such changes make diving very dangerous.

Lakes, Ponds, and Quarries

In fresh water, underwater weeds and other plant life pose potential danger. The plants themselves are not dangerous, but they catch swimmers by surprise. A swimmer who panics at contact with weeds could become entangled as a result of frantic and erratic attempts to escape. The panic, not the entanglement, is the real danger.

If you encounter weeds yourself, remain calm and use slow, subtle shaking movements to escape the entanglement. If you must rescue someone who has become entangled, your first task will be to calm the victim and get him or her to stop thrashing about. Give the victim your rescue tube or buoy to provide some flotation assistance; it will provide some security and give you a chance to untangle the victim's feet. When swimming out of an area of underwater weeds, modify your crawl or breaststroke by kicking minimally to avoid entanglement.

Review Questions

1. What conditions indicate that a storm is approaching?
2. What procedures should you follow when bad weather is detected?
3. List the tornado safety procedures.
4. How can you avoid sunburn?
5. What should you look for when examining yourself for possible skin cancer?
6. What two issues are of concern in assessing water conditions?
7. Why are tides of concern to open water lifeguards?
8. List the different kinds of currents you might encounter in an open water environment.
9. How do you provide first aid for a jellyfish sting?
10. How do you reduce your chances of being attacked by a shark?
11. How would you swim out of a strong current in a river?
12. How would you escape from being tangled in weeds?

CHAPTER 11

Lifeguarding on the Waterfront

Although most YMCA-certified lifeguards work in pool settings, some guard in open water environments, such as oceans, lakes, ponds, or rivers. As you just learned, these environments present some concerns not found in pools. To handle the changing conditions of open water and to cope with disadvantages of lifeguarding outdoors, such as larger areas to guard, greater distances to communicate over, and delays in obtaining EMS assistance, waterfront lifeguards need to know additional special procedures.

IN THIS CHAPTER YOU'LL LEARN ABOUT

■ waterfront procedures,

■ scuba safety, and

■ search and rescue operations.

NEED FOR ADDITIONAL TRAINING

As stated in the *United States Lifesaving Association Manual for Open Water Lifesaving* (1995), lifeguarding in open water requires a high level of fitness and additional training. Beach lifeguards need extensive experience in swimming in open water. They may be stationed in remote locations where advanced medical support can be delayed, and they may have other responsibilities such as aiding distressed boaters, law enforcement, cliff rescue, flood rescue, marine firefighting, and scuba search and rescue. In addition, they may need to operate emergency vehicles, rescue boats, and other technical equipment. Because of this, they require more in-depth training.

Open water presents guards with different conditions than a pool:

- Water temperature and clarity depend on the natural environment.
- Long distance swimming in adverse conditions may be necessary.
- Natural hazards, such as surf, currents, and severe weather, can cause problems.
- Attendance levels and hours are not controlled.

The United States Lifesaving Association (USLA) provides a certification specifically for surf lifeguards. For more information, contact the USLA, P.O. Box 366, Huntington Beach, CA 92648.

WATERFRONT PROCEDURES

Having learned about open water environments in the previous chapter, you now need to consider how those environments change your role as a lifeguard. To this point we have discussed primarily procedures that are most appropriate for lifeguarding at a pool. If you will be working at an open water area, beach areas, conditions, and equipment require some additional specific training. We'll address these in a surf environment, with some variations for lakes, rivers, and ponds.

Selection of a Beach Area

Many beautiful beachfront areas are not acceptable for recreational swimming. For a waterfront area to be designated as a swimming beach, various factors must be considered:

- Shoreline
- Water conditions and purity
- Bottom conditions
- Marine life
- Obstructions (sandbars, shipwrecks, etc.)
- Boat traffic
- Local current and tide conditions

Shoreline.   To be selected as a beach site, an open water area must have a relatively unobstructed stretch of shore that allows lifeguards a clear view of all swimming areas and has adequate access for emergency vehicles. Piers, wharfs, and other such obstructions create hazards for both swimmers and lifeguards. The shoreline must have suitable locations for elevated lifeguard stands. On an ocean beach these stands may be fixed or may be movable to allow lifeguards close access to the water at both high and low tides.

Water conditions and purity.   Both the height of waves as they come ashore and water depth are factors in selecting a swimming beach. Large crashing waves are certainly not conducive to recreational swimming. The best open water swimming areas are also not very deep. Shallow water offers several advantages:

- Waves tend to break farther from shore.
- More people enjoy shallow water because they know they can stand up if they are knocked over by a wave.
- Area markings are more consistent because tethers anchored to the bottom are not as long, keeping markers from drifting as much.

Water purity is also important—any swimming area should be reasonably free of pollution from nearby industry and shipping channels. The local health department should run appropriate tests over several weeks to gather conclusive data about water cleanliness.

Bottom conditions. Avoid areas with sharp drop offs, which in addition to catching swimmers unaware can accentuate the effects of tides, rip currents, and winds. In shallow water, sandbars may build, which can create steep dropoffs and troughs. Gently sloping conditions are best, both for swimmers' comfort and for anchoring lifelines and markers.

Marine life. Virtually every open water area will have some marine life. People selecting swimming beaches must evaluate the types of life in the area, their effect on swimmers, and the swimmers' effect on the marine life. For example, areas where seaweed is common should be avoided; swimmers could become entangled, panic, and drown. Similarly, areas that tend to collect jellyfish, sea urchins, and microscopic bacteria are not suitable for swimming.

Some marine life will not harm humans, but the presence of people threatens the marine life. For example, swimming areas should not be set up in spawning areas.

Obstructions. Rocks, sandbars, ledges, pilings, piers, and sunken or partially submerged wrecks can be dangerous to swimmers and lifeguards. These obstructions can create rip currents and modify the flow of water unpredictably. Swimmers could be pulled into such obstructions and be injured or entangled, and lifeguards are placed at a disadvantage in dealing with such objects. They obstruct the lifeguard's view and then endanger life during a rescue. Such conditions should be avoided in selecting swimming areas.

Boat traffic. Any swimming area should be relatively free of intrusion by boats of any size. In addition to the obvious danger associated with a boat moving through a group of swimmers, the pollution from oil and wastes and the wake left as the boat moves on are hazardous.

Currents. The best open water swimming areas are those that are relatively unaffected by currents and tides. Bays and inlets offer excellent conditions, as do protected areas well inside a breakwater. Although some current is unavoidable, try to stay away from areas with a history of strong currents. On rivers, be especially careful of areas near low-head dams.

Other considerations. Other factors should be taken into account in selecting a beach area:

- The availability of funds and personnel to build and maintain the necessary facilities and equipment
- The age and experience level of those expected to use the area
- The proximity of rescue and first aid facilities and the means to call for assistance (phone, radio links)

Marking the Swimming Area

Once the decision has been made to designate a swimming area, it should be marked by flags, buoys, and lifelines. These items serve somewhat standardized roles at all beaches.

Flags. Flags are used to identify boundaries predominantly in ocean settings. The outside boundaries of the guarded area of a beach are marked by flags posted on the beach. The international convention is to plant two flags—at one end a flag with a red horizontal stripe, at the other end a flag with a yellow horizontal stripe—on 12-foot poles to designate the swimming area. The poles are movable and allow lifeguards the flexibility to change the designated swimming area to avoid strong currents.

A second type of flag, to signal the present conditions, should appear on every beach. Such flags are usually attached to posts at the entrance to the beach area and on each lifeguard stand. One example of the flag system operates on the following color coding:

- Red: Dangerous conditions. No swimming allowed.
- Yellow: Lifeguard on duty. Hazardous conditions require some caution; only experienced swimmers should enter the water.
- Green: Lifeguard on duty. It is safe for all swimmers to enter the water.

An explanation of your facility's color coding should be posted.

Buoys. Brightly colored buoys may also be used to mark the swimming area. Large buoys anchored to the bottom can be spaced along the perimeter of the swimming area. On beaches using the buoy system, lifeguards must check a diagram of the swimming area regularly to be sure that wind, surf, and storm conditions have not caused a change in the location of the buoys. Buoys are used not only in surf conditions but also on freshwater beaches. Even in these areas, the lifeguard should regularly verify the placement of the buoys.

Buoys must be maintained properly in ocean environments. If they are not cleaned regularly, various marine organisms will attach themselves to the buoys, making the buoys dangerous to touch.

Buoys and their anchors should be removed from the water at the end of the season. The long winter months can damage the buoys or anchor lines, cutting short their lifespan.

Lifelines. Some beach areas use lifelines to designate the outer boundaries of the swimming area. The lines are generally set to angle in away from shore. As a result, the shoreline boundary is wider than the one opposite. Lines are anchored on shore and attached to a weighted anchor in the water. The angle of the lifeline will vary somewhat due to the wind and tide action.

Although some areas also provide a lifeline at the edge of the swimming area farthest from shore, this demarcation is not recommended because swimmers are often tempted to "swim to the rope." During low tide that may be no problem—the swimmer can still touch the bottom if necessary—but during high tide the water may be considerably deeper, making the swim to the rope unwise.

Lifeguard Stations

In waterfront situations, two types of lifeguard stations may be useful: lifeguard towers and floating lifeguard stands. Each has certain advantages.

Lifeguard towers. Depending on the prevailing conditions, lifeguard stations may be enclosed or simply elevated chairs. Enclosed lifeguard stations offer protection from the elements, fewer distractions by beach patrons, good visibility, and a storage area for rescue equipment. They are also highly visible to those on the beach who need assistance. Enclosed stations do have a disadvantage though, in that they are usually erected at a point near the water during high tide, and thus at low tide they are farther from the water line.

One solution to that problem is to erect a high, sturdy lifeguard chair that is portable—the lifeguard moves the chair to be close to the water's edge. This chair, however, does not offer storage space. In almost all instances a stationary tower is preferable to a portable chair.

Floating lifeguard stands. On a waterfront it may be useful to have lifeguards designated to patrol an area from a paddleboard, boat, or floating deck. The advantage of a floating lifeguard stand is that the guard is already in the water should a problem arise. The guard is also more able to enforce rules if she or he is closer to the swimmers.

Boats are a bit more difficult to use than paddleboards or floating decks, but they have some advantages. Boats can provide a safety barrier by sandwiching swimmers between the guard in the chair and the guard in the boat. They also put the guard in the water in a position to help keep other boats away from the swimming area. Special training is required for using a boat in rescue operations.

Equipment for Open Water Beaches

The equipment required to operate a safe open water beach is significantly different from what is needed at a pool. You will need a more sophisticated communication system; paddleboards; mask, fins, and snorkel; boats; and vehicles, in addition to other specialized rescue equipment.

Communication system. Because lifeguard stations are more spread out at a beach than at a pool and because the area patrolled there is much larger, it may be impossible to communicate by whistle blasts. For communicating with beach patrons, power megaphones and public address systems are excellent options.

On a beach each lifeguard should have a telephone or a two-way radio to communicate with other guards and emergency personnel. The radio systems are often linked to a local emergency frequency so that help can be summoned immediately.

In an emergency, the lifeguard should not have to spend much time communicating the problem. For that reason, a code system has been developed by many agencies. Check with your local police and fire departments and EMS to determine how they want you to quickly communicate your needs.

When sending a message on the radio, proceed with guidelines similar to those used in calling for emergency assistance at a pool:

- Give your name and the name of the person or service being called.
- Await acknowledgment by that person or service.
- State your location.
- Speaking slowly, give your message as distinctly as possible.
- Await acknowledgment of your message.
- Sign off with your name.

Paddleboards. Paddleboards (Figure 11.1), also known as rescue boards or rescue surfboards, are versatile. Because of their buoyancy, they can be used as floating lifeguard stands or for quick transportation to a victim in light to moderate surf. They also can be used to carry a victim back to shore, and their flat surfaces make in-water rescue breathing easier.

Figure 11.1

Paddleboard.

Paddleboards should be kept near the water and checked daily for any needed repairs. The surfaces should be kept smooth for maneuverability and for the comfort of the rescuer and victim. Boards should be kept waxed to avoid slippage during a rescue.

Be careful when using a paddleboard in a crowded surf zone or a swimming area. Its size and weight can cause serious injury to a patron who is knocked into the board or is hit by it as it cuts through the water. In rough surf you should stay prone to reduce the chances of losing your balance and being knocked off the paddleboard.

Masks, fins, and snorkels.   The masks, fins, and snorkels shown in Figure 11.2 are used both recreationally and in rescue situations. They should be standard equipment at lifeguard stations for open water and deep water pools (pools with depths greater than 12 feet). Whatever the intended use, this equipment requires special fitting and instruction.

Figure 11.2

Masks, fins, and snorkels.

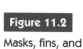

• *Masks.* The air space between your eyes and the water provided by a mask enables you to see clearly underwater. Several styles of masks are available, varying in the amount of peripheral vision they allow and the ease with which you can block off your nostrils to equalize pressure in your ears. Avoid masks that do not cover the nose and eyes because they do not allow you to clear water out of your mask efficiently.

Whatever mask you select, try this test to determine whether it fits properly: Without putting the strap over your head, position the mask on your face, enclosing your eyes and nose. Inhale through your nose. If the mask stays firmly in place, it fits your face properly.

Even the best-fitting mask will sometimes become filled with water. Should that happen, don't panic. In some instances you can simply pull the mask away from your face, surface, drain the mask, and start over again. There is, however, no need to surface to clear the mask. Simply submerge yourself, press the top of the mask against your forehead, look toward the surface, and exhale through your nose. This should force the water out. To avoid getting water from the mask up your nose, begin exhaling before you tip your head to look to the surface.

• *Fins.* Using fins will extend the power and strength of your kick. Several styles are available, so be sure to select one that fits you comfortably. The style that is best for you depends on your size and strength and the situation in which you will be using the fins. Fins used by open water lifeguards for swimming through rough surf have heel straps and short blades and are fairly rigid. Because more strength is needed for large, rigid fins, most swimmers will want fins with moderate rigidity and medium-size blades.

Put fins on in the water to prevent tripping while on land. To use the fins, kick naturally, slightly exaggerating your knee bend. Fins let you cover more distance in less time while expending less energy. This ability, which is what makes wearing fins fun, also makes them useful in searching for submerged victims.

• *Snorkels.* The snorkel should be attached to your mask strap with a "snorkel keeper" (see the loop on the snorkel pictured in Figure 11.2) to ensure proper positioning when you surface and try to clear the snorkel. As your snorkel goes underwater, water will fill it. You'll need to learn how deep you can go without pulling your snorkel underwater. Once you have submerged past that level, do not breathe in. When you surface, blow out forcefully to clear the snorkel (the "blast" method). You can also use the "displacement" method: As you begin to surface, tilt your head so that the snorkel is at a 45-degree angle to the surface. Beginning about 2 feet from the surface, exhale gently through your mouth. By the time you clear the surface, your snorkel will be clear and ready for surface use.

Boats.   The type of boat needed at a particular beach depends on the kind of service it will see. Boats are often used as lifeguard stands in the water, as rescue tools, and to perform a variety of daily maintenance checks. They are also used in search operations.

If the boat is needed simply to assist swimmers and perform daily checks, an inflatable rescue boat is recommended (see Figure 11.3). In surf situations this craft is less dangerous to swimmers. In lake or river environments, not only is the inflatable rescue boat safe in a swimming area, it is an excellent in-water lifeguard stand.

Figure 11.3

Inflatable rescue boat.

Wave runners (Figure 11.4) and jet skis are also useful rescue tools that allow the lifeguard at any open water area to reach a victim quickly. Because of their size and maneuverability, these vehicles are less dangerous to swimmers than motorboats are.

Figure 11.4

Wave runner.

If the boat is to be used in rescuing other small craft, a motorized boat is necessary. Operation of such power vessels requires additional training. Patrol boats should be equipped with the following:

- Motor
- Gas can
- Oars
- Anchor and extra line
- PFDs
- Rescue equipment
- Bailers and tools
- Fire extinguisher
- Flashlight
- Mask, fins, and snorkel
- First aid kit

For safety, the motor can be equipped with a protective prop guard and a kill switch.

Vehicles. At a pool a victim can be brought to a first aid station with little difficulty, but on the beach a victim may be quite far from treatment. It is essential that the lifeguard have some sort of vehicle to transport the victim to a first aid center immediately. The vehicle may also be used to transport rescuers, first aid equipment, and a public address system for crowd control to the scene of an accident.

A four-wheel-drive vehicle is most appropriate. The vehicle must be equipped with lifesaving equipment, first aid equipment (including a backboard), a radio for emergency communication, and a siren and flashing lights to identify it as an emergency vehicle and to clear a path during an emergency.

Any lifeguard vehicle should be operated at a low speed for routine duties. In an emergency, however, the siren and lights should alert beach patrons that there is an emergency and that the vehicle is moving fast.

Helicopter. The distance from many open water beaches to an emergency medical facility is considerable. In such instances, helicopters offer speedy transportation. Train with local helicopter services to determine landing zones and transportation procedures before you try to use this option.

Additional equipment needs. Here is a checklist of equipment that should be available at all open water facilities.

Equipment Checklist

_____ Plastic molded rescue buoy with handle grips (known as a *rescue can*)

_____ Rescue tube

_____ Area-specific rescue equipment

_____ Megaphone or public address system

_____ Telephone or two-way radio

_____ Binoculars

_____ First aid kit (including blood-borne pathogen prevention kit)

_____ Universal spill kit (for cleaning up blood and body fluids)

_____ Oxygen kit

_____ Blankets

_____ Extra towels

_____ Scuba gear (if any staff are certified)

_____ Masks, fins, and snorkels

_____ Extra rope

_____ Backboard (with head immobilizer and cervical collars)

_____ Paddleboard

_____ Boat

_____ Coast Guard–approved PFDs

_____ Oars or paddles

_____ Vehicles

Accident Prevention

Accidents can be caused by any number of circumstances at any swimming facility. If you will be working at a beach, become familiar with the following causes of accidents in open water and consider how you can help swimmers avoid becoming victims.

To help keep the beachfront safe, follow these rules when lifeguarding:

- Do not permit play with rescue equipment at any time.
- Monitor the swimming area for floating debris.
- Never leave your area of the waterfront unguarded.
- Know what you are to do in the event of an emergency and understand all emergency plans.
- Keep rescue equipment on the swimming dock for immediate access.
- Post rules, regulations, and hazardous condition warnings in prominent locations.

15 Frequent Causes of Beach Accidents

- Being unable to swim
- Diving into shallow water
- Rough play in the water and on the shore
- Inability of untrained would-be rescuers
- Hypothermia
- Drop off from shallow to deep water
- Currents (rips and parallel currents instigate 80% of surf rescues)
- Changing bottom conditions
- Being pulled over rocky areas or into piers and jetties
- Overestimating one's swimming ability
- Being intoxicated
- Using an unapproved flotation device (e.g., air mattress, tube)
- Not wearing a PFD while boating
- Stepping on broken glass or other sharp debris
- Swimming outside the marked area

If there is a floating dock in your area, suggest that the following regulations be posted:

- Keep the dock clear of all unnecessary equipment (bicycles, gas cans, etc.).
- No running or pushing on the dock.
- No fishing from the dock.
- No swimming under the dock.

Encourage waterfront swimmers to follow these guidelines:

- Swim only in designated areas and only near a lifeguard.
- Always swim with a buddy.
- Stay within your ability.
- Avoid staying in the water too long. When you are cold or tired, get out!
- Avoid long exposure to the sun.
- Never swim in an unlighted area after dark.
- Never go on a long swim without being escorted by someone in a boat or on a paddleboard.
- Never swim during an electrical storm.
- Never call for help unless you need it.
- Dive only in designated diving areas where you know the depth of the water.
- Obey all rules and regulations.

RESCUING SCUBA VICTIMS

Interest in the sport of skin and scuba (self-contained underwater breathing apparatus) diving has been growing. This has meant increased involvement of YMCAs across the country in training their members to dive (first in swimming pools and later in open water), placing a new emphasis on the need for related lifeguarding skills. You must expand your thinking about lifeguarding to include rescue operations that are suitable for the type of equipment and gear used by the scuba diver (see Figure 11.5).

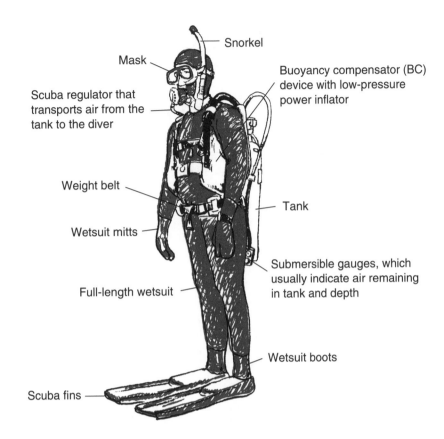

Figure 11.5

Scuba gear.

Labels: Snorkel, Mask, Buoyancy compensator (BC) device with low-pressure power inflator, Scuba regulator that transports air from the tank to the diver, Weight belt, Tank, Wetsuit mitts, Submersible gauges, which usually indicate air remaining in tank and depth, Full-length wetsuit, Wetsuit boots, Scuba fins

It is best to segregate scuba and skin divers from other swimmers so that all groups of aquatic enthusiasts can enjoy safe, adequately supervised experiences. In open water, make sure that the diving area is marked with a flag as illustrated in Figure 11.6. In some states such flags are required where boat traffic is possible.

Figure 11.6

Diving flag.

The YMCA and other national organizations have certification standards for scuba divers. Facility management will set policy to determine which "C" (certification) cards will be accepted for admission to their facility. Only divers with current C cards should be admitted.

If you will be guarding a scuba area regularly, you may want to get training in scuba lifesaving and accident management/rescue (SLAM/Rescue). The YMCA offers such a certification course for certified scuba divers.

Scuba Diving Emergency Procedures

Scuba diving emergencies require special attention. Air embolism (see p. 195) and decompression sickness accidents, in which gas bubbles get into tissues or blood, both require immediate treatment in a recompression chamber, so time is of the essence. Where scuba diving is permitted, you may need to know the location of the nearest recompression chamber and how to get a diver there. Special rescue procedures will vary depending on the area where you are guarding, but the basics for determining those procedures can be developed through *CARE*—cognizance, assessment, rescue, and evacuation.

Cognizance.   The signs exhibited by a scuba diver needing assistance are often subtle. An exhausted diver at the surface may suddenly and quietly slip beneath for no apparent reason. It is possible that a potential victim's ego may impede the ability to express anxiety, illness, or other distress to diving partners or to others. Also, scuba equipment often conceals facial expressions and other gestures that signal stress or anxiety, and it reduces the possibility of verbal communication. Signs of distress often are not easily recognizable, but the following behaviors can be considered indicators of trouble:

- High treading or finning with sufficient vigor to lift a portion of the body and equipment out of the water
- Rejecting the mask or regulator mouthpiece, or both
- Clinging and clambering (pulling the body toward the high point of any object on the surface)
- Diving alone
- Not moving—apparent unconsciousness
- Struggling on or below the surface
- Giving distress signals—raising one arm, whistling, yelling for help, and so on

Assessment.   To assess the problem, you must continuously monitor all conditions that might help or hinder you in preventing trouble or performing a rescue. In assessing the severity of the problem, consider the following issues:

- The nature of the problem (the environment, physical distress, equipment problems, anxiety, etc.)
- The status of the victim (conscious or unconscious, rational or irrational)
- The training and physical conditioning of the potential rescuers
- The availability of rescue personnel and equipment
- The distance to safety

If after assessing the situation you determine that a swimming assist is necessary, determine which rescuer is best qualified to make the rescue.

Rescue.   An advantage to rescuing a scuba diver is that you can use the diver's equipment to establish positive buoyancy, to assist in breathing, and generally to stabilize the victim while still in deep open water. However, diving equipment can be dangerous and difficult to use if you are unfamiliar with it. For example, if you overinflate the diver's buoyancy compensator (BC; see Figure 11.5), it may be more difficult to assist the diver.

When you are establishing contact with the victim of a scuba diving accident, certain priorities should determine your actions:

- Establishing contact
- Establishing positive buoyancy
- Establishing the victim's airway, breathing, and circulation (ABCs) as quickly as possible when needed
- Stabilizing and towing

If the victim is on the surface and is conscious, proceed in the following manner:

1. Activate the EMS.
2. Move toward the victim while giving verbal encouragement.
3. Call to the victim, "Drop your weight belt and inflate your BC." Don't expect a verbal response.
4. Use the procedure for approaching an active victim from the front with a rescue tube or buoy (p. 82).
5. Remove the victim's weight belt and inflate the victim's BC if either is not yet done. Use the power inflator if there is still air in the tank or orally inflate if necessary.
6. Tow the victim to safety by grabbing the tank valve or using an armpit carry.
7. Always stay behind and to the left of the victim and monitor him or her continuously.

If the victim is on the surface and unconscious, take the following steps:

1. Activate the EMS.
2. Reach the victim in the shortest time possible.
3. Check for signs of spinal injury. If there are signs, use the procedures in chapter 9; if not, and if the victim is lying facedown on the surface, turn the victim faceup.
4. Remove the victim's weight belt.
5. Inflate the victim's BC with the power inflator or orally inflate. If no BC is present, use the rescue tube or buoy as in the rescue of a passive victim from the front by either supporting yourself or placing the tube under one or both arms of the victim.
6. Remove the victim's mask and remove the regulator from the mouth.
7. Check the ABCs and proceed with rescue breathing immediately if necessary.
8. Tow the victim to shore and continue resuscitation efforts if needed.
9. Remove the victim's tank and BC, move the victim to shore, and continue rescue breathing or begin CPR if necessary.

Although it is unlikely to happen, you may be called upon to recover and rescue a submerged scuba diver. Thus, you should be trained and prepared for this specialized type of rescue, especially if you guard a pool in which scuba activities are conducted. In most such rescue situations, the use of a mask, snorkel, and fins would help you perform the recovery and rescue.

Be sure to use caution and prudence in doing such a rescue. Don't dive too deep or too long and jeopardize your own safety. Also, don't use scuba equipment to rescue unless you have been properly trained and certified in its use.

If the victim were underwater and unconscious, your priority would be to locate and bring him or her to the surface. The sooner this is accomplished, the better the victim's chances of recovery. Once you bring the victim up to the surface, you can assess the person's ABCs and initiate rescue breathing if necessary (see Figure 11.7).

If you are called upon to rescue a submerged diver, follow these procedures to bring the diver to the surface:

Figure 11.7

Rescue breathing
for scuba diving
victim.

1. Activate the EMS.
2. Reach the victim in the shortest time possible. If you suspect the victim has a spinal injury, follow the procedures in chapter 9.
3. Establish positive buoyancy by using the power inflator of the BC. If the regulator was in the victim's mouth, secure it there; if not, leave it out.
4. Position yourself on the victim's left side. Keep the victim's head level during the ascent by holding the chin and head in a neutral position with your left hand and grasping the tank valve with your right hand. By towing the victim to the surface with the tank valve, you will leave your left hand free to control buoyancy and stabilize the head (see Figure 11.8).

Figure 11.8

Bringing a diver
to the surface.

5. If you have not inflated the victim's BC before or during the ascent, inflate it at the surface by operating the power inflator or by blowing into the oral inflator valve mouthpiece.

6. Tow the victim to the shore or surface platform (such as a boat, pier, or dock) with a "do-si-do" tow (see Figure 11.9). For this tow, get on the victim's left side, near the head. Slide your left arm between the victim's left arm and body, and secure the tow by grasping the BC straps or tank valve on the victim's back. Use a strong kick to transport the victim.

Figure 11.9

Do-si-do tow.

7. If you must do rescue breathing, partially inflate the victim's BC and roll his or her head toward you as you seal your mouth over the victim's mouth to provide breaths (see Figure 11.7). Call for surface support and assistance from other individuals.

8. Especially if the towing distance is long, consider removing the victim's tank and BC. Do so only if the victim is wearing a wetsuit, which provides some flotation assistance during the tow. The victim's weight belt must be removed before the BC. Remove whatever equipment is necessary in order to perform rescue breathing, transport the victim to shore, and get him or her out of the water.

9. Once the victim is out, recheck the ABCs and perform rescue breathing or CPR if necessary while waiting for the EMS. If you are trained to administer oxygen, provide 100% medical oxygen as soon as possible. As a rescuer, you can provide first aid, but medical experts will need to give definitive care.

The skills necessary to successfully complete a rescue of a scuba diver are somewhat different from typical rescue skills. You'll need to practice scuba rescue carefully if you are assigned to an area where scuba diving is done. Be sure to learn the procedures your facility has developed.

Evacuation. Once you have rescued a scuba diver, the after-care of this victim will differ from the care given to a nondiver in one important respect. An injured or unconscious scuba diver may be suffering from an air embolism, also known as an arterial gas embolism or AGE. An air embolism occurs when a diver holds her or his breath while ascending. This causes the small air sacs of the lungs (alveoli) to rupture.

Symptoms of an air embolism may include

- coughing a bloody froth,
- confusion,
- staggering,
- collapsing,

- having difficulty breathing,
- blue color,
- convulsions and paralysis, and
- unconsciousness (may be the first and only sign noticed).

The victim's condition will worsen quickly. Be sure to activate the EMS immediately.

The victim should be transported while lying flat. Keep the victim flat while lifting him or her onto a boat or into a vehicle for transport to a medical facility. If vomiting occurs, roll the victim onto the left side and wipe the mouth clean. Then maintain an open airway. If you are trained to administer oxygen, provide 100% medical oxygen to the victim if it is available as you provide other first aid measures.

Victims of scuba accidents may need special facilities for treatment. Management should ensure that all lifeguards know where the nearest recompression chamber is or how to locate it. DAN—the Divers Alert Network—is located at the Duke University Medical Center in Durham, North Carolina. The agency is open 24 hours a day to answer questions regarding diving accidents. In an emergency, you can reach them at 919-684-8111. For more routine questions during regular business hours, call 919-684-2948.

Missing Diver Procedure in Open Water

If you suspect that a scuba diver is missing and not simply separated from a diving buddy, take the following steps immediately:

1. Activate the EMS. This is a medical emergency. Send for additional help (lake patrol, emergency personnel, law enforcement personnel, underwater search and recovery team or others).
2. Identify the missing diver's buddy; ask the buddy where the missing diver is or where he or she was last seen.
3. Determine from others where the diver was last seen.
4. Move to that area and look for bubbles.
5. Put a search group of at least two certified scuba divers into the water immediately to search the area. Use a predetermined search pattern (see pp. 198-199).
6. Determine whether the diver could have left the diving area without notifying anyone.

Be aware of currents that could alter the missing diver's location. Where currents are present, conduct the search working in a downstream direction.

SEARCH AND RECOVERY OPERATIONS

Time is critical when you are searching for a submerged victim. The increased mobility and visibility with mask, fins, and snorkel will allow you to search more area more quickly. In some open water areas, however, the visibility is unavoidably limited. Groups of volunteers or guards can assist in shallow water, and groups of lifeguards can search in deep water.

The following procedures should be used by the person in charge, such as the head guard or lifeguard supervisor, to initiate a search for a swimmer believed to be missing in open water.

1. If a swimmer is suspected to be missing, alert all staff immediately.
2. Encourage the person who reported the missing swimmer to remain calm, to give a complete description of the missing swimmer—including where he or she was last seen—and to stay in one location.

3. Make an announcement specifying the name, description, and last location of the missing swimmer; tell patrons where additional information about the swimmer should be reported.

4. If the swimmer does not report, clear the swimming area and begin search procedures.

5. Instruct designated lifeguards to check the water, bathrooms, showers, locker rooms, snack bars, and adjacent areas.

6. Depending on the personnel available, have someone call the swimmer's home (or check living quarters if the person is vacationing).

Shallow Water Search Method

In shallow water with poor visibility, instruct volunteers or guards to link arms or hold hands and wade in a line across the area. (Volunteers should not be used in water deeper than chest level.) The line should progress forward slowly, with searchers making careful sweeping motions with their feet as illustrated in Figure 11.10 and trying not to disturb the bottom. When the shortest member of the search line is unable to continue, the coordinator should reform the search line with lifeguards capable of continuing the search through the use of surface dives. A guard should coordinate each search group.

Figure 11.10

A search line using sweeping foot motions.

Line advancing

Deep Water Search Method

In deeper water, standardized search patterns are suggested for specific circumstances. No search can be completed in an orderly manner without planning and practice, but these standard patterns should simplify the organization of a rescue effort. If a search is prolonged, the chances of a rescue are diminished, and the search instead becomes a recovery.

In searching, adjust the extent of each sweep of the pattern to the current level of visibility in order not to skip any area. Also, keep in mind that the victim may not be lying on the bottom. In a line, guards should surface dive to the bottom and complete a predetermined number of strokes before surfacing. They should use sweeping, semicircular motions with their arms just above the bottom to search. Such movements will avoid stirring up the bottom sediment. To cover low visibility areas completely guards must stay close enough together to slightly overlap each other's sweeps.

Guards should complete the designated number of strokes, surface almost straight up, and move back about 6 feet before reforming their line and diving down again. A guide line formed with one guard on the surface will allow directional control because the guards will be able to see the guide when they come to the surface. The guard on the surface is responsible to see that the other guards move back to the designated surface dive location, an important task in ensuring that the entire area is searched thoroughly.

Where visibility is better, extend a rope between rescuers to maintain spacing. In clearer water, rescuers can rely on sight rather than on touch to locate the victim, so they can remain closer to the surface and expand their field of vision and the area covered. Each facility should have a set of hand signals that all guards and experienced rescue personnel know to indicate recovery or the need to surface.

Search Patterns

Using one of four standard search patterns—circular, grid, parallel, and diagonal—lifeguards can search virtually any area efficiently. Each pattern has its own benefits.

Circular pattern. From a fixed center point, search a progressively widening circle (see Figure 11.11) using the surface dive and reforming procedures already described. The distance from the center point of each circular sweep depends on the water clarity. Expand the circle with each revolution, and make certain that a marker is placed at the starting point to assure complete coverage of the circle. The distance from the center can be readily controlled by a line held by the guards that is attached to the center point. In murky water, the hand not holding the line may be used to search by touch. Guards should try not to disturb the bottom while searching.

A post stuck into the river or lake bottom can serve as a center point. The anchor line of the boat also can be used for the center, or a weight may be placed on the bottom, providing it is heavy enough to remain in a fixed position. The rope attached to the center should be kept taut on each sweep at the distance desired for searching.

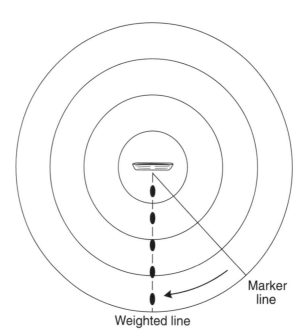

Figure 11.11

Circular search pattern.

Grid pattern. Divide the area into a grid to be searched by tying ropes to fixed anchors. The pattern, illustrated in Figure 11.12, allows the area to be covered thoroughly. Guards can search one unit and then move to another. The size of the units should not be greater than twice the visibility distance each guard has on one sweep. Two or more guards can be assigned to search a unit before moving to another sector of the grid.

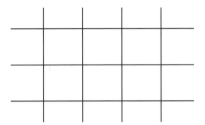

Figure 11.12

Grid search
pattern.

Parallel pattern. The guide or controller should walk along the shore holding a line extended to a guard or line of guards searching the visibility range from the shore. By keeping the line taut and at right angles to the shoreline, the guards can search the area thoroughly. Space each search pass to the limit of visibility, and complete the search.

Diagonal pattern. Swim diagonally to the shore (because the current naturally carries you on an angle, this will eliminate the need to fight the current). After crossing the current, return using a diagonal path (see Figure 11.13). Upon reaching the shore, step upstream 6 feet and start a second search. Be sure to keep your search parallel to your initial entry point. It is important to search quickly where currents are involved because the victim may drift.

Figure 11.13

Diagonal search
pattern.

Choosing a search pattern. It is important that lifeguard staff understand each pattern so that the correct one can be selected in an emergency. The chart here highlights the situations for which each pattern is most valuable.

Selecting a Search Pattern	
Pattern	**Appropriate Situation for Use**
Circular	Flat-bottomed areas with little current (Large areas can be searched quickly.)
Grid	Areas with irregular bottoms (This method is the surest search method, but it takes a great deal of time and equipment to set up and execute.)
Parallel	Areas of irregular shoreline
Diagonal	Areas where currents are likely to have influenced the position of a victim

Review Questions

1. List 7 considerations in selecting a beach site.
2. How are beachfront swimming areas identified?
3. List the additional equipment required on beaches.
4. How can you tell if a mask fits you properly?
5. How do you clear a snorkel of water?
6. List 10 of the frequent causes of accidents on beaches.
7. Why do scuba diving emergencies require special attention?
8. Explain the rescue of a diver using CARE.
9. Describe the rescue techniques for the active and the passive scuba victim.
10. If you suspect a diver is missing, what should you do?
11. Describe the search methods for shallow water and deep water.
12. Briefly explain the search and recovery patterns for a flat-bottomed lake, a lake with an irregular bottom, an irregular shoreline, and a river current.

CHAPTER 12

Lifeguarding Water Recreation Attractions

Water recreation attractions started to become really popular in the 1970s, and today you may find anything from a single water fume in a camp lake or community pool to multi-attraction indoor water recreation parks and 50-acre outdoor water parks. They are all meant to give patrons fun, thrilling rides, but special lifeguarding precautions are necessary to ensure the ride is safe, too.

IN THIS CHAPTER YOU'LL LEARN

■ the main causes of accidents at water recreation attractions,

■ the characteristics of specific attractions, along with the most common accident situations on those attractions and the appropriate lifeguarding positions,

■ the recommended operational safety standards for lifeguarding water recreation attractions, and

■ the general areas of concern for rules and safety and the use of signs and recorded messages to communicate those concerns to patrons.

UNDERSTANDING HOW TO GUARD WATER RECREATION ATTRACTIONS

Today, American water recreation areas include not only pools and diving areas but also a wide variety of water recreation attractions (see Figure 12.1). In most of these attractions, water helps control the speed of the rider, reduce friction between the rider and the activity surface, and restrain or cushion the rider in a landing area at the end of a ride.

For you to do a good job of lifeguarding water recreation attractions, you need to understand the main causes of accidents on attractions. You also need to learn the characteristics of some specific attractions, the most common accidents on those attractions, and where lifeguards should be stationed on each. We will also give you some fundamental operation safety standards to follow for water recreation attractions, as well as information on how to communicate rules and safety concerns to patrons using signs or taped messages.

Figure 12.1

American water recreation today includes a wide variety of water recreation attractions like this one.

CAUSES OF ACCIDENTS AT WATER RECREATION ATTRACTIONS

Over the past 20 years, enough information has been acquired to provide a clear picture of the primary causes of accidents at water recreation attractions, which include the following:

1. Unsafe design—Many attractions are manufactured and put into use without proper safety testing that uses appropriate research design and experimental testing.
2. Facility operations—After attractions have been installed on site, some owners and operators do not operate them properly. Sometimes owners and operators increase water flow rates or do not maintain proper water depths for slides, runouts, and catch pools. Maintenance may also be substandard.
3. Poor supervision—Lifeguards are sometimes inattentive to their dispatcher and ride supervision, rule enforcement, and catch pool duties.
4. Patron behavior—Water recreation area patrons who come to have fun may have medical problems, such as a heart condition, that may affect their safety on

attractions. Many patrons also are first-time visitors, unfamiliar with the rules or the attraction's characteristics. In their excitement, they often fail to read signs or listen to recorded announcements. Some patrons also choose to disobey rules.

5. Poor communication by management—Often patrons fail to read signs at attractions because of the large number of signs or improper signage. Signs may be difficult to read because of the color of the letters or numbers, background colors, or the height, thickness, or style of the font used. Placing signs where they are hard to read, failing to provide pictorial and bilingual signs, or failing to consistently use signal words such as "Danger," "Warning," and "Caution" often render a sign ineffective; in other words, such signs simply do not communicate properly. Recorded statements played while patrons wait in line may also fail to communicate because the tape wears out, the message is too long or is played too frequently, or the words are not clear.

LIFEGUARDING TIPS FOR INDIVIDUAL ATTRACTIONS

Each attraction has its own specific hazards. As a lifeguard, you need to know the characteristics of each attraction, those situations likely to lead to accidents, and where you and other lifeguards should be stationed. The attractions covered here include wave pools, deep-water activity pools, free-fall and speed slides, serpentine slides and rapids, coaster rides, and lazy or winding rivers.

Wave Pools

Waves in wave pools (see Figure 12.2) are created by one of two methods: compressed air or moving paddles.

- In the compressed air method, air is forced into half of the water chambers located within the end wall simultaneously (the odd-numbered ones), pushing the water out through the bottom of the chambers. After the water has escaped from the odd-numbered chambers, it is then released from the even-numbered chambers.
- In the paddle-operated method, a large mechanically operated paddle moves in a chamber in which a cascade of water is released from the back wall to displace water in a filled chamber.

Figure 12.2

Wave pools are popular attractions at water parks, but they have the potential for many different kinds of accidents.

A wave pool may produce waves on a cycle of small waves for 20 minutes followed by a 20-minute off-cycle period or one large wave every 5 to 10 minutes.

Wave Pool Accidents.   Wave pool hazards relate directly to the size and frequency of waves, as well as the cement bottom of the pool. Common wave pool accidents include the following:

- Weak swimmers in the four- to five-foot depth zone who are knocked over by waves
- Weak swimmers or nonswimmers who become buoyant as a wave lifts them off the bottom, causing them to panic
- Swimmers who are injured when waves push them into recessed wall ladders in the deep end
- Patrons in shallow water who are knocked down by people riding the waves on inflatable rafts
- Weak swimmers floating on inner tubes in deep water who fall off the tube, submerge, and cannot return to the surface due to the number of tubes covering the surface
- Weak swimmers hanging onto pool railings who are not strong enough to swim safely through the waves to shallow water

Patrons who suffer impact injuries from contact with the bottom or who are struck by other patrons riding on rafts may bleed. Be prepared to follow the blood-borne pathogen procedures identified in chapter 8.

Lifeguard Positions.   The number of sitting lifeguards and standing lifeguards depends on the size of the pool and the number of patrons in the water. Lifeguard chairs should be placed only near water depths over five feet along the sides of the pool. Standing or moving guards should be placed between chairs, along the back wall, and in shallow water.

Deep-Water Activity Pools

Deep-water activity pools are associated with a variety of attractions. Sometimes they are used as a landing area for patrons exiting from a "shotgun slide," five to six feet above the surface of the water. They also provide entry areas for diving boards, diving platforms, cable or rope swings, zip lines, nets, or rings on cables, along with inflatables or walking and play surfaces anchored to the bottom. Depending on the activity, the water depth may vary from 11.5 to 18 feet.

Deep-Water Pool Accidents.   Accidents in this type of pool are related to entries. Entries from objects high above the water are sometimes unplanned falls or sudden drops, and impact with the water can be painful. Accidents common to deep-water pools are the following:

- An injured or weak swimmer suddenly entering deep water
- A person losing consciousness who ends up lying face down in the water due to impact with the water, another person, or some part of the attraction

Be ready to use blood-borne pathogen procedures with impact injuries.

Lifeguard Positions.   The number of lifeguards and their locations should be determined by the activity:

- For shotgun slides, a lifeguard dispatcher is needed at the top of the slide. Another lifeguard must be stationed near the drop zone where patrons enter the water.

- For pools with 7.5- and 10-meter platforms, water depths will range from 15 to 18 feet. In case they have to rescue a submerged victim, lifeguards should have mask, fins, and snorkel handy. They should receive in-service training on how to use this equipment in victim recovery from the bottom and practice rescue procedures regularly.

For most of these deep-water activities, a lifeguard must be stationed near the entry point. Other lifeguards should be situated where they have an unobstructed view of the sides.

Free-Fall and Speed Slides

Free-fall and speed slides are similar in design. Free-fall slides are long slides with very steep drops. Some are so steep that the top of the slide is enclosed, giving the rider the sensation of falling straight down (see Figure 12.3). Speed slides have a more gentle slope and sometimes have a bump halfway down. These slides may end in a catch pool or a long run-out, which is generally where accidents occur.

Free-Fall and Speed Slide Accidents. Because of the speeds attained on these slides, riders should stay in a position in which their legs are crossed at the ankles and their arms are folded across their chest. Injuries on these attractions usually result from a combination of speed and improper body position, as in these situations:

1. Soft tissue injuries, such as strains and sprains affecting the limbs.
2. Serious internal injuries from entering the catch pool or run-out with legs apart.
3. Broken bones or dislocated joints from impact with the slide after becoming airborne from sliding over a speed bump. Impacting water in the catch pool or

Figure 12.3

Riders of free-fall slides should stay in a position in which their legs are crossed at the ankles and their arms are folded across their chest.

hitting the wall or steps at the end of a slide run-out or catch pool that is too short can produce similar injuries.

Lifeguard Positions.   Lifeguards for free-fall and speed slides should be stationed at the top of the slide to control the dispatch of riders and at the bottom in the run-out area or adjacent to the catch pool.

Serpentine Slides and Rapids

Serpentine slides are generally long slides that wind their way down a hillside or super structure much like a rollercoaster (see Figure 12.4). They are constructed of fiberglass or cement. Riders slide on mats or in one- or two-person tubes or they body-slide feet-first with arms and legs crossed (as when using a speed slide). Rapids-type rides simulate tubing in a creek or river. Such rides wind downhill and may have one or two catch basins at points between the top and bottom where the ride funnels riders into a cave or to the next drop level.

Serpentine Slides and Rapids Accidents.   Accidents may occur anywhere from the top to the bottom of these slides. Common accidents include the following:

- Falling off a mat and losing body control, producing soft tissue injuries, broken bones, or head injuries.
- Stopping on the way down and blocking the following riders, causing impact injuries.
- Riding in one- or two-person tubes and hitting the walls of the slide with the head, arms, or feet. The rider cannot control the tube as it spins and turns on its downhill course.
- Sliding and getting caught in a hydraulic formed at the end of the ride. Hydraulics are the result of water cascading from the slide into the catch pool, which forms a waterfall effect that produces a reverse circular current. A hydraulic can make it extremely difficult to stand up, especially for young children or weak swimmers and may even hold a person on the bottom.

Figure 12.4

Lifeguards for serpentine slides should be stationed at the dispatch positions, the catch pool, and appropriate locations in between.

- An excessive number of tubes collecting in a rapids' catch basin where some tubes may be overturned, causing injury or even drowning.

Lifeguard Positions.   Riders may need assistance or rescue at any point from the top of the ride to the catch pool. Standing lifeguards need to be stationed at the dispatch positions, the catch pool, and appropriate locations in between.

Coaster Ride

Coaster rides are similar to, but shorter than, speed slides. They often are constructed in pairs. Riders sit on plastic sleds that glide down on small metal rollers or water-lubricated surfaces. When the rider and sled leave the slide, they skim along the surface of a long catch pool, gradually slowing down until coming to a stop.

Coaster Ride Accidents.   Accidents common to coaster rides include the following:

- Collisions between two sleds discharged simultaneously
- Sleds flipping over, resulting in a rider hitting a side wall or the bottom

Lifeguard Positions.   Lifeguards assigned to coaster rides should be positioned at the top of the slide to dispatch riders and adjacent to or in the catch pool to assist injured or disoriented riders. Lifeguards in the catch pool should be ready to use blood-borne pathogen protocols.

Lazy or Winding Rivers

The paths of lazy or winding rivers may be oval in shape or they may wind their way through a water recreation area, sometimes encompassing the entire area. They generally are three to four feet in depth and float patrons along on inner tubes at two to three miles per hour (see Figure 12.5).

Figure 12.5

Lazy or winding rivers are generally three to four feet in depth and float patrons along on inner tubes at two to three miles per hour.

Lazy or Winding River Accidents.   Lazy or winding rivers generally have a low incidence of accidents. Those that do occur are often the following:

1. Patrons slipping or falling at the point of entrance or exit
2. Patrons who injure themselves by getting out of the river and then jumping or diving back in
3. Patrons who hit their head after falling from an overturned tube caused by horseplay and other patrons blocking the progress of riders

Lifeguard Positions.   Lifeguards must be stationed at the entrance and exit points in order to assist riders in getting into and out of tubes. They also must be positioned sitting or standing along the river, so that no part of the river is out of the sight of a lifeguard at any time.

OPERATIONAL SAFETY STANDARDS FOR LIFEGUARDS

As water recreation areas have many different types of activities, ensure that each attraction is supervised and guarded according to its individual characteristics. We recommend the following operational safety standards for water recreation attractions:

- Always emphasize accident prevention.
- Get orientation and in-service training specific to each attraction you guard.
- Have some means of communication and signaling provided by your facility, such as an intercom system, FM radio, public address system, signal lights, radio telephones, CB radios, air horns, or whistles.
- Completely inspect and test each attraction according to manufacturer's instructions each day before use. Then fill out a daily checklist specific to the attraction to record findings. After inspection and testing, have a lifeguard ride the attraction as it would normally be used by patrons. If maintenance needs to be performed, do it before the attraction is opened for use or close the attraction until the required maintenance can be completed. Record all maintenance procedures in the log.
- Inspect first aid, safety, and rescue equipment, including first aid kits, HIV precautionary kits, and pocket masks, and record the results of the inspection in a log.
- Test and adjust the water chemistry balance each time the filters are cleaned, and test and adjust the disinfectant levels hourly.
- Expect your facility to have developed written emergency and accident management procedures (which should be practiced) specific to each attraction as well as an emergency procedure for an unplanned shutdown of each attraction.
- Remember that the keys to accident prevention are to
  - stay at a high level of physical conditioning,
  - pay constant attention to scanning and lifeguard duties, and
  - consistently enforce rules.
- Be ready to respond quickly when you see a patron
  - slip and fall,
  - collide with another rider, side wall, end wall, or bottom,
  - lose body control on an attraction,
  - fall from an attraction,
  - become airborne and hit a hard surface,
  - fail to read signs or listen to recorded messages and warnings,

- act as if he or she is under the influence of drugs or alcohol,
- appear to be suffering from a medical condition, such as a heart attack, epilepsy, diabetes, or heat exhaustion,
- fail to heed warnings such as height, weight, or age restrictions, or
- act disoriented or unstable.

COMMUNICATION AT WATER RECREATION ATTRACTIONS

You must communicate often and clearly with all patrons, especially those who are visiting for the first time, as they are more likely to be injured than those who frequent the attractions regularly. Keep in mind that patrons are excited and eager to ride as many attractions as possible. As a result, they sometimes don't read the rules and warning signs or listen carefully to recorded messages. Some children may also be unsupervised by an adult. You may have to repeat warnings and rules verbally in a dispatch area, even though patrons have been presented with signs and recorded messages along the way into or up to an attraction. The following list represents general areas of concern for which your facility should develop, communicate, and enforce warning and safety rules.

Warning Signs

Personal Health

Fear of heights or sudden immersion
Fatigue and exhaustion
Heart problems

Proper Use of Equipment

Tubes, rafts, mats, sleds, and PFDs

Slowing and Stopping

Extending arms and legs to slow
Extending arms and legs to stop
Holding on to wave pool rails

Rider Behavior

Changing body positions
Multiple riders, trains
Weaving back and forth

Activity Use Prohibited

For people on certain prescription drugs or those using recreational drugs or alcohol

Water Depth

At entrance and exit of attractions
On the coping of all pools

General Warnings

Failure to follow the rules or instructions can result in paralysis or serious or fatal injury.
Lifeguards must always be obeyed.
Failure to obey can result in dismissal.

Safety Signs

Bathing and Personal Attire

Bathing suits
Clothing—T-shirts
Glasses, sunglasses
Jewelry
Dentures, hearing aids
Prosthetics

Patron Limitations

Age
Height
Weight or overweight
Height and weight for large patrons

Body Position

Head-first
Feet-first
Prone position
Supine position
Sitting position

Entry Positions

Jumping
Diving
Running
Swinging
Pushing off

Exit Rules

Approved behavior
Where exit is allowed

Special Rules

Unique to special attractions

As mentioned, besides posting signs, you may want to have recorded messages on warnings and rules announced through loudspeakers located along entrance paths and stairs. When you record such a message, make sure to do the following:

- Speak clearly and slowly.
- Use inflections, avoiding a monotone.
- Make the message brief and concise.
- Use language that everyone can understand.
- Use positive messages, avoiding sarcasm and profanity.
- Consider multilingual messages in languages, such as Spanish, French, German, and Japanese, consistent with the languages and nationalities of those who frequent your facility.
- Be sure the message is loud enough to be heard, but not obnoxiously loud.

Review Questions

1. What are the primary causes of water accidents at water recreation attractions?
2. What are the common accidents in a wave pool?
3. What are the common accidents in deep-water activity pools?
4. What are the common injuries resulting in the use of a speed slide?
5. What are the common accidents from using a serpentine slide?
6. What are the common accidents from using a lazy or winding river?
7. What are the common accidents resulting from a coaster ride?
8. What are the lifeguard's keys to accident prevention?
9. When should a lifeguard be ready to respond?
10. What are the general warning signals in which warning and safety signs should be developed, communicated, and enforced?

CHAPTER 13

Legal
Obligations

In addition to developing physical skills to be a good lifeguard, you must accept responsibility for your actions. As a professional lifeguard, you accept the duty to provide patrons of your facility a safe environment in which to enjoy aquatic activities. This means that you must maintain the pool and surrounding area to meet basic health and safety codes, provide adequate supervision for all areas in the facility, provide appropriate direction to patrons regarding the rules, anticipate potential hazards and act to reduce the resulting risks, provide necessary emergency first aid, and proficiently perform the skills described in this lifeguarding manual.

IN THIS CHAPTER YOU'LL LEARN ABOUT

- common legal terms,
- the legal process,
- aquatic liability, and
- liability defenses.

COMMON LEGAL TERMS

Take some time to familiarize yourself with the following legal terms, applied here to lifeguarding. They will be important to your understanding of the legal responsibilities of being a professional lifeguard.

duty: A duty is a legal obligation to act in accordance with a prescribed standard of conduct in order to protect others from unreasonable risk.

breach: If a patron is owed a duty and the lifeguard does not perform it, the lifeguard is said to have breached the duty.

common law: Under this general principle of law, which all states follow in the absence of a specific law, an individual owes no general duty to help another person in danger, even if the individual has the skills and ability to provide assistance. But the doctrine of common law is negated when a lifeguard is *on duty*. A lifeguard on duty must help a person in danger or may be considered negligent if an injury occurs.

ordinary standard of care: The performance considered by law or practice within a profession as the action likely to be taken by an average, reasonable, and prudent professional is the ordinary standard of care.

negligence: Actions that fall below the standard of care established by law for the protection of others against unreasonable risks are considered to be negligent. Such actions could be an unintentional breach of a legal duty, causing foreseeable damage that could have been avoided had the individual performed his or her duty.

liability: An individual can be held legally responsible for actions or lack of action intentionally designed to harm another as well as for negligent acts that harm another.

proximate cause: When a reasonably close causal connection is drawn between the failure to provide a legal duty and an injury, the breach is considered a proximate cause.

Good Samaritan laws: These statutes provide protection from legal liability to a trained person acting in good faith while off duty to provide emergency medical assistance at the scene of an accident or emergency. Good Samaritan laws differ from state to state, and lifeguards should know the law for their state.

nuisance: Anything that causes hurt, inconvenience, annoyance, or damage is considered a nuisance.

plaintiff: The plaintiff is the individual or group of individuals claiming a wrongdoing and filing a lawsuit.

defendant: The defendant is the individual or group of individuals accused of committing a wrong.

THE LEGAL PROCESS

Following any accident there is a possibility that the victim, or a relative of the victim, will initiate action against the aquatic facility and the lifeguards on duty at the time of the accident. The process usually follows the same general path, illustrated in Figure 13.1.

In our society, a lawsuit can be brought against anyone for any reason, so the filing of a complaint doesn't mean a facility or lifeguard is guilty of any wrongdoing. It means rather that the plaintiff's attorney has gathered information on the case and that the plaintiff is willing to present the case to a court for a decision.

Before a trial, attorneys for the plaintiff and for the defense continue to gather information and to secure sworn testimony from experts on the standard of care for the

Figure 13.1

Lawsuit process.

particular situation under examination. This is called pretrial discovery. The plaintiff must prove that the defendant's actions caused the injury sustained and that the injury was foreseeable and therefore preventable.

Such court cases may be heard by a jury or by a judge alone. In either situation, both sides of the case are presented. After a deliberation or discussion period the judge or jury decides whether the defendant is guilty of the charges and, if so, what damages should be awarded.

AQUATIC LIABILITY

Most lawsuits concerning aquatic activities involve a perceived wrong. Liability arises when an injury results from a lifeguard's either failing to perform an action that should have been performed or performing an incorrect action. Most lawsuits filed against aquatic facilities focus on two elements that give rise to liability: negligence and nuisance. Because specific laws regarding aquatic liability vary from state to state, we will consider general principles in this chapter. Check with the appropriate departments in your local government to learn about the laws governing aquatic facilities in your area.

Negligence

In the law of negligence, the person bringing suit—the plaintiff—must prove

- that the defendant owed a duty to the plaintiff,
- that the defendant breached that duty,

- that the plaintiff suffered some injury or loss, and
- that the injury or loss was caused by the defendant's breach (proximate cause).

All four elements must be proved for the lawsuit to advance.

Negligence can take many forms. *Willful negligence* is performing an action intended to cause someone harm. Unintentional acts of negligence that cause harm are considered *slight*, *ordinary*, or *gross negligence*, depending on their severity. Examples of unintentional negligence include failure to foresee a potential hazard, carelessness, poor judgment, excitement, inattention to duty, inexperience, ignorance, stupidity, and forgetfulness.

In your role as a professional lifeguard, you assume a legal duty to provide the services you were trained to provide to each patron of your facility while you are on duty. That doesn't mean that you ensure the safety of patrons. Rather, it means that if an accident occurs while you are on duty you must function competently. In other words, as a lifeguard you must respond by providing the standard of care outlined by the organization that certified you and that is expected of professional lifeguards. If you perform according to those standards, you would not be found negligent.

Constructive notice.   The facility owner should know of any potentially dangerous conditions that may exist, regardless of whether or not he or she has actual knowledge of them. In other words, if an employee or a patron sees a hazardous condition but fails to report it to the owner, the owner is considered to have *constructive notice* because he or she should have been aware of the condition. If an injury occurs because of this hazardous condition, the owner can be held liable due to negligence.

In any pool facility, the owner must ensure the following conditions:

- Chemical and storage areas are safely and properly used.
- Rescue equipment is in good working order and readily available.
- Ladders and diving structures are safe and in good repair.
- Lighting, including underwater lighting, is safe and adequate.
- Pool water is disinfected, and pH levels are correctly adjusted.
- Water is clear.
- Water depth is clearly marked at all places, especially in shallow and deep water.
- Regular checks are made for hazards such as broken glass, equipment that has not been put away, or cracked cement around posts supporting the diving structure and lifeguard chairs.

Ordinary standard of care.   You can be found negligent if you do not fulfill the ordinary standard of care you owe a patron; you are obligated to use the care that circumstances would indicate to a prudent and careful person. Negligence would be based on the plaintiff's demonstrating that your actions fell below what could be expected of other similarly trained individuals in similar circumstances.

Nuisance

Nuisance is not the same as negligence. Rather, in the legal sense, a nuisance is something that causes hurt, inconvenience, annoyance, or damage. The operation of a swimming facility is not by itself a nuisance if it is done without disturbing the surroundings. Large floodlights, loud music, and inadequate parking, however, could be judged nuisances.

LIABILITY DEFENSES

To avoid legal liability, you must exercise reasonable care. Although there are numerous ways to be held liable for an injury, the only sure way to avoid liability is to see that an injury doesn't occur. By taking the appropriate actions to ensure the safety of your patrons and by adhering to state and local regulations for aquatic facilities, you will be doing as much as you can to prevent accidents.

Many organizations suggest that you obtain liability insurance for your lifeguarding activities. Most facilities have liability insurance to protect themselves and their employees, and many personal general liability insurance policies include such liability coverage. Take time to learn about the insurance available to you before you accept any lifeguarding position.

If a liability suit against an aquatic facility should come to trial, the following are some types of defenses that the defendants might use.

Governmental or Sovereign Immunity

In some states, government employees involved in liability actions can claim immunity because of their positions as "agents" of the state.

Assumption of Risk

In the assumption-of-risk defense, the defendant combats the plaintiff's charges by claiming that the plaintiff assumed or accepted a certain level of risk by entering the aquatic facility and by participating in the activity that led to the injury. For example, a patron who dove from the diving board and hit her head on the end of the board could be said to have assumed that risk by deciding to attempt a dive.

Contributory Negligence

The contributory-negligence defense is somewhat weak in that it admits negligence. However, it also places some of the burden on the plaintiff, indicating that he or she contributed to the overall negligence. If, for example, a patron was injured by participating in rough play in the shallow end of the pool, the lifeguard might admit negligence by not having stopped the activity. However, the lifeguard would claim that the plaintiff contributed to the cause of the injury by knowingly participating in an activity that was against the facility rules.

Comparative Negligence

This defense, too, admits some degree of guilt on the part of the lifeguard. In deciding the award to be given to the plaintiff, the judge or jury would assign relative amounts of negligence to the lifeguard and to the injured party. Say, for example, a lifeguard had cleared the water because of an impending electrical storm and a patron sneaked back into the water and was struck by lightning. Under the comparative negligence defense, the plaintiff might be awarded no damages because the lifeguard fulfilled her or his initial duty by clearing the water. Although it might have been negligent not to have noticed that the patron went back into the water, the plaintiff bore greater negligence by not obeying the lifeguard.

Last Clear Chance

In many accidents the injured party could have stopped some action before the injury occurred. If the plaintiff had a clear chance to avoid the accident and did not, the lifeguard might not be found negligent.

RECORD KEEPING

In many facilities patrons must sign waivers of liability. By signing such forms, they agree that they will not hold the facility liable for injuries they receive while participating in specific activities. These waivers do not remove liability resulting from faulty or damaged equipment or any intentional or willful negligence by staff.

Other records that may be of use in aquatic facilities include staff manuals, emergency plans, posted rules governing the facility, accident and incident reports, and chemical safety logs. These records can establish the standard of care that your facility provides, and they include information that will be vital to your defense in the event of a lawsuit. Be sure you complete these records systematically and file them carefully. If you usually keep excellent records but cannot provide them for a particular situation, you would appear to have failed to meet the standards your organization has set. It is not generally necessary to keep records for longer than 5 years.

Review Questions

1. Describe the Good Samaritan law.
2. Describe the legal process when a lawsuit is initiated.
3. Define liability and explain why it is of concern to aquatic facilities.
4. Define negligence and list the 4 elements required to determine it.
5. Could a pool owner be liable if a patron is injured when a piece of equipment breaks but the owner didn't know it was in poor condition?
6. What is the ordinary standard of care?
7. Define nuisance.
8. Name 5 types of liability defenses.

CHAPTER 14

Pool Management Basics

As a lifeguard, you will most commonly be assigned to monitor the pool area to help prevent accidents and to respond to situations as necessary. It is likely that you will also be asked to assist in several other operations essential to the success of the aquatic facility. This chapter is designed to give you an introduction to pool management. For more in-depth coverage, take the YMCA P.O.O.L. (Pool Operator on Location) course.

IN THIS CHAPTER YOU'LL LEARN ABOUT

- safety inspections and precautions,
- signage,
- filtration,
- pool chemistry,
- common water problems, and
- spas.

SAFETY INSPECTIONS

Each facility must be routinely inspected for potential hazards. A complete inspection should be performed regularly throughout the season. The findings of these inspections are the basis for major maintenance work to be completed.

The regulations governing your facility may provide a timetable for systematic inspection of the water and the surrounding areas. Be sure you are aware of the procedures to be followed.

Most inspections cover not only the pool or the waterfront but also include any structures on the facility grounds, and the results should be reported to the managers of the facility. As a general guideline, the following areas should be checked:

- Bottom
- Water clarity
- Chemical readings
- Air and water temperature
- Deck
- Ladders
- Lifelines and lane lines
- First aid and safety equipment
- Lights
- Filtration system

- Diving area
- Diving boards
- Diving stands
- Radio or phone system
- Entry and exit areas
- Shower and locker room areas
- Water fountains
- Deck chairs or furniture
- Drain areas

If a problem is noted in any of these areas, maintenance is required. That maintenance must be performed to remove the risk associated with the conditions and to protect the facility from legal action in the event of a related injury. Patrons should not be allowed in areas with problems until the hazards are removed or fixed.

The inspection forms, together with maintenance reports indicating when and how the noted safety problems were handled, should be filed in a secure location and kept for at least 5 years.

Daily maintenance is also vital to the well-run aquatic facility. Testing pool chemicals, sweeping walkways and locker room floors, emptying trash cans, and disinfecting floors, benches, toilet seats, and fixtures are all important to the cleanliness and healthfulness of your facility.

SAFETY PRECAUTIONS

Pool chemical safety, electrical safety, and maintenance of non-slip surfaces are areas of particular concern in pool management.

Chemical Safety

Although you are not likely to be solely responsible for the management of pool chemistry, you may be asked to assist in this task. You must be aware of the potential dangers of pool chemicals; handling them is hazardous.

To better understand the dangers and proper handling of the chemicals used at your facility, ask your pool operator or manager for copies of the material safety data sheets (MSDS) for those chemicals. By OSHA (Occupational Safety and Health Administration) standards, your employer must have these informational sheets available. Your employer should train you in the handling of pool chemicals before you work with them.

First Aid for Chemical Accidents

For any chemical accident, have someone call EMS immediately.

• *Chlorine gas*—Remove the victim from the area; keep him or her warm and quiet. Lay the victim on the back with the head elevated. If the victim is breathing, administer oxygen if you are trained to do so. If the victim is not breathing, begin rescue breathing or CPR immediately, supplementing it with oxygen if you are trained to do so.

• *Liquid chlorine*—Flush skin with cold water. Flush eyes with cold water for 15 to 30 minutes. If clothing is splashed with the chemical, remove the clothing and wash the skin with cold water. If the victim has swallowed the chemical, have someone call the poison control center in your area after calling EMS.

• *Hydantoin bromine*—If the liquid mixture gets in your eyes, flush with cold water for 15 to 30 minutes. If clothing is splashed with the chemical, remove the clothing and wash the skin with cold water. For contact with skin, flush with cold water. If the victim has inhaled fumes from a dry chemical fire, give oxygen if you are trained to do so. If the victim has swallowed the chemical, have someone call the poison control center in your area after calling EMS.

• *Dry chlorine compounds (calcium or lithium hypochlorite and chlorinated cyanurates), sodium bisulfate*—Flush skin with cold water. Flush eyes with cold water for 15 to 30 minutes. For contact with clothing, remove the clothing and flush the skin with cold water. If the victim has inhaled fumes from a chemical fire, give oxygen if you are trained to do so. If the chemical was swallowed, have someone call the poison control center in your area after calling EMS.

• *Muratic acid*—Flush skin or eyes with cold water for 15 to 30 minutes. If clothing is splashed, remove the clothing and flush the skin with cold water for 15 to 30 minutes.

• *Soda ash, diatomaceous earth*—Flush skin with cold water. Flush eyes with cold water for 15 to 30 minutes. If the victim inhaled large amounts of the substance, have someone call EMS.

• *Test kit reagent*—Flush skin with cold water. Flush eyes with cold water for 15 to 30 minutes. For contact with clothing, remove the clothing and flush the skin with cold water. If the chemical was swallowed, have someone call the poison control center in your area after calling EMS.

Use the following general safety precautions when handling chemicals:

• Never smoke near chemicals.
• Avoid inhaling the fumes or dust of any chemical.
• Avoid spilling chemicals on your clothes or body.
• Wear a dust mask or breathing apparatus, rubber gloves, and a rubber apron when handling chemicals.
• Never mix chemicals together.
• Always add acid to water—never add water to acid.
• Divide a chemical into three equal units and apply a third of the chemical every 3 to 4 hours.
• Dissolve powders or crystals in water before adding them to the pool.
• Use chemical feed pumps, and change output levels slowly if possible.
• Add chemicals dissolved in water to the pool when the pool is not in use.

- Avoid adding chemicals to vacuum filter tanks, skimmers, or gutters.
- Make sure chemicals are stored properly.

Before you help move or apply any chemical, be sure you know how to work with that substance. Your pool operator should provide you adequate instruction before you attempt to assist in chemical operations.

Your facility should have a plan for chemical emergencies. In the event of a chemical accident, contact EMS immediately. These professionals will provide advanced care for the victim. While awaiting the EMS, you can provide some emergency first aid. The chart here indicates what steps you can take in the event of a chemical accident.

The phone number of the poison control center in your area should be posted by your phone. Call the center as well as EMS whenever chemicals have been inhaled, absorbed, or swallowed.

Electrical Safety

Any pool environment poses the potential for electrical shock because electrical outlets and fixtures in this area often come in contact with water. For your protection, the National Electrical Code has established stringent requirements for the location of electrical fixtures in pool areas. Outlets are typically required to have covers and ground-fault interrupters.

Your facility must meet safety requirements, but you must also exercise caution and common sense in preventing electrical accidents. Don't use tape recorders, video cameras, or other electronic devices near the water's edge. And don't stand in water as you reach into the electrical box of the pool filter compartment.

Non-Slip Surface Maintenance

Pool lifeguards often are required to perform maintenance jobs prior to pool opening, while off duty, or during relief breaks. One job that is frequently performed incorrectly, and which could cause an accident, is the cleaning of non-slip surfaces. Such surfaces can be found on places such as springboards, diving mount steps, starting block surfaces and steps, lifeguard chair steps, steps leading to water slides and flumes, and steps to diving platforms. At outdoor facilities where these surfaces are constantly wet and are shaded, green algae can cause the surface to become slippery. In indoor pools, especially those with high humidity or poor air handling, or in which the air handling system is turned off overnight (which is improper), black mildew may collect on these surfaces, which also can cause slipperiness.

In an effort to clean these surfaces, lifeguards or maintenance personnel often are told to scrub the surface with detergent and a stiff bristled brush. However, frequent scrubbing with such a brush will loosen the silica in the paint or loosen the sand put on top of the wet paint (as is done in homemade resurfacing). If the gritty material is removed by scrubbing, the surfaces become smooth and slippery when wet, and are then hazardous.

A better way to clean non-slip surfaces is to apply household bleach, full strength, to the entire surface to be cleaned. After letting it stand for up to five minutes, rinse the bleach off with a hose. This type of cleaning removes the slime while leaving the grit material in place. It also is less effort than scrubbing!

SIGNAGE

Along with adequate safety inspections, every aquatic facility should have signs with rules, warnings, and information about water depth and other potential hazards. These signs should be large enough to be read from a distance, written in language that is easy to understand, and placed in the proper visible location. Where possible, use universal symbols, and in multilingual areas, signs should be multilingual. All depth markings should be at least 4 inches high and be posted in both feet and meters. They must appear on the pool deck and on the vertical wall at or above the water's surface, and they must be of a contrasting color with the background.

FILTRATION

Each aquatic facility has its own system and procedures for maintaining the water environment. Although these systems vary, all should meet the standards set by the appropriate local and state public health and safety organizations. Additional information regarding your facility's system can be obtained from your manager. You also can receive additional training by taking the YMCA P.O.O.L. (Pool Operator on Location) course. Be sure to follow manufacturer's instructions relating to care and use of the equipment.

Filtration Equipment

In general, the filtration system in a pool is designed to recirculate the water continually, keeping it clean, safe, and enjoyable for all swimmers. The system serves a number of important functions:

- Removes hair, lint, leaves, and other items that would otherwise interfere with the water treatment process
- Adds fresh water to replace water lost through leakage, splashing, evaporation, cleaning, and skimming
- Recirculates water so that all pool water is filtered every 6 to 8 hours (check your state code on required filtration rate)
- Adds chlorine or bromine to disinfect the water
- Adds soda ash or acid when necessary to maintain the appropriate pH level
- Filters out any materials suspended in the water
- Cleans itself with a backwash system

The catcher that removes foreign matter from the water protects the pumping unit. Having debris flow through the system would cause unnecessary wear and reduces the pumps' effectiveness.

Repairs on the pumps and motors that run the filtration system should always be made by competent technicians who are familiar with the manufacturers' instructions for the equipment. Normal maintenance consists of:

- protecting the pumps and motors against water and chemical corrosion,
- lubricating the pumps and motors, and
- adjusting the pump packing to ensure a slight water leak, thus avoiding overtightening the adjustment bolts.

Most pools use one of two types of filtration systems: sand-and-gravel or diatomaceous earth.

Sand-and-gravel filtration systems.   Dirt and other suspended particles must be removed from pool water to provide maximum clarity. Sand-and-gravel filters are one type of filter system used in many pools. There are three common types of sand-and-gravel filters.

- *Vacuum sand filters* consist of a bed of several layers of gravel topped with sand in an open tank. Water flows through the layers of sand and gravel, which trap the dirt, and is recirculated by a combination of gravity and vacuum forces.
- *Pressure sand filters* are closed filter tanks containing several layers of sand and gravel. Water is forced through the layers, which trap the dirt, usually in the first layer of sand.

- *High-pressure sand filters* combine two or more small closed filter tanks, usually consisting of a few feet of sand. This setup is used to speed the filtration. Dirt particles are removed throughout the entire bed of sand as the water moves through the filter from top to bottom.

Diatomaceous earth filtration systems.   These filters also remove small particles from the water, but diatomaceous earth differs from sand in being made up of fossilized marine plant life, or *diatoms*. When diatomaceous earth is applied to the system's filter elements, water passes through and around the tiny spaces in the diatoms, which trap the dirt particles. Diatomaceous earth filters, because of the size of their individual particles, can remove smaller particles than sand-and-gravel filters.

Cleaning the Pool Bottom

Filters remove the fine dirt that is suspended in the water, but a certain amount of matter settles to the pool bottom. Removing this residue takes some of the strain off the filters and makes for a more attractive pool.

The extra dirt can be picked up by a pool vacuum. Two common types are a portable pump and motor, which can be rolled to the edge of the pool, and a vacuum line hooked directly to the filter system.

The vacuum line is perhaps the most popular method because it operates without any loss of water. Connections to the vacuum hose are made at various points around the pool by outlets a few inches under the surface. Other models and methods for cleaning the pool bottom are on the market.

The best time to vacuum is in the morning when no one is in the pool, after the sediment has settled overnight. In smaller pools, the operation can be done from the deck by using a long pole with a vacuum head attached to vacuum along the bottom of the pool. In larger pools, automatic vacuums move across the pool bottom.

REMOVING FECAL MATTER FROM THE POOL

Because fecal matter carries the possibility of transmitting blood-borne pathogens to others (see p. 114), it needs to be removed immediately. If you see feces in the pool, clear the pool and close it until the pool has been cleaned. Notify your aquatic director or pool manager so he or she can put your facility's cleanup policy into action.

Cleanup should start with removal of as much fecal material as possible with a leaf skimmer. If the pool bottom is vacuumed, waste water should be channeled directly to a sewer or approved waste disposal system, not through the filtration system. The vacuum equipment and leaf skimmer will have to be cleaned and disinfected with sodium hypochlorite before they can be used again. The pool water and filtration system also will need to be disinfected according to your facility's procedures.

POOL CHEMISTRY

Maintaining safe, clean water for swimming requires the use of chemicals to kill bacteria and to keep the proper pH balance. The correct balance helps ensure that water isn't irritating to swimmers and, in outdoor pools, that algae won't form in the water and on pool surfaces. The amount of chemical to be used is determined in part by the facility's capacity.

Disinfecting Water

Chlorine is the most common water disinfectant, although bromine has become more popular recently; they work in similar ways. For our purposes, we'll consider how chlorine functions. If your facility uses bromine, ask about proper testing procedures.

Chlorine acts quickly and can be maintained in the water to provide for continuous disinfection. Although chlorine can be corrosive and poisonous, it does not pose any great difficulty in distribution or handling.

Water can be chlorinated in several ways. One method is using pure chlorine gas contained in cylinders under pressure. A chlorinator is needed to feed the gas into the pool in a controlled manner. Another common method of chlorination is using hypochlorites in liquid, granular, or powder form. Such substances are applied by a chemical feeder that must operate constantly to maintain a steady amount of chlorine suspended in the water, or a *residual*.

Water must be tested for the residual value of chlorine; it is considered safe if a minimal value of .4 ppm (parts per million) can be maintained. The recommended level is 1.0 ppm. The acceptable level of chlorine residual varies among states, so check with your health department to learn about local standards.

One common method used to test residual chlorine is the colorimeter test. A sample of water to be tested is mixed with the test solution in a test tube, and the coloring immediately produced indicates the amount of residual chlorine present. By comparing the color to a fixed scale, you can make an accurate reading in seconds. Another test uses a test strip, whose coloration is also compared to a fixed scale.

Acid-Base Balance

Water molecules are constantly breaking up into positive or negative ions. An excess of positive ions make the water more acid, which can cause skin irritation and corrode metal surfaces. An excess of negative ions makes the water more basic, which can lead to cloudy water and form scale on filters and plumbing. Thus, a proper balance of acid to base is sought for effective filtration, for effective use of chlorine, and for swimmers' comfort.

This balance is maintained by testing for pH, a measurement of how basic or acid the water is.

A pH test is used to monitor the water. You can determine the pH with a colorimeter test or test strips: A rating below 7.0 is considered acidic; above 7.0, basic. The recommended pH range is 7.4 to 7.6. At this level the water is suitably alkaline (basic) for the filtration system to operate. Soda ash (sodium carbonate), added through a chemical feeder, is the generally accepted material used to raise the pH level when necessary.

Algae Control

Algae is slimy-looking green or brown plant life that makes pools look and smell uncared for. Because wind and rain can introduce algae to water, growth of algae is more of a problem in outdoor than indoor pools. If conditions are right, algae can multiply enough within 24 to 48 hours to grow on the pool walls and make water appear green or brown.

Warm water encourages the growth of algae as well as of bacteria. Control of algae has been a perplexing problem for outdoor pool operators. The best method to control algae is to prevent its growth. Once algae begins its growth cycle, the chief method for control is superchlorinating the water. During this procedure, which must be done when the pool is not in use, the chlorine residual is raised to 3.0 ppm, three times the recommended amount of residual.

Pool Volume

Whatever chemical is to be applied, the pool volume (sometimes known as *facility capacity*), is an important determinant of the amount to be used. A variety of formulas exist to determine the volume of water in the pool. Once you know the capacity, check the manufacturer's instructions for proper chemical application.

In general, you can determine the volume of a rectangular pool by using the following formula:

Volume in gallons = length 3 width 3 average depth 3 7.5
(7.5 is the number of gallons in a cubic foot of water)

COMMON WATER PROBLEMS

Water problems begin when the water is not tested systematically. When the water chemistry becomes unbalanced, the following problems may result:

- Turbidity or cloudiness
- Algae growth
- Hard water
- Colored water

Turbidity

Cloudy water means that impurities have not been filtered out. The problem may be caused by contamination of the water, a malfunctioning filter, or unbalanced water chemistry. The best solution is to prevent turbidity in the first place. If it does occur, check to see that you have maintained the pool according to the recommended water chemistry values. Here are the steps to preventing and overcoming cloudy water:

- Maintain appropriate water chemistry levels (see the "Water Testing" section later in this chapter).
- Maintain the appropriate water level.
- Backwash filters on a systematic schedule.
- Keep pool entrances and deck areas clean.

Algae Growth

Although algae themselves are not life-threatening, they should be eliminated immediately to avoid odors, slippery surfaces, decreased visibility, and a stale taste to the water. Good pool maintenance—routine superchlorination and meticulous attention to filtration and vacuuming—will reduce the likelihood of developing algae problems.

Hard Water

In many areas of the U.S., hard water—water high in calcium—is a typical complaint. Although it doesn't negatively affect patrons, the water damages plumbing and filtration systems. Hard water problems can easily be averted by treating the water with sodium hexametaphosphate or a water softener when the pool is filled.

Colored Water

Colored water is caused by the presence of metallic ions. Each metal gives a different color; for example, copper makes the water appear more blue, and iron gives a reddish-brown tint. You can remove the coloration by adjusting the pH to the appropriate level, superchlorinating, vacuuming the pool, cleaning the filter system, and readjusting the residual chlorine levels.

WATER TESTING

It is vital that the water in any aquatic facility be tested systematically. Faulty procedures or lack of adherence to standards can increase the risk of spreading communicable diseases, damaging the filtration system, and promoting algae growth. Your facility should have a commercial grade testing kit available for testing disinfectant levels, pH, alkalinity, and calcium hardness (hard water). The facility should also test for the amount of total dissolved solids in the water—the sweat, body lotion, hair spray, disinfectant, and other solids that would be left if all of the pool water evaporated. If the chemicals used in testing the water are over 1 year old (6 months for phenol red), they should be replaced; they must be fresh to ensure valid testing. In fact, chemicals stored incorrectly may not last even 2 weeks.

Your facility procedures should call for the water to be tested at regular intervals during the day. The need for more frequent testing depends on the number of swimmers, the temperature, and numerous other factors.

Table 14.1 identifies six tests that should be conducted, what tests should be used, and acceptable levels for each.

Table 14.1 Water Quality Tests		
Element tested	**Type of test**	**Appropriate level**
Residual chlorine	Colorimeter or test strip	1.0 ppm
Residual bromine	Colorimeter or test strip*	2.0 ppm
pH	Chemical tests or test strips	7.4 to 7.6
Alkalinity	Chemical test kit	80 to 100 ppm
Calcium hardness	Chemical test kit	80 to 200 ppm
Total dissolved solids	Chemical test kit	200 to 600 ppm

*You can also use chlorine colorimeters and test strips to determine the amount of residual bromine by doubling the chlorine reading.

You may also calculate the Langelier Saturation Index weekly to ensure pH balance at a specific pool temperature. This index is important because the pH can affect both patron comfort and the pool system. Ideally, the Langelier Saturation Index should equal zero. A positive index means that a deposit may form on the valves, pipes, and pumps. A negative index means that the water may begin to corrode metal surfaces. Both circumstances can be corrected by adding corrective chemicals: muriatic acid or sodium bisulfate for positive readings and soda ash, bicarbonate of soda, or calcium chloride for negative readings.

The Langelier Saturation Index uses five variables to calculate water balance: pH, temperature, calcium hardness, alkalinity, and total dissolved solids. Temperature, calcium hardness, and alkalinity must be converted to factor weightings for use in the formula. Factor information is presented in Table 14.2. Simply look up your test scores and use the related factor weighting in the formula.

Saturation index = pH + temperature factor +
calcium hardness factor + alkalinity factor − total dissolved solids

Table 14.2 Langelier Saturation Index					
Section 1 Temperature (°F)	Temperature factor	Section 2 Calcium hardness (ppm)	Calcium factor	Section 3 Total alkalinity (ppm)	Alkalinity factor
32	0.0	5	0.3	5	0.7
37	0.1	25	1.0	25	1.4
46	0.2	50	1.3	50	1.7
53	0.3	75	1.5	75	1.9
60	0.4	100	1.6	100	2.0
66	0.5	150	1.8	150	2.2
76	0.6	200	1.9	200	2.3
84	0.7	300	2.1	300	2.5
94	0.8	400	2.2	400	2.6
105	0.9	800	2.5	800	2.9
128	1.0	1000	2.6	1000	3.0

For additional information about the saturation index, consult the *YMCA Pool Operations Manual*.

SPAS

Hot tubs and whirlpools, which are becoming popular at many aquatic facilities, pose some hazards—electrocution, drowning, and the transmission of disease seem to be the most common. A few rules and common sense will help make spas safe for patrons to enjoy. Review the rules listed on page 59 for some suggestions to make the spa at your facility hazard-free.

The health-related problems associated with spas can be reduced if the management

- maintains the spa at a temperature between 98° and 104° F,
- keeps the water chemistry balanced, and
- tests for the presence of bacteria and treats the water as necessary.

Review Questions

1. How often does the YMCA recommend safety inspections be conducted?
2. What steps should you take in the event of a chemical accident?
3. What is the role of the filtration system?
4. Describe how a vacuum sand filter functions.
5. What chemicals are used to disinfect water?
6. Define residual chlorine.
7. What is pH? What pH level is deemed appropriate for a pool?
8. What are algae?
9. What factors influence the amount of chemical used?
10. What is the best way to avoid water problems?
11. What 6 water tests should be conducted?

CHAPTER 15

Job Training and Opportunities

It is often a challenge to the newly trained lifeguard to get that first lifeguarding job. In this section you'll learn how to prepare for a job search. Once you have been hired, there are still ways to improve your skills.

IN THIS CHAPTER YOU'LL LEARN ABOUT

- getting a job and
- additional training opportunities.

GETTING A JOB

Like everything else you have done in preparing to become a lifeguard, getting a job requires some systematic work. Many qualified people are looking for the same kind of position as you. Fortunately, the skills you learn in preparing to find your first lifeguarding job will be helpful as you look for jobs in the future.

Preparing a Resume

The first step in getting a job is to prepare your resume, a brief history of your background. This information tells prospective employers what kinds of experience you have and forms the basis for their decisions on who to interview and what questions to ask.

Your resume gives a prospective employer a first impression about you, so you need to be very careful in your presentation. In general a resume should

- be neat;
- be as complete as possible;
- use accurate grammar, spelling, and punctuation;
- provide your name and address prominently;
- organize information into clear categories; and
- be as short as possible (2 pages maximum).

Include the following information in your resume:

- Name, address, and phone number
- Birthdate
- Educational background, including dates of attendance and grade average
- Awards and honors you have earned
- Current certifications and their expiration dates
- Job-related experience, including employers' names, dates of employment, and positions or roles (listed with the most recent job first)
- Volunteer activities
- References

The people you select as your references are very important. First, think about the people you know who could tell a prospective employer about your reliability and your ability to perform the tasks the position would require. Teachers, previous employers, and ministers are commonly listed as references (don't use family members).

Before you list someone as a reference on your resume, as a courtesy ask if she or he is willing to be one for you. It will save you embarrassment if the answer is no, and it will alert your references to your job search. Most people serving as references want time to formulate what they would say about you to a prospective employer.

On your resume list your references' names, addresses, telephone numbers, and how they know you. You want to make it easy for employers to reach people who will tell them about your abilities. Listing how the reference knows you helps tell what kind of information the reference can supply. A neighbor will provide different information than a previous employer.

Job Searching

Once your resume is ready, you can begin looking for job opportunities. Think about where you want to work, then contact your local YMCA, park district, county recreation department, or other aquatic facilities to see if they have openings. Talk with current lifeguards or aquatic supervisors if you can to let them know you are interested in working at their facility. Ask friends who have connections with aquatic facilities you are interested in whether they know of any positions.

Check newspaper ads for job listings, but don't stop there. You can also find job listings in places such as community bulletin boards and the public library or through school counselors, public or private employment agencies, and personnel offices at large companies.

Applying for a Job

The first time you apply for a job, you'll be nervous. Don't worry—you're in good company. What is important is that you leave a positive first impression. Most job applications are done in person, so dress neatly for your visit to a prospective employer and use your best manners.

Although job application forms differ from employer to employer, most include the same types of information. Bring your resume with you to the employer's office. You'll find it helpful in completing the form. Some employers may even accept your resume rather than having you complete the application.

When you complete an application form, keep the following guidelines in mind:

- Complete any application in ink.
- Write or print neatly so the employer can read your application easily.
- Fill in all blanks to the best of your ability. Leaving an area unanswered may make the employer think you were careless.
- If a question does not apply to you, mark it *NA* (not applicable).
- Be honest; don't try to present yourself as someone you are not.

Preparing for an Interview

When a prospective employer contacts you for an interview, you must then prepare for it. Consider the interview an opportunity to learn more about the position and the employer as well as to present yourself and your abilities.

Before any interview, take these steps:

- Learn all you can about the employer and the type of facility he or she operates.
- Think about the qualities you have that will make you a good employee at such a facility.
- Prepare a list of questions you would like to ask about your responsibilities and the procedures at the facility.
- Practice answering interview questions. Ask a parent or an adult friend to play the role of the interviewer and to conduct a practice interview. Typical questions include these:
  a. What led you to apply for this job?
  b. What do you think you can add to our organization?
  c. What would you consider your greatest strength?
  d. What do you think your weaknesses are?
  e. What have you learned from your previous work experiences?
- Select a neat outfit to wear to your interview.

Interviewing

The most important thing to remember as you enter an interview is that you want to present yourself in a favorable light. Arrive a little early—it tells the prospective employer that you will be on time if you are hired. Dress neatly, and don't chew gum when you enter the office.

When the interviewer comes to get you, stand up and greet him or her with a firm handshake. Establish eye contact and smile. It's amazing how confident those actions can make you feel. They also present the image of a confident candidate. Try to maintain your eye contact throughout the interview. And try to avoid any distracting habits you might have. Biting your fingernails, drumming your fingers, scratching your head, and tapping your feet are not good ways to present a positive image!

Listen carefully to the interviewer's complete question—never interrupt. Then think before you speak. Provide a clear answer to the question without rambling. When your opportunity to ask questions arises, be sure to ask questions that show you are interested in the job and that you are interested in progressing with the organization.

As you leave, thank the interviewer for contacting you. Indicate that you are interested in the position and hope that you will be considered. Then simply shake the interviewer's hand, thank him or her, and leave in a dignified manner. When you get home, write a note thanking the interviewer for the opportunity to interview.

You may not get the first job you apply for. Learn from each experience and your interviewing skills will improve. Eventually you will land your first job. Congratulate yourself—you're on your way. But don't get complacent. Be a good employee—keep trying to learn as much as you can about your position and about the facility.

TRAINING OPPORTUNITIES

Remember that your certification as a lifeguard depends on keeping your CPR and first aid certifications current. More importantly, your moral and legal duties call for you to have adequate first aid and CPR training. Your local American Heart Association, National Safety Council, and American Red Cross branches offer programs that can be of value to you.

The YMCA also offers a variety of aquatic leadership and management courses that you might find valuable. For example, certification courses are available for the following positions:

- Pool Operator on Location
- Competitive Swim Coach
- Competitive Swim Official
- Aquatic Facility Manager
- Specialist Instructor/Trainer (Progressive Swimming, Skippers, Arthritis, Water Exercise, Water Polo/Wetball, Synchronized Swimming, Special Populations, Lifeguard)

In-service training at your facility is also a valuable tool in your ongoing training and development. Each time you review a procedure or learn a new technique, you are becoming more valuable as a professional lifeguard and more capable of taking on additional responsibility.

Keep in mind, too, that if you enjoy aquatics or just working with people, you can have a lifetime career at the YMCA. Ys across the country offer full-time job opportunities in many different aspects of aquatics and other areas of social service and recreation. If you care about others and want to make a difference in their lives, consider working for the Y.

Review Questions

1. List the steps to getting a job as a professional lifeguard.
2. What should you do to prepare yourself for an interview?
3. What should you do during an interview?
4. List other training you can get to improve your lifeguarding and aquatic skills.

APPENDIX A

Child Abuse Identification and Prevention: Recommended Guidelines for YMCAs

STATEMENT OF THE YMCA OF THE USA MEDICAL ADVISORY COMMITTEE:

Child abuse is damage to a child for which there is no "reasonable" explanation. Child abuse includes nonaccidental physical injury, neglect, sexual molestation, and emotional abuse.

The increasing incidence of reported child abuse has become a critical national concern. The reported incidence of physical abuse, sexual abuse, and neglect has tripled since 1980. It is a special concern of the YMCA because of the organization's role as an advocate for children and its responsibility for enhancing the personal growth and development of both children and adults in all YMCA programs.

Each YMCA is encouraged to develop a written policy that clearly defines management practices related to prevention of child abuse. This policy should include approved practices for recruiting, training, and supervising staff; a code of conduct for staff relationships with children; reporting procedures for incidents when they do occur; and the responsibility to parents on this issue.

To assist YMCAs, the YMCA of the USA has developed a *Child Abuse Prevention Training* manual. This manual includes two three-hour training designs, one for staff who hire and supervise and a second for front-line program staff. Sample policies and procedures are included in both designs. Each YMCA received a copy of the manual in 1994. Additional copies are available from the YMCA Program Store (Item no. 5268). YMCAs are encouraged to offer these trainings on a regular basis for all staff.

The following guidelines have been developed to stimulate thinking about the potential for child abuse in YMCA programs and the need to develop a YMCA policy related to this important issue. Common sense and good judgment should guide the development of required procedures. Good management policies and practices will vary based on local situations. Laws differ from state to state. YMCA administrators need to be aware of changing state and local requirements and monitor YMCA programs to ensure that they are in compliance.

GUIDELINES FOR LOCAL YMCAS FOR STAFF RECRUITMENT, TRAINING, AND SUPERVISION

1. Reference checks on all prospective employees and program volunteers will be conducted, documented, and filed prior to employment.

2. Fingerprinting and criminal record checks of adults who work in programs such as child care and camping, where authorized or required by state law, are included in the employment process.

3. Photographs will be taken of all staff and attached to personnel records for identification at a later time if needed.

4. All new staff and volunteers must participate in an orientation program including written materials explaining YMCA policies, procedures, and regulations. They should be aware of legal requirements and by their signature acknowledge having received and read appropriate policies, standards, and codes of conduct. Documentation of attendance in the Child Abuse Prevention training should be added to the employee's personnel file.

5. Staff and volunteers working directly with children will be provided information regularly about the signs of possible child abuse. They should be educated about "high-risk parents" and "high-risk families" (for example, drug-addicted, alcohol-addicted, mentally ill, unemployed, or teenage parents, and parents who were abused themselves as children). Staff training will include approved procedures for responding to the suspicion of abuse.

6. Administrative staff supervising programs involving the care of children will make unannounced visits to each program site to assure that standards, policies, program quality, and performance of staff are being maintained. Written reports on these visits will be completed.

GUIDELINES FOR STAFF RELATIONSHIPS WITH CHILDREN

7. In order to protect YMCA staff, volunteers, and program participants, at no time during a YMCA program may a program leader be alone with a single child unobserved by other staff.

8. Young children will never be unsupervised in bathrooms, locker rooms, or showers.

9. Staff members and volunteers are not encouraged to relate to children in YMCA programs in non-YMCA activities, such as babysitting or weekend trips, without the knowledge of the responsible YMCA executive.

10. Adult YMCA staff and volunteers are not encouraged to socialize with program participants under the age of 18 outside of YMCA program activities.

11. YMCA staff and volunteers will not discipline children by use of physical punishment or by failing to provide the necessities of care, such as food and shelter.

12. YMCA staff or volunteers will not verbally or emotionally abuse or punish children.

13. Staff and volunteers providing direct care for very young children will be identified by a badge/name tag or uniform that is familiar to the children with whom they work. Children will be instructed to avoid any person not so identified.

14. Staff and volunteers should be alert to the physical and emotional state of all children each time they report for a program and indicate, in writing, any signs of injury or suspected child abuse.

GUIDELINES FOR THE YMCA'S RESPONSIBILITIES TO PARENTS

15. Invite parents to serve on interview committees to screen and select staff and volunteers. Caution should be taken in the selection of parents for this function. They should have a thorough understanding of, and be in agreement with, the YMCA's philosophy and operating procedures.

16. Ask parents to sign a Parent Statement of Understanding, which includes a statement limiting staff and program volunteers in their conduct with children and families outside of the YMCA program and which informs parents of the YMCA's mandate to report suspected cases of child abuse or neglect.

17. Conduct an intake/orientation with all parents to share the program's policies and procedures. Be sure to include the pre-employment screening, supervision, code of conduct, training, and other child abuse prevention policies established to protect children.

18. Daily communication should inform parents of their child's health, behavior, positive anecdotes from their day, etc.

19. The YMCA should maintain an open door policy that encourages parents to drop by and observe or share in the program with their child—at any time.

20. The YMCA should offer information and assistance to parents through workshops, counseling, book and video lending libraries, etc.

21. The YMCA should try to identify families in stress and offer referral information to agencies that can assist them.

22. Through newsletters, conferences, and modeling appropriate interaction skills, the YMCA should inform and educate parents about age-appropriate expectations and discipline.

23. The YMCA curriculum should stress children making choices, developing positive self-esteem, sharing feelings, and practicing their assertiveness skills. The YMCA should encourage parents to reinforce these skills at home, as they leave children less vulnerable to maltreatment.

24. The YMCA should sponsor guest speakers who address the issues of child abuse, child abuse prevention, teaching personal safety to children, etc. Administrators should screen all individuals and their material before allowing them to present.

REPORTING PROCEDURES

25. At the first report or probable cause to believe that child abuse has occurred, the employed staff person it has been reported to will notify the program director, who will then review the incident with the YMCA executive director or his/her designate. However, if the program director is not immediately available, this review by the supervisor cannot in any way deter the reporting of child abuse by the mandated reporters. Most states mandate each teacher or child care provider to report information they have learned in their professional role regarding suspected child abuse. In most states, mandated reporters are granted immunity from prosecution.

26. The YMCA will make a report in accordance with relevant state or local child abuse reporting requirements and will cooperate to the extent of the law with any legal authority involved.

27. In the event the reported incident(s) involve an employed program volunteer or employed staff, the executive director will, without exception, suspend the volunteer or staff person from the YMCA.

28. The parents or legal guardian of the child(ren) involved in the alleged incident will be promptly notified in accordance with the directions of the relevant state or local agency.

29. Whether the incident or alleged offense takes place on or off YMCA premises, it will be considered job related (because of the youth-involved nature of the YMCA).

30. Reinstatement of the program volunteer or employed staff person will occur only after all allegations have been cleared to the satisfaction of the persons named in #25 above.

31. All YMCA staff and volunteers must be sensitive to the need for confidentiality in the handling of this information, and therefore, should only discuss the incident with the persons named in #25 above.

POSSIBLE INDICATORS OF ABUSE

Sexual Abuse—Behavioral Indicators

1. Is reluctant to change clothes in front of others.
2. Is withdrawn.
3. Exhibits unusual sexual behavior and/or knowledge beyond that which is common for his/her developmental stage.
4. Has poor peer relationships.
5. Either avoids or seeks out adults.
6. Is pseudo-mature.
7. Is manipulative.
8. Is self-conscious.
9. Has problems with authority and rules.
10. Exhibits eating disorders.
11. Is self-mutilating.
12. Is obsessively clean.
13. Uses or abuses alcohol and/or other drugs.
14. Exhibits delinquent behavior such as running away from home.
15. Exhibits extreme compliance or defiance.
16. Is fearful or anxious.
17. Exhibits suicidal gestures and/or attempts suicide.
18. Is promiscuous.
19. Engages in fantasy or infantile behavior.
20. Is unwilling to participate in sports activities.
21. Has school difficulties.

Sexual Abuse—Physical Indicators

1. Has pain and/or itching in the genital area.
2. Has bruises or bleeding in the genital area.
3. Has venereal disease.
4. Has swollen private parts.
5. Has difficulty walking or sitting.
6. Has torn, bloody, and/or stained underclothing.
7. Experiences pain when urinating.
8. Is pregnant.
9. Has vaginal or penile discharge.
10. Wets the bed.

Emotional Abuse—Behavioral Indicators

1. Is overly eager to please.
2. Seeks out adult contact.
3. Views abuse as being warranted.
4. Exhibits changes in behavior.
5. Is excessively anxious.
6. Is depressed.
7. Is unwilling to discuss problems.
8. Exhibits aggressive or bizarre behavior.
9. Is withdrawn.
10. Is apathetic.
11. Is passive.
12. Has unprovoked fits of yelling or screaming.
13. Exhibits inconsistent behaviors.
14. Feels responsible for the abuser.
15. Runs away from home.
16. Attempts suicide.
17. Has low self-esteem.
18. Exhibits a gradual impairment of health and/or personality.
19. Has difficulty sustaining relationships.
20. Has unrealistic goal setting.
21. Is impatient.
22. Is unable to communicate or express his/her feelings, needs, or desires.
23. Sabotages his/her chances of success.
24. Lacks self-confidence.
25. Is self-deprecating and has a negative self-image.

Emotional Abuse—Physical Indicators

1. Has a sleep disorder (nightmares or restlessness).
2. Wets the bed.
3. Exhibits developmental lags (stunting of his/her physical, emotional, and/or mental growth).
4. Is hyperactive.
5. Exhibits eating disorders.

Physical Abuse—Behavioral Indicators

1. Is wary of adults.
2. Is either extremely aggressive or withdrawn.
3. Is dependent and indiscriminate in his/her attachments.
4. Is uncomfortable when other children cry.
5. Generally controls his/her own crying.
6. Exhibits a drastic behavior change when not with parents or caregiver.
7. Is manipulative.
8. Has poor self-concept.

9. Exhibits delinquent behavior, such as running away from home.
10. Uses or abuses alcohol and/or other drugs.
11. Is self-mutilating.
12. Is frightened of parents or going home.
13. Is overprotective of or responsible for parents.
14. Exhibits suicidal gestures and/or attempts suicide.
15. Has behavioral problems at school.

Physical Abuse—Physical Indicators

1. Has unexplained* bruises or welts, often clustered or in a pattern.
2. Has unexplained* and/or unusual burns (cigarettes, doughnut-shaped, immersion-lines, object-patterned).
3. Has unexplained* bite marks.
4. Has unexplained* fractures or dislocations.
5. Has unexplained* abrasions or lacerations.
6. Wets the bed.

(*Or explanation is inconsistent or improbable.)

Neglect—Behavior Indicators

1. Is truant or tardy often or arrives early and stays late.
2. Begs or steals food.
3. Attempts suicide.
4. Uses or abuses alcohol and/or other drugs.
5. Is extremely dependent or detached.
6. Engages in delinquent behavior, such as prostitution or stealing.

7. Appears to be exhausted.
8. States frequent or continual absence of parent or guardian.

Neglect—Physical Indicators

1. Frequently is dirty, unwashed, hungry, or inappropriately dressed.
2. Engages in dangerous activities (possibly because he/she generally is unsupervised).
3. Is tired and listless.
4. Has unattended physical problems.
5. May appear to be overworked and/or exploited.

Family Indicators

1. Extreme paternal dominance, restrictiveness, and/or overprotectiveness.
2. Family isolated from community and support systems.
3. Marked role reversal between mother and child.
4. History of sexual abuse by either parent or by children.
5. Substance abuse by either parent or by children.
6. Other types of violence in the home.
7. Absent spouse (through chronic illness, depression, divorce, or separation).
8. Severe overcrowding.
9. Complaints about a "seductive" child.
10. Extreme objection to implementation of child sexual abuse curriculum.

Source: Becca Cowan Johnson. 1992. *For Their Sake: Recognizing, Responding to, and Reporting Child Abuse.* Martinsville, IN: American Camping Association. Reprinted by permission of the publisher. For permission to reprint please contact the publisher at (317) 342-8456.

Family Indicators section from Committee For Children.

Note. These indicators can also be indicative of emotional dysfunctions that merit investigation for emotional problems and/or being the victims of abuse.

YMCAs are urged to share copies of their management policies related to child abuse with other YMCAs and the YMCA of the USA. A bibliography of printed and audiovisual educational resources for use with parents and children is included in the *Child Abuse Prevention Manual,* or available from the Program Development Division, YMCA of the USA, 101 North Wacker Drive, Chicago, Illinois 60606.

June, 1989

Revised April, 1996

APPENDIX B

Risk Management Involving Starting Blocks or Platforms, Water Depth, Deep Diving Starts, and Supervision

Research has proven that it is dangerous to dive in water less than 5 feet deep. Key factors in preventing diving injuries are swimmer/diver supervision, correct training and instruction, and participant awareness of the hazards of diving in shallow water.

STARTING BLOCKS OR PLATFORMS

Starting blocks or platforms

- are to be placed at the deep end of the swimming pool only. They are never to be placed in the shallow end or in water less than 5 feet in depth.
- are removed from the pool area, capped off to avoid any unintended use, or use is regulated by signage.
- are inspected regularly for stability, surface characteristics (traction), and any sign of wear.
- are considered competitive swimming equipment ONLY, to be used with proper supervision and safety instruction. They are not to be used as recreational devices or toys.
- are to have safety warnings posted regarding starting block or platform use.

WATER DEPTH

In order to minimize the risk of injury, conduct diving instruction from the deck in no less than 9 feet of water* and from a 1-meter board in no less than 11 feet, 6 inches of water.

Long shallow dives should be taught in no less than 9 feet of water. Once participants are proficient in such dives, warn them that they are allowed to perform these dives only in water at least 5 feet deep **and** when participating in a competitive swimming or lifeguard training program. Standing front dives should be performed in no less than 9 feet of water.

DEEP DIVING STARTS

This type of dive has been called the scoop start, pike start, spoon start, hole-in-the-water start, and no-resistance start. This start causes a swimmer to enter the water at a steeper angle than the traditional long shallow water dive or flat start.

This particular dive is being used more frequently by competitive swimmers. It is of questionable value and presents a potentially dangerous dive unless the water is 5 feet deep or more.

The water, unfortunately, may be deep enough in one pool, but not in another. This presents a

---

*Height and weight of the participant and the design of the pool bottom are factors to be considered in determining the safety of the diving area.

problem for swimmers and coaches in determining when the "scoop" dive can be safely used. During the excitement of a swimming meet, the competitor may forget, use the scoop start in a shallow pool, and suffer injury. **Due to the potential danger of serious injury, it should be eliminated in water less than 5 feet deep.**

SUPERVISION

Starting blocks or platforms are to be used only by trained swimmers under supervision in the deep end and in water at least 5 feet deep. They are removed or capped off to prevent use in all other situations or their use is regulated by posted rules.

Coaches and instructors will use proper sequential training techniques and enforce safe starting skills.

Swimmers will be instructed not to abort a poor start during its execution. Somersaulting, tucking, or jerking to one side may increase the risk of hitting the pool bottom.

Shallow water areas and starting blocks are controlled by lifeguards, instructors, and aquatic personnel.

Lifeguards will be alert and strictly enforce all rules.

REFERENCES

American Red Cross basic water safety. (1988). Oklahoma City: American National Red Cross.

American Red Cross safety training for swim coaches. (1988). Oklahoma City: American National Red Cross.

Aquatics. (1988, Winter). *YMCA Risk Report*, p. 2.

BFS Architectural Consulting and Interior Design. (1988, December 7). *Pool depth.* [Memorandum]

Bunnell & Co. (1984, August 21). *Safety group warns swimmers about Labor Day diving accidents.* [News release]

Counsilman, J., Nomura, T., Endo, M., & Counsilman, B. (1988, Spring). A study of three types of grab start for competitive swimming. *National Aquatic Journal*, pp. 2-6.

Gabriel, J. (Ed.) (1992). *Diving safety, a position paper.* Indianapolis: U.S. Diving, Inc.

Gabrielsen, M.A. (1984). *Diving injuries: A critical insight and recommendation.* Indianapolis: Council for National Cooperation in Aquatics.

Gabrielsen, M.A. (1987). *Swimming pools: A guide to their planning, design, and operation.* Champaign, IL: Human Kinetics.

Hunsaker, D.J. (1986). *Design compendium for competition swimming and diving pools.* San Antonio: National Swimming Pool Foundation.

National Collegiate Athletic Association. (1990). *1991 NCAA swimming and diving men's and women's rules.* Overland Park, KS: Author.

Pennsylvania Interscholastic Athletic Association. (1990, April 12). *Major rule revisions in swimming and diving.* [Memorandum]

Pennsylvania Interscholastic Athletic Association. (1990, April 20). *Water depth requirement in swimming.* [Memorandum]

Pennsylvania Interscholastic Athletic Association. (1990, April 24). *Swimming and diving rule revisions for 1990-91.* [Memorandum]

Prigitano, A. (1988, September). The cost of poor diving safety: Great incidence of paralysis. *Perspective*, pp. 30, 31.

Think twice before you dive. (1989). *For Kids' Sake*, **7**(2), p. 5.

YMCA of the USA. (1986). *On the guard: The YMCA lifeguard manual.* Champaign, IL: Human Kinetics.

YMCA of the USA. (1986). *YMCA progressive swimming instructor's guide.* Champaign, IL: Human Kinetics.

YMCA of the USA Aquatic Director. (1989, July 7). *Warning notice.* [Memorandum]

APPENDIX C

Sample Accident Report Form

Sample Accident Report Form

Date of report: _____

Name of injured person: _____ Age: _____ Sex: _____

Address: _____

Date of accident: _____ Time: _____ Number of people in water: _____

Water condition: _____ Weather condition: _____

Describe the accident. Include where the accident occurred, what happened, and how many people were involved in the accident.

List the names of those involved in the accident and comment on their swimming skills if such skills contributed to the accident.

Did those involved disregard rules or orders of the lifeguard? _____ If so, explain.

Identify who, if anyone, was injured and describe the injuries.

Describe the first aid given.

Was CPR used? _____ For how long? _____

Were law enforcement or EMS squads called? _____ What time did they arrive? _____

Was additional medical attention required? _____ If so, indicate where individuals were taken, who provided treatment, and what treatment was given.

Blood-borne Pathogen Program Exposure Incident

Employee name: _____ Soc. sec. no.: _____

Was the source the injured person listed above? _____ Yes _____ No

If not, give source's name: _____

Address: _____ Phone no.: _____

Document route of exposure: (mucous membrane, puncture, etc.) _____

_____

_____

Was protective equipment used? _____ Yes   Describe equipment. _____

_____

_____

Was protective equipment used? _____ No   Give reason it was not used. _____

_____

_____

Describe post-exposure cleanup procedures that were used: _____

_____

_____

_____

_____

Lifeguard Information

Name: _____   Position: _____

Years of experience: _____   Assignment location: _____   Hours on/off duty: _____

List names, addresses, and phone numbers of at least two witnesses on the back of this sheet.

Sketch the area of the accident, showing unusual conditions (if any) and assignments of personnel.

General comments of employees:

Signature: _____   Date: _____

APPENDIX D

YMCA Lifeguarding and the United States Lifesaving Association

The YMCA of the USA is proud of its heritage in lifeguard training and water safety. It began with the first lifesaving corps, organized at Camp Dudley in 1904, the first National Lifesaving Service in 1912, and the first lifesaving textbook, *Water First Aid*, by George Goss in 1913. For almost 100 years YMCA-certified lifesavers and lifeguards have staffed America's swimming pools, the lake and river beaches, and camp waterfronts. However, training has not included surf lifeguarding.

After briefly attempting to certify surf lifeguards in the mid-1970s, the YMCA soon discovered that they lacked the surf beach facilities to train and certify surf lifeguards. However, many students who complete YMCA lifeguard courses would like to use their lifeguarding skills at surf beaches. That is why the YMCA aquatic program is pleased to have developed a linkage with the United States Lifesaving Association (USLA).

The USLA is the oldest, most experienced surf lifeguard training agency in America today. Its mission is to establish and maintain high standards for open water (beach) lifeguards, to educate the public, and to promote actions intended to result in the saving of human life in and around the aquatic environment. The USLA is made up of groups of individuals who form chapters locally. The chapters then join together to create regions of the USLA, within which they can exchange local and regional information relevant to their activities and needs. Currently there are eight regions of the USLA.

This appendix was developed in cooperation with the USLA to provide YMCA lifeguards with the information and fundamental steps necessary to link up with USLA programs from coast to coast.

Because USLA training includes the use of cervical collars for spinal cord injured victims, the use of a rescue buoy in rescue skills, and the use of in-water assessment and rescue breathing, just as YMCA training does, Y-trained lifeguards have an advantage in training for surf lifeguarding.

If you are a certified YMCA lifeguard with an interest in becoming a surf lifeguard at a USLA-certified beach, you must satisfy the following basic requirements to be eligible for entry-level open-water lifeguard training:

1. Age—Be a minimum of 16 years of age.
2. Swimming ability—Demonstrate the ability to swim 500 meters over a measured course in 10 minutes or less.
3. Health and fitness—Possess adequate vision, hearing acuity, physical ability, and stamina to perform the duties of an open water lifeguard, as documented by a medical or osteopathic physician.
4. First aid certification—Be certified as having successfully completed a first aid course accepted by the federal government or by the state government in the state of employment. Total formal first aid training, including the certified first aid course, shall be no less than 21 hours.
5. CPR certification—Be certified as having successfully completed a course in providing one-person adult, two-person adult, child, and infant CPR, including obstructed airway training, accepted by the federal government or by the state government in the state of employment.

6. Lifeguard training—Be certified as successfully completing a course consisting of no less than 40 hours in open water lifesaving that meets the curriculum requirements of USLA. This shall not include the minimum training hours required for first aid and CPR.

7. Scuba training—Any lifeguard who will be required to utilize scuba in the course of employment must, at a minimum, be certified as a scuba diver at the basic level by a nationally recognized certifying agency.

Because the USLA realizes that differences in environmental conditions will impact specific training issues, variations to the USLA curriculum requirements may be permitted under very specific situations.

If you can meet the first six requirements of the seven just identified, then you are considered to be a viable candidate for USLA surf lifeguard training. Your next step would be to obtain and study a copy of *The United States Lifesaving Association Manual of Open Water Lifesaving*, as well as other USLA publications. In the meantime, you should stay in peak physical condition by swimming and participating in a resistive exercise program, and you should contact the USLA chapter in the beach town where you would like to gain employment as a beach lifeguard.

Other standards exist for Open Water Lifeguard Trainees, Full Time Open Water Lifeguards, and Open Water Lifeguard Instructors. Information on the USLA's certification programs may be obtained by ordering their *Lifeguard Agency Certification Program* booklet which, along with *The United States Lifesaving Association Manual of Open Water Lifesaving*, is the association's response to the need for standardization in the profession of open water lifesaving.

To order copies of *The United States Lifesaving Association Manual of Open Water Lifesaving* (ISBN 8359-4919-2), write or call Brady Publishing at the following:

Brady Publishing (Division of Prentice-Hall)
113 Sylvan Avenue
Englewood Cliffs, NJ 07632
800-374-1200

(For customer service, call 201-767-4993.)

APPENDIX E

Safety Guidelines for Inflatables and Permanent Equipment

This appendix is an excerpt from a YMCA of the USA paper, "Fun, Function, and Safety: Improving and Expanding Your YMCA Aquatic Center." The excerpt focuses on safety guidelines for non-permanent equipment, or inflatables, and permanent equipment such as permanent slides.

NON-PERMANENT EQUIPMENT (INFLATABLES)

Inflatables are a popular addition to pools these days, and many Ys have used them successfully to increase participation during recreational swims. Inflatables are large objects or animals usually made of a reinforced PVC fabric with a tough polyester mesh bonded between two layers of PVC to allow for stretching and flexing. Inflatables come in many models, shapes, and sizes. They range in price from $600 to $13,000 and are available from a number of vendors.

Inflatables can be put into your pool or taken out with relative ease. They can add a new look and provide great fun for your members and participants. Some associations have bought more than one inflatable, then shared them among their branches. If you decide to buy one, be sure you know what age group you are targeting before you decide which kind to buy. Take the time to be sure you purchase one that is the appropriate size for your pool and can be put in the appropriate depth. Have the manufacturer confirm that the particular play structure you want to purchase will fit your YMCA's intended use, pool size, and water depth.

Inflatables come in two types:

- **Sealed inflatables** are play structures that can support one or more persons above the surface of the water. They are capped once they are filled with air. There are many different designs.
- **Constant-blow inflatables** have an air blower permanently connected and constantly running while the inflatable is in use. These tend to be used differently than the sealed inflatables. For example, participants try to run the length of aqua fun runs and use them as obstacle courses. There also are inflatable water slides.

As always, it is the Y's responsibility to ensure the safety of users of this equipment. When using inflatables, consider the following precautions in addition to the manufacturer's safety recommendations and applicable state and local codes. Include the cost of these in your cost analysis before buying an inflatable.

Sealed Inflatables

Figure E.1 shows how a sealed inflatable should normally be anchored.

Any inflatable used should not cover a continuous area more than one square meter (39 square inches) wide of water and should be no more than one meter in height above the water's surface. Wherever possible the depth should be consistent on all sides of the inflatable.

Limited product safety research is available on the appropriate depth at which inflatables should

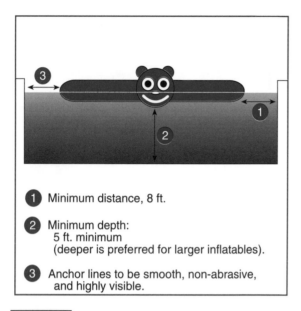

1 Minimum distance, 8 ft.

2 Minimum depth:
   5 ft. minimum
   (deeper is preferred for larger inflatables).

3 Anchor lines to be smooth, non-abrasive,
   and highly visible.

Figure E.1

Normal method for anchoring a sealed inflatable.

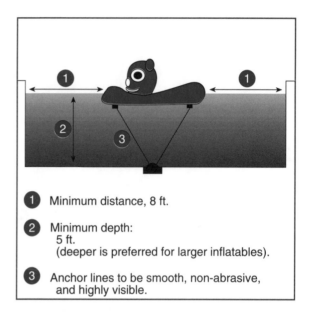

1 Minimum distance, 8 ft.

2 Minimum depth:
   5 ft.
   (deeper is preferred for larger inflatables).

3 Anchor lines to be smooth, non-abrasive,
   and highly visible.

Figure E.2

Bottom method for anchoring a sealed inflatable.

be placed. Due to the variety of activities for which inflatables can be used, a minimum of five feet is recommended for sealed inflatables (and an even greater depth would be preferable). As new research becomes available, this depth should be adjusted. Due to the five-foot depth recommendation, a deep-water swim test should be required for all swimmers before allowing them to play on the structure.

These play structures are not recommended for use by children or adults who cannot swim. If your Y chooses to allow young children and their parents to play on the structure and they are not proficient swimmers, parents should be aware that accidental falls can be frightening for a child and can cause a fear of the water. You might want to consider using lifejackets for children and establishing a separate play period for parents and their young children.

Sealed Inflatable Installation.   Figure E.2 shows the bottom method for anchoring a sealed inflatable.

- The inflatable should be inspected each time before being used. Pay particular attention to seams, anchorage points, and other potential areas of weakness. These checks should be recorded in a log book.

- An electrical receptacle with a ground-fault interrupter is required and should be placed in a convenient location for safe inflating and

deflating. Electrical cords should not cross traffic areas.

- Prior to using an electric blower for inflation or deflation, check the blower for safety and make sure it is plugged into an outlet with a ground-fault interrupter. Before each use, check the blower for any damage and make sure that the mesh guards over the air inlet and outlets are secured and that cables, plugs, sockets, and switches are not damaged.

- When the inflatable is being filled with air, it should not obstruct the movement of people onto the pool deck or block emergency exits. The pool should be closed during inflation or deflation of the inflatable if on-duty guards are responsible for doing it.

- The inflatables should be transported carefully, carried, not dragged along the pool deck. Inflatable lifespans fluctuate due to variations in care, use, and storage, but an average is three years. With the proper care, they will last longer.

- Nylon or other water-resistant tether lines with a minimum diameter of 3/8 inches should be used to tether all pool inflatables. Five-inch "lok-on" rope floats should be placed every two feet on the tether line, with a brass swivel clip on one end to attach to the pool side. The tether lines should not be pulled on, played with, or used to climb on the inflatable. Anchor lines should be smooth, non-abrasive, and highly visible.

- There should be a minimum clearance of eight feet on all sides of the sealed inflatable.

Sealed Inflatable Operation.   Figure E.3 illustrates how to position a sealed inflatable.

- An emergency plan should be developed and staff trained on the following: dealing with unruly behavior, collapse or partial collapse of the inflatable, failure of the tether ropes, or serious injury of a swimmer.
- At least one lifeguard should be stationed on the deck on each side of the inflatable structure. Additional guards might be needed to help supervise in the water depending on the number, age, and abilities of the swimmers using the inflatable. This does not include the general duty guards for other swimmers using the pool.
- A small age range should be allowed to play on the inflatable at one time (for example, 10- to 12-year-olds should not play at the same time as 5- to 7-year-olds). Recommended playing

time for each group is between 15 and 20 minutes.

- Head-first dismounts should be forbidden.
- Standing on the object should not be allowed unless it is specifically designed for this activity.
- Swimmers should not be allowed to push or throw each other onto or off of the inflatable.
- Swimmers should not be allowed to deliberately swim under the inflatable or lift it to try to knock others from the inflatable.
- Swimmers should not swing, hang, or pull on the anchor ropes.
- Consider having an age minimum, depending on the size of the inflatable you purchase.
- No swimsuit pins or sharp objects should be allowed near the inflatable.

Constant-Blow Inflatables

Two common types of constant-blow inflatables are inflatable slides and aqua runs.

Inflatable Slides.   Inflatable slides are attached to a three-meter diving platform or a customized frame. The active sliding length is about 26 feet. The air blower works continuously so that the proper air pressure is delivered. The user safely slides between two large air-filled side tubes.

Inflatable Slide Installation.   The positioning of an inflatable water slide is shown in Figure E.4.

- Constant-blower-filled slides should be used and secured to a platform or frame three meters above the water surface area to ensure the correct angle of descent.
- A designated "splash area" should be established and should extend out at least 15 feet from the bottom of the slide. Ropes with floats every two feet or inflatable booms should be used to form the boundary lines of the splash or non-swimming area.
- Appropriate daily inspections of the slide, supporting structure, and electrical equipment should be logged and reported properly.
- Stairs with landings should be used instead of ladders. The diameter and height of the handrails should be appropriate for the age group using the slide.
- There should be plenty of empty space above the platform (at least eight feet ceiling clearance).

1 Anchorage lines at 30 degree to the line of the inflatable.

2 At least 8 ft. clearance.

Figure E.3

Positioning of sealed inflatable.

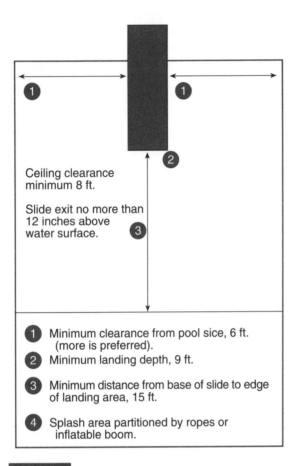

Ceiling clearance minimum 8 ft.

Slide exit no more than 12 inches above water surface.

1. Minimum clearance from pool sice, 6 ft. (more is preferred).
2. Minimum landing depth, 9 ft.
3. Minimum distance from base of slide to edge of landing area, 15 ft.
4. Splash area partitioned by ropes or inflatable boom.

Figure E.4

Positioning of inflatable water slide.

- All sides of the platform must be completely enclosed.
- The exit of the slide should not be more than 12 inches above the surface of the water.
- Deck obstruction must not exceed state and local codes.
- If water is needed to operate the slide, a hose attachment should be in place. An adequate water flow down the slide is needed to minimize friction burns to users.
- At least 6 feet clearance from either side of the pool tank is needed (10 feet is preferred).
- Limited research is available on the appropriate depth in which inflatable slides should be placed. It is recommended that at least 9 feet (2.8 meters) of pool depth is needed, and 15 feet of clearance is needed in front of the exit point of the slide. As new research becomes available, this depth should be adjusted.
- The sliding surface will wear out with usage and require patching and repairing. Some slides

have available a replaceable sliding surface, which should be inspected and patched or replaced as needed. This can increase the lifespan of the slide.

Inflatable Slide Operation. Guidelines for operating an inflatable slide include the following:

- Heed weight limits recommended by the manufacturer.
- No one who is less than four feet tall should use the slide.
- Only one person should be allowed down the slide at one time.
- The feet-first sliding position is the only one that should be allowed.
- Do not let participants run or jump on the slide.
- One guard should be positioned at the top of the slide to make sure the rider is in the proper slide position. This guard also controls the flow of participants using the slide and climbing the stairs.
- Another guard should be stationed on the deck to supervise the exit point of the slide and the swimmers' clearance of the splash area.

Aqua Fun Runs. Aqua fun runs are constant-blow structures that can run up to 40 feet in length and a maximum of 4 feet, 9 inches wide. There are many safety concerns to be aware of with aqua fun runs. For instance, fun runs that are more than one square meter (39 inches by 39 inches) of covered water surface area shouldn't be used because of the increased risk that someone could become trapped underneath. The play elements of the structure should be no more than one meter in height of playable surface above the water. A number of aqua fun runs do meet these recommendations.

The purpose of aqua fun runs is for swimmers to traverse (walk or run) the structure like an obstacle course. We recognize that some Ys will choose to use the structure as a sealed inflatable instead of as a fun run. In this case, staff need to realize that different operating procedures and rules need to be established and that the sealed inflatable recommendations should be followed. A word of caution: Having two sets of rules can confuse your swimmers and make enforcement of rules more difficult.

Check your pool carefully before buying an aqua fun run. Some pools won't be able to accommodate the safety recommendations for this type of inflatable.

Aqua Fun Run Installation. The proper anchoring for aqua fun runs (constant-blow inflatables) is shown in Figure E.5.

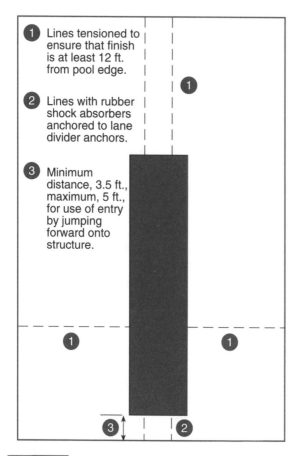

① Lines tensioned to ensure that finish is at least 12 ft. from pool edge.

② Lines with rubber shock absorbers anchored to lane divider anchors.

③ Minimum distance, 3.5 ft., maximum, 5 ft., for use of entry by jumping forward onto structure.

Figure E.5

Anchoring for aqua fun runs.

- The structure should be in deep water (at least 9 feet) with no other users around the structure.
- The inflatable purchased should be appropriate to the depths and dimensions of the pool.
- The finish should have at least 12 feet of clearance from the edge of the pool.
- There should be at least 12 feet of clearance on each side of the pool. The end of the run should allow participants to exit into the deep end of the pool.
- The air blower will be in constant operation while the structure is in use. Full compliance with electrical codes and regulations is necessary.
- The pool area should be cleared when the inflatable is being put in or taken out.

Aqua Fun Run Operation. Rules of operation are similar to those for sealed inflatables, plus the following:

- At least two designated guards are needed—one to supervise participants getting on the

inflatable and then dispatching swimmers, the other to supervise the run and dismount and clearing of the dismount area.

- Only one participant should be dispatched onto the inflatable at a time.
- The flow of participants should be controlled by a lifeguard.
- At the far end, swimmers must slide off feet first and then swim to the nearest side.
- Swimmers should be instructed to fall off the fun run if they lose their balance, not try to dive off it.
- If the aqua fun run is being used as a sealed inflatable (for play and not as a run), then participants should not be allowed to stand on it, but should be allowed to crawl only. The type of play on the inflatable should be posted so the designated rules can be understood by swimmers and the rules enforced.
- No substantive research has been done on the best entry of the swimmers onto the run. Until more research is completed, use your best judgment as to how your swimmers should get onto the structure. Two methods are possible:

1. One method is to have a lifeguard stationed at the beginning of the run, with its starting point against the edge of the pool. The lifeguard helps users step carefully onto the structure before they traverse the obstacle course.

2. The other method is to have the lifeguard closely supervise the swimmers as they jump onto the unit (rather than step onto it) to ensure forward projection and to reduce the danger of falling back and hitting the poolside. The unit should be placed so that there is a minimum clearance of three-and-a-half feet and a maximum clearance of five feet from the edge of the pool to the start of the structure.

PERMANENT EQUIPMENT

Interactive or creative-play water playgrounds and slides are among the most popular family aquatic center elements. But there are additional precautions to be considered if you purchase some of these types of equipment. These should be implemented in addition to all the safety and operating guidelines available from the manufacturer.

Interactive Playground Safety Recommendations

Follow these safety precautions:

- Post the rules by each piece of aquatic equipment and at pool entrances.
- Make sure that the rules are clearly written and easily understood by all.
- Have special guarding policies in writing for each piece of equipment.
- Strictly enforce all policies and rules.
- Station an additional lifeguard on a play structure to monitor slides and potentially hazardous play.
- Have smooth surfaces on all objects (walls and pipes).
- Have contour lines to show increases in depth.
- Make sure that it's clear that the playground is intended for children under four feet tall.
- Make sure slides have an open tube at the end of the slide so visibility is clear.
- Ensure that the angle and exit of slides are not dangerous and conform to Consumer Product Safety Commission standards.

Permanent Slide Safety Recommendations

Here are recommendations for installing and operating a permanent slide.

Permanent Slide Installation. The following are guidelines for installing permanent slides:

- Follow the same standard for pool depth at the mouth of a drop slide as you would use for a one-meter board.
- Install closed steps with landings instead of ladders (according to industry standards).
- Make sure that there is plenty of empty space (at least nine feet) above the platform.
- Make sure that deck obstructions meet codes.
- If the pool has a diving board and a slide in the deep end, make sure there is a space at least 10 feet wide between them.
- Have permanently enclosed sides on the platform.
- Post signs to identify assumption of risk for riders. Parental releases are recommended before those under 18 years of age use the equipment.

Permanent Slide Operation. Follow these guidelines for permanent slide operation:

- Have written emergency procedures for this area and rehearse them.
- Station lifeguards at the top and bottom of the slide. The guard at the top has dispatching duties and the guard at the bottom supervises proper exiting of the participants.
- Don't allow children on the equipment if they are shorter than 48 inches. This is because it is recommended that children be six inches taller than the water depth in the catch pool, or other modifications should be in place (e.g., deep water swim test, use of lifejackets, or a guard in the catch pool). Be sure to discuss this with the manufacturer to ensure that the slide will be properly positioned so that the groups you want to serve will exit into the appropriate water depth.
- Heed weight limits established by the manufacturers. A weight limit used by some manufacturers is about 250 pounds for a basic serpentine slide.
- Don't use members as safety testers.
- Stop water flow and the dispatch of participants during a major rescue (such as when multiple guards are involved in the assistance and care of an injured swimmer). Have a water shut-off button close by so the guard can stop water flow quickly.
- Allow only feet-first sliding.
- Perform a safety inspection prior to opening each day.
- Keep a detailed log of any maintenance and safety inspections.
- Review and analyze an injury chart and incident reports for any corrective measures that can be taken to reduce the possibilities of repeat occurrences. Note and date any actions taken.

Serpentine Slide Installation and Operation. These recommendations relate to the serpentine slide:

- Follow the manufacturer's recommendations on water depth for a serpentine slide with a low-grade discharge (a 10 percent grade is recommended). Slides that do not have a safe deceleration to near zero velocity at the point of discharge should have a minimum depth of 9 feet and would preferably meet one-meter board guidelines for water depth.

- Be aware of conditions in the catch pool, such as currents created from the water flow.
- The lifeguards stationed in the catch pool should always have their rescue tubes. It is also helpful for them to wear deck shoes to minimize slipping.
- Some catch pool areas have a pad to help absorb any impact from the landing. Check with your manufacturer on their recommendation based on the slide you are considering.

OTHER COSTS TO REMEMBER

Adding equipment probably will mean added costs as well. Check these areas for possible expenses:

- For permanent equipment, time the completion of installation so that you can benefit from a full season of activity; otherwise you need to make appropriate downward budget adjustments. Consult your architect for a schedule that includes planning, design, construction documents, bidding, construction permits, start-up, punch lists, and move-in.
- Be prepared for increased electrical, water, and chemical expenses from pumping water on the equipment and increased evaporation rates.
- Review maintenance guidelines carefully. These can add to your staff time and operating costs.
- Increased supervision will be required when equipment is in use.

A FINAL WORD ON EQUIPMENT

Just adding a slide will not necessarily give you long-term participation and program growth. You will find it necessary to make continual improvements to the pool areas to maintain a positive growth rate after your initial investment. It's the same with Y fitness centers: One Stairmaster or new program won't make a long-term difference in membership, but regular additions to the fitness area and its programs will. No matter how ambitious you want your aquatic center to be, a good plan with comprehensive research will help you build it successfully.

RESOURCES USED IN WRITING "FUN, FUNCTION, AND SAFETY: IMPROVING AND EXPANDING YOUR YMCA AQUATIC CENTER"

We would like to thank those who contributed to this project:

YMCA of the USA Staff

Eileen Carroll, Purchasing Service
Vernon Delpesce, Mid-America Field Office
Rod Grozier, BFS/PM
Marv Reinke, YSC
Glenda Short, YSC
Laura Slane, Program Development
Bill Smith, YSC
George Stazin, BFS/PM
Lynne Vaughan, Program Development

Volunteers

Dr. Jerry DeMers, California Polytechnic University

Dr. Ralph Johnson, Indiana University of Pennsylvania

Denise Menke, Milwaukie, Oregon

Allen Wagner, East Allegheny (Pennsylvania) School District

We also would like to thank the following YMCA preferred vendors for their help with research and assistance in developing our guidelines:

Airspace, USA, Inc., 80-872-1319
Whitewater USA, 614-621-2440
SCS Company, Interactive WaterPlay Systems, 619-459-4649

The Use of Play Equipment and Water Features in Swimming Pools: A Recommended Code of Practice, published by the Institute of Sport and Recreation Management, Giffard House, 36/38 Sherrard Street, Melton Mowbray, LE13 1XJ, U.K., telephone: 0664 65531.

Swimming Pool Slides Safety Standard, published by the Consumer Product Safety Commission.

APPENDIX F

Procedures for Cleanup and Disposal of Medical Waste

Your facility should have steps for cleanup and disposal of medical waste in its facility operation or lifeguard manual, and these steps should be practiced during in-service training. The following recommendations meet or exceed the universal precautionary procedures (see p. 116) established by the Centers for Disease Control of the United States Public Health Services. They are consistent with OSHA requirements.

When involved in a rescue or cleanup that might put them in contact with an individual's body fluids, lifeguards should wear at least one pair of latex gloves and learn how to take them off using the following procedures:

a. Grasp the top or wrist part of one glove, being careful to touch only the glove.

b. Then pull the glove down toward the fingers, turning it inside out. Continue to hold onto the glove.

c. Insert one or two clean fingers into the top of the other glove. Be careful not to touch the outside surface.

d. Pull the glove off, turning it inside out while pulling it over the first glove. Now the first glove taken off is inside the second glove, both turned inside out.

e. Discard the gloves into a red plastic, medical waste bag with the biohazard symbol on it.

f. Dispose of the medical waste bag in accordance with the protocols established by your Department of Health, local hospital, EMS service, or local municipal code.

When performing a rescue, lifeguards should begin assessment of the victim and resuscitation in the water with a pocket mask and change to a bag valve mask resuscitator when the victim is brought out of the water.

When performing a water rescue, lifeguards should follow these steps:

1. Attempt to determine during the approach if blood is visible in the water.

2. If the victim is bleeding and active, avoid swimming in the blood-contaminated water if possible. Approach from the front if blood is visible behind the victim. If blood is visible in front and the victim does not appear to be in danger of submerging, swim around behind and use a rear active approach.

3. Avoid contact with the bleeding victim as much as possible during the approach and while towing an active victim.

4. During rescues of both passive and active victims, keep the routes of entry into your body (eyes, ears, nose, and mouth) above water at all times.

5. If you are the single guard at your facility, you will not be able to avoid direct contact when assisting a conscious victim or removing a passive victim from the pool or waterfront. If two or more lifeguards are available, your accident management procedure should be structured so that a second lifeguard equipped with barrier protection is ready to assist you in removing the victim

from the water. You (the rescue guard) should then apply the necessary precautionary barriers (as described earlier) before assisting with first aid or resuscitation.

6. When first aid and/or CPR has been completed and the EMS personnel have taken the victim to the hospital, wash your hair and entire body with soap and water. Rinse your mouth with an antiseptic mouthwash if you performed resuscitation with a pocket mask.

The pool area and pool equipment will need to be disinfected after an incident in which body fluids were released. These are the appropriate procedures for disinfection:

- The best defense against contamination of swimming pools and spas from exposure to blood-borne pathogens is sustaining appropriate free chlorine or bromine levels. The best range for a pool is 1.0 to 3.0 ppm of free residual chlorine or 2.0 to 6.0 of free residual bromine. For spas, a free chlorine residual of 3.0 to 5.0 ppm or a free bromine residual of 6.0 to 10.0 ppm is necessary.

- If blood contaminates the pool deck, coping, or walkways made of cement, granite, rock, or other porous surface material, they will have to be disinfected. Mix 4 ounces of calcium hypochlorite or 16 ounces (one pint) of sodium hypochlorite with 1 gallon of water. Be sure that either type of chlorine is fresh. Clear the area of aquatic staff members and pool patrons. Then apply the solution on all contaminated surfaces with a garden sprayer and let it stand for five minutes. Rinse the surface with water from a hose toward a swimming pool deck drain. Repeat applying and rinsing the solution, and allow the surface to

dry completely before permitting anyone to walk on it or use it in any way. This same procedure can be used to sanitize diving boards, starting blocks, and wood surfaces.

- To disinfect grass, dirt, and sand surfaces contaminated by blood, mix a solution of chlorine and water using 4 ounces of fresh calcium hypochlorite or 16 ounces (one pint) of sodium hypochlorite with 1 gallon of water. Apply the chlorine solution until the area where the blood spill occurred is thoroughly saturated with the chlorine solution. Rope off the area and prohibit sunbathing or other uses of the area until the area is completely dry. If the contaminated area consists of dirt or sand, turn it over with a shovel and rake it. Saturate the sand or dirt again, and continue to prohibit use of the area until it dries and is raked a second time. As grass will be killed by the chlorine solution, waterfront and outdoor pool operators may want to remove small quantities of sod and dispose of it in medical waste bags to be incinerated. Be sure to decontaminate any shovels, rakes, brooms, or other tools used in the cleanup with the same strength chlorine solution, and rinse them thoroughly.

- Any personal equipment used in rescue, first aid, CPR, or oral suction that is reusable must be properly sanitized before it is used again. This includes, but is not limited to, rescue tubes, rescue buoys, masks, fins, snorkels, backboards, straps, head immobilizers, and hard cervical collars. These items should be cleaned with a quaternary ammonia disinfectant. Be sure to follow the instructions on the label. Disposable equipment such as pocket masks and first aid materials must be disposed of in medical waste bags.

REFERENCES

Brewster, C. (Ed.). (1995). *United States Lifesaving Association manual for open water lifesaving*. Englewood Cliffs, NJ: Brady (division of Prentice-Hall).

Canadian Red Cross Society. (1983). *Cold water survival*. Victoria, BC: Author.

Johnson, R., G. DeMers, A. Wagner, and R. Clayton. (1997). *Swimming pool operations*. Ft. Collins, CO: Professional Aquatic Consultants, Inc.

United States Coast Guard, Department of Transportation. (1977). *Hypothermia and cold water survival—Instructor's guide*. Washington, DC: Government Printing Office.

ADDITIONAL RESOURCES

American Red Cross. (1991). *First aid: Responding to emergencies*. St. Louis: Mosby.

American Red Cross. (1992). *Swimming and diving*. St. Louis: Mosby.

Bergeron, J.D., & Greene, H.W. (1989). *Coaches guide to sport injuries*. Champaign, IL: Human Kinetics.

Ellis, J. (1985). Drowning: Mechanism and causes. *National Aquatics Journal*, **1**, 10-13.

Golden, F. (1985). Hypothermia and survival. *NationalAquatics Journal*, **1**, 2-10.

Johnson, R.L. (1989). *YMCA pool operations manual*. Champaign, IL: Human Kinetics.

Mebane, G.Y., & Dick, A.P. (1985). *DAN underwater diving accident manual*. Durham, NC: Duke University Press.

Pia, F. (1974). Observations on the drowning of non-swimmers. *Journal of Physical Education*, 164-167, 181.

Pia, F. (1984). The RID factor as a cause of drowning. *Parks and Recreation*, 52-55, 67.

Smith, D.S. (1984). Notes on drowning. The misunderstood, preventable tragedy. *Physician and Sportsmedicine*, **12**, 66-73.

Smith, R.W. (1985). *The new science of skin and scuba diving* (6th ed.). Champaign, IL: Human Kinetics.

Strykowski, J. (1974). *Diving for fun* (4th ed.). Northfield, IL: Dacor Corp.

Wagner, A. (1985). Emergency procedures for aquatic facilities. *Parks and Recreation*, 56-69.

YMCA of the USA. (1986). *On the guard*. Champaign, IL: Human Kinetics.

YMCA of the USA. (1987). *Aquatics for special populations*. Champaign, IL: Human Kinetics.

YMCA of the USA. (1993). *YMCA aquatics program and leadership training*. Champaign, IL: Human Kinetics.

Yorkshire, B. (1982, November). Wave pools and lifeguarding. Paper presented at the conference of the Council for National Cooperation in Aquatics, Columbus, OH.